Off the
Beaten Path®

the dakotas

Help Us Keep This Guide Up to Date

Every effort has been made by the author and editors to make this guide as accurate and useful as possible. However, many changes can occur after a guide is published—establishments close, phone numbers change, facilities come under new management, and so on.

We would love to hear from you concerning your experiences with this guide and how you feel it could be improved and be kept up to date. While we may not be able to respond to all comments and suggestions, we'll take them to heart, and we'll make certain to share them with the author. Please send your comments and suggestions to the following address:

The Globe Pequot Press
Reader Response/Editorial Department
P.O. Box 480
Guilford, CT 06437

Or you may e-mail us at: editorial@GlobePequot.com

Thanks for your input, and happy travels!

INSIDERS'GUIDE®

OFF THE BEATEN PATH® SERIES

Off the Beaten Path®

FIFTH EDITION

the dakotas

A GUIDE TO UNIQUE PLACES

ROBIN McMACKEN

INSIDERS'GUIDE®

GUILFORD, CONNECTICUT
AN IMPRINT OF THE GLOBE PEQUOT PRESS

The prices, rates, and hours listed in this guidebook were confirmed at press time. We recommend, however, that you call establishments to obtain current information before traveling.

INSIDERS'GUIDE®

Copyright © 1996, 1998, 2000, 2002, 2004 by The Globe Pequot Press

Text design by Linda Loiewski
Text illustrations by Marty Grant Two Bulls,
except pages 57, 116, and 173 by Carole Drong
Maps created by Equator Graphics © The Globe Pequot Press
Spot photography throughout © Glen Allison/Photodisc

ISSN 1540-4382
ISBN 0-7627-3016-1

Manufactured in the United States of America
Fifth Edition/First Printing

I have traveled along many of the roads in this book geographically and spiritually with family and friends. I dedicate this book to them, especially to my father and mother, for always believing.

WESTERN
NORTH DAKOTA
Bismarck ★

Missouri R.

EASTERN
NORTH DAKOTA

Fargo ■

WESTERN
SOUTH DAKOTA
■ Rapid City

ALONG
THE
MISSOURI
RIVER
Pierre ★

NORTHEASTERN
SOUTH DAKOTA
Watertown ■

SOUTHEASTERN
SOUTH DAKOTA
Sioux Falls ■

Missouri R.

Contents

Acknowledgments

Special thanks to South Dakota Tourism, North Dakota Tourism, Kimberley Johnson and Norma McMacken for their assistance, and all the chambers of commerce that so graciously accommodated my requests.

Introduction

As a fourth-grader at Horace Mann Elementary School in Rapid City, South Dakota, I was certain Mount Rushmore National Memorial was the bedrock of the nation and perhaps of all civilization. George, Abe, Teddy, and Tom still ruled America. The flags from all fifty states were—and are still—flown at the base of the monument, making a second shrine, or at least a fluttering canopy, of democracy. Whenever family or friends visited, we took a trip to Mount Rushmore. I was beguiled each time.

In my small world, everything seemed big in North Dakota and South Dakota—the homelands of my family for several generations. In fact, a small town in North Dakota's Slope County (population 907, I am told) is named DeSart, after my maternal grandfather's family. I feel I live and breathe a rural story worthy of Garrison Keillor's *Prairie Home Companion*.

I tell my friends I am an "Ota" girl and now an "Ota" writer. I am able to relive some of my childhood memories when friends visit the Dakotas for the first time. A few years ago, I took a good friend, a photographer from big, ultra-hip Los Angeles, to Mount Rushmore, and he was instantly enchanted. I loved his first sense of the plains, the Black Hills National Forest, and the Badlands.

I mentioned this to my mother. "Ah, yes, the Dakotas have cast their spell," she said knowingly.

For newcomers and dyed-in-the-wool Dakotans like me, the mysteries of the land—as well as the earnestness of the people—beckon time and time again. Corn, cowboys, and cattle are the obvious calling cards of North Dakota and South Dakota, but the states cast a spell in roundabout ways too. The sweet, singsong accent of the Dakota people. The ease of downtown parking. The cozy cafes. The small-town parades and rodeos that liberally fill summer calendars. The powwows' strong rhythm. And the stunning sense of history chiseled into Mount Rushmore—and nailed into the very foundation of the Maltese Cross cabin in North Dakota's Theodore Roosevelt National Park.

ruraldistinctions

North Dakota has 642,200 people, while South Dakota boasts a population of 754,844. To put that in perspective, consider the city of Los Angeles, which has a population of 3.6 million—and that's metro only. New York City has more than 7.5 million residents.

The Dakotas offer a smidgen of everything that makes up the glorious United States: natural beauty, arts, culture, outdoor recreation, shopping (from upscale department stores to the thrift shops bulging with Americana), the Native Americans, and the ethnic charm of the Germans in South Dakota or the Russians in North Dakota.

Once in the Dakotas, it's nearly impossible to shake that Heartland spirit. A close friend of mine from Pennsylvania, who has spent part of his military career in South Dakota, was so besotted with the state that he later purchased land near Deadwood, South Dakota. No matter where Uncle Sam sends him, he knows the safeness and beauty of America in that small plot of land.

ruraldistinctions

Kuchen is the official state dessert of South Dakota.

Dakota is in my blood, too. I never really liked to fish, but when my siblings and I went out with Grandpa DeSart on the Missouri River it was always magical, starting with the ritual stop at the bait and bottle shop. Grandpa would buy Nesbitt's orange soda for me, my sister, and two brothers. At the river, we would open Grandpa's tackle box and marvel at the wooden lures, their colors faded from countless hours in the chocolate waters of the Mighty Mo.

When we lost interest in fishing, we would scour the banks of the Missouri River, collecting pieces of driftwood. We etched our names into the driftwood with a wood-burning kit and threaded the pieces together with rope. We proudly hung our primitive folk art on the front door.

As an adult, I still have many attractions and activities to check out. I look forward to testing my luck at the nickel slot machines in Deadwood with my ninety-six-year-old Grandma Mac. Recent reports indicate she is still on a winning streak—$150 one evening. I hike the peaceful hills that surround our family cabin near Custer, South Dakota. I find simple pleasure in taking a Sunday drive to see the fall colors in Spearfish Canyon.

North Dakota covers 69,299 square miles, while South Dakota weighs in as the bigger twin with 75,956 square miles. Sometimes I think if I dared to travel a Dakota country road long enough—an unfailingly straight and simple road—I could touch a sunset. Geographically, both North Dakota and South Dakota are generously endowed with pristine lakes, clay-streaked buttes, thick forests, blue-tinged prairies, and, of course, the mighty Missouri River. The Mighty Mo splits both states into East River and West River, with the flatlands of East River coveted for their agriculture, and the hills and forests of the West River praised for their beauty and frontier inspiration.

Dakota weather can be unforgivingly cold in the winter, especially in North Dakota, with windchill factors that send the effects of the thermometer plummeting. The wise traveler, always mindful that long stretches of road in these states can be quite desolate, will pack lots of warm clothes and have the car serviced and stocked with provisions. My mother always made sure we had M&Ms packed in an old coffee can and placed in the trunk of our car, "for quick energy," she explained, if the car were to break down.

Agriculture is a mainstay of the economies in North Dakota and South Dakota, but there are other avenues of economic strength as the states build on tourism, gaming, and other resources.

In North Dakota, the discovery of oil in 1957 heightened natural resource development. The oil crisis of the 1970s spurred increased exploring and development, as well as the mining of the state's immense lignite reserves. Meanwhile, the Northern Hemisphere's largest underground gold mine is found in the Black Hills of South Dakota.

History binds North Dakota and South Dakota. Both were part of the Dakota Territory, which was organized on March 2, 1861. Both became states on November 2, 1889. The lands that explorers Lewis and Clark so dauntlessly traveled are today part of not only the Great Plains but also the Midwest and the West. The settlers' stories are assuredly familiar, especially in my own Norwegian-Irish-French family, but Native American voices also are clearly heard. Indeed, Dakota means "friend" or "ally" in Sioux.

As you might expect, Dakotans are fiercely independent, hard-working people. The Midwest work ethic is as real and sturdy as the sunflowers that stretch toward the summer sky. Immigrant groups of Germans, Scandinavians, and Czechs flocked to South Dakota, where these folks traveled to find a piece of land to call their own. In North Dakota, settlers, the biggest group of which was Norwegian, were lured by the promise of fertile land.

Native American people, too, have endured displacement, turmoil, and change. Yet today the tribal culture here still resonates in such events as the spectacular powwows, and in the exquisite beadwork, quillwork, and star quilts of Native American artists.

Essentially, the Dakotas are a seamless terrain, and maybe that is why visitors sometimes have a hard time telling them apart. But the Dakotas are hardly carbon copies of one another.

North Dakota, for instance, borders two Canadian provinces: Saskatchewan and Manitoba. The International Peace Garden on the North Dakota/Canadian border recognizes the friendship of the United States and Canada in a most becoming way.

Long before the Four Faces were carved in South Dakota, the lure of gold in the Black Hills enticed fortune seekers, and lively frontier towns were established with equally colorful inhabitants. Visitors today can walk in the footsteps of characters such as Calamity Jane and Wild Bill Hickok for an instant trip back into the Old West.

Appreciating the Dakotas is a state of mind, especially when crossing the broad, clean landscape of the West. This is a place to unfold the mind. Driving across the Dakota prairies encourages serious thinking time and, if you're not alone, meaningful conversation.

The Dakota spell begins with the down-to-earth quality of these two states. And it never ends.

Northeastern South Dakota

By an incredible accident of nature, the northeastern area of South Dakota, also known as the Glacial Lakes Region, features prime boating and recreational areas, with sixteen state parks and two national wildlife refuges. Serendipity appeared in the form of glaciers some 20,000 years ago, and more than 120 lakes and miles of prairies were left when the glaciers retreated. This area is referred to as the Young Drift Plains by geologists, but residents simply call it the Lakes Region. For the most part the area is swampy plain, dotted with lakes and marshes. The notable exception is the wide, flat valley of the James River. Interstate 29, which runs north-south, and U.S. Highway 12, which runs east-west, help keep travel and commerce flowing from Sioux Falls, in the southeastern corner of the state, to Rapid City, in the west.

Fertile Valley

We'll begin on U.S. Highway 12 in the northwest corner of the Fertile Valley region. Aberdeen lies in the fertile valley of the James River. The area was first settled by the Arikara Indians, who introduced farming to the region. Others were to follow

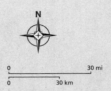

N

0   30 mi

0   30 km

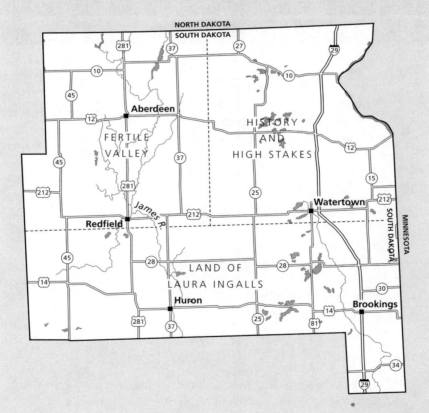

by train and wagon and on foot. Settlers came to forge new lives from eastern states, the Scandinavian countries, Germany, Russia, and the British Isles.

Established in 1881 near the Milwaukee Railroad, the town was named for Aberdeen, Scotland, the hometown of Alexander Mitchell, president of the railroad. Aberdeen soon became known as the Hub City in recognition of the network of rail lines that converged there. Culture flourishes today in this community of more than 24,658 people. Northern State University, established in 1901, and Presentation College, the state's newest four-year college, bring history, higher learning, and the arts to the region.

The Highlands Historical District is located on Main Street between Twelfth and Fifteenth Avenues North. Seventeen homes were built here between 1907 and 1969. The district earned the lofty title of Highlands because it rose 3 feet higher than the commercial sector, which was located in a slough. When the first houses were built, only prairie grass covered the area, so young trees were brought up from along the James River and transplanted here to line the sedate streets. Many architectural styles have melded in the district over the years, and the result is a fascinating study in both modern and classical structures. Compare the stately 1909 Georgian Revival home at 1206 North Main Street with the sturdy yet elegant lines of the 1929 Neocolonial brick residence at 1404 North Main Street. Although these are still private homes, some are open for tours. Call the chamber of commerce at (605) 225–2860 for more information.

For a refreshing change of pace, stop by the ***Red Rooster Coffee House*** at 202 South Main Street. In addition to the java fare, the coffeehouse offers croissant sandwiches, soup, bagels, hummus sandwiches, nachos, and baked goods. Here, you can learn the fundamentals of espresso drinks. For instance,

NORTHEASTERN SOUTH DAKOTA'S TOP HITS

Bramble Park Zoo	Mellette House
Dacotah Prairie Museum	Moody County Museum and Complex
Easton's Castle	Redlin Art Center
Gladys Pyle Historic Home	South Dakota State Fair
The Highlands Historical District	Storybook Land
Laura Ingalls Wilder Pageant	Wauneta's Gardens

did you know cappuccino is a shot of espresso with equal parts steamed milk and foamed milk? (I didn't.) In true coffeehouse fashion, Red Rooster also features live performances. For more information, call (605) 225–6603.

When you reach the dead end of Second Avenue Northwest, you have arrived at an isolated, strangely ominous home called **Easton's Castle.** You can tour the home by making an appointment thirty days in advance (605–225–2045) and inspect the Jacobean style of architecture that was popular in England in the 1830s. Multiple windows, peaked roofs, and gables distinguish this style. Samples of the home's French-made wallpaper, which remains intact, have been documented in the Cooper Hewitt Museum of Design of the Smithsonian Institution.

In March 1973, Easton's Castle was added to the National Register of Historic Places. The current owners, Sam and Jacintha Holman, adapted the home and barn as a veterinary clinic in 1967. Their loving care is evident throughout the castle. Jacintha recalls the home's restoration in a brochure: "Much has been written about the joys and tribulations of owning an old house. Nothing can compare to the gradual intrusion of a thriving, twenty-four-hour service business into a twenty-room house with the comings and goings of five hippie children and friends during the 1970s. From the road to the top of the chimneys and barn cupola, the rehabilitation turned into constant maintenance and repair. Eventually, the aura and wonder of the place took over."

trivia

The annual Oz Festival during the summer celebrates L. Frank Baum's writings and the Oz heritage. Learn the history of the story through a weeklong series of events, including an arts fair and theatrical presentations of Baum's writings. For more information call (605) 626–3310.

The longest residents of the home were the C. F. Easton family, who bought the property in 1889. Matilda Gage, a secretary in Mr. Easton's banking business, was a frequent visitor, and she recorded her memories of the castle. Matilda was the inspiration behind the character of Dorothy in the *Wizard of Oz* stories, which were penned by her uncle, L. Frank Baum (there were fourteen Oz books). When Matilda died in 1986 at the age of 99, she left her Baum memorabilia to the local **Alexander Mitchell Library** in Aberdeen.

"Basically, it's a collection of some of the Baum books—some are autographed and some are reprints," library director Dave Rave said. "We have some pictures and scrapbooks that Matilda had collected through the years and some of the letters that Baum had written to Matilda and her family. There are lots of odds and ends, but the big item that we have is the original copy of the newspaper Baum published, *The Aberdeen Saturday Pioneer.*" Since the paper is in a fragile state, library patrons can only read it on microfilm. T. Clarkson

Gage, Matilda's father, also assembled a scrapbook of life in early Aberdeen, and it, too, can be viewed on microfilm. If you're interested in visiting the Baum collection, contact the library in advance.

The library was founded by Andrew Carnegie, a boyhood friend of railroad president Alexander Mitchell. It's located at 519 South Kline Street and is open from 9:00 A.M. to 8:45 P.M. Monday through Thursday, 9:00 A.M. to 5:45 P.M. Friday, and 1:00 to 4:45 P.M. on Saturday. Call (605) 626–7097 for more information.

The Land of Oz extends beyond the recollections of Matilda in Aberdeen. L. Frank Baum was enamored with the Wild West and moved here from New York in 1888. He opened a variety store called Baum's Bazaar that fall, but he was dismally lacking in business acumen. After closing the store, he purchased the town newspaper, renamed it *The Aberdeen Saturday Pioneer,* and proved to be a top-notch journalist. Baum's stories were witty, satirical, and sometimes controversial, but the town's happenings were always reported with great passion. Scholars suggest that the populist prairie might have inspired the Land of Oz, a fairyland where the common man and woman become hero and heroine.

Those too young to care about literary analysis can join in the Oz fun at **Storybook Land,** located one mile north of Aberdeen on Highway 281. The park features characters from *The Wizard of Oz.* Other larger-than-life stories re-created here are "Jack and Jill Went Up the Hill," "Cinderella," "Jack and the Beanstalk," and "Humpty Dumpty."

The entrance to the park features Dorothy's farmstead, including her house, a petting zoo with farm animals, a barn and silo, a windmill, an antique farm tractor, and a pony ride concession. There's even Munchkin Land (a small cornfield that is planted and harvested annually), the Yellow Brick Road, and other beloved sites from the Oz books and from the movie. Storybook Land is free; open April 15 through October 30, from 10:00 A.M. to 9:00 P.M. daily. Call the park at (605) 626–7015.

ROBIN'S FAVORITES

Dakota Sioux Casino,
Watertown, (605) 882–2051

Ingalls Homestead,
De Smet, (800) 776–3594

Easton's Castle,
Aberdeen, (605) 225–2045

Pickler Mansion,
Faulkton, (605) 598–4285

Gladys Pyle Historic Home,
Huron, (605) 352–2528

Just outside the gates of Storybook Land you'll find **Wylie Park.** With more than 200 acres of grassland, the park features a spectacular variety of wildlife. You can camp, swim, picnic, and golf. The park is open year-round and is free.

The park's man-made lake, with more than 1,000 feet of shoreline, features an unsupervised swimming area. The lake is stocked with fish each year, and paddleboats and canoe rentals are available.

The park's pavilion—built in 1912—was once the stage for Lawrence Welk. The pavilion was added to the National Register of Historic Places in 1978.

Wylie Park Campground offers paved roads and camp pads, ninety-three sites, and modern rest rooms and shower facilities. For reservations, call (605) 626–7015 or (888) 326–9693.

Aberdeen's newest theme park is the **Land of Oz,** a ten-acre park northwest of Storybook Land in Wylie Park. It expands on the *Wizard of Oz* themes already so lovingly and gaily presented in Storybook Land. Open 8:00 A.M. to 10:00 P.M. April 15 through September 1. Admission is free. For more information log on to www.aberdeencvb.com/sbl.htm.

If you want to see more of the prairie life that so enthralled Baum, stop by the **Dacotah Prairie Museum.** The building, located at 21 South Main Street in Aberdeen, is a designated landmark on the National Register of Historic Places. Banker Henry Maple built this impressive three-and-a-half-story edifice, completed in 1889, in the popular Romanesque style. Inside are exhibits on the prairie, early settlers, the railroad, and native tribes. The Hatterscheidt Wildlife Gallery displays more than fifty-five mounted specimens from North America, Africa, and India. On the second floor the Lamont Gallery features the work of local and regional artists. About six art shows are planned for each year. Educational opportunities include the History-in-a-Trunk program, which takes a hands-on approach to learning: Grade-schoolers can spend an afternoon reliving the past by dipping candles, churning butter, or laundering with a washboard and lye soap. Museum hours are 9:00 A.M. to 5:00 P.M. Tuesday through Friday and 1:00 to 4:00 P.M. Saturday and Sunday. Tours and special openings are available by appointment. Call the museum at (605) 626–7117. The Web site is www.brown.sd.us/museum. Admission is free. Donations are appreciated.

While you're on South Main Street, don't forget gifts from the Heartland for friends and family. **Baskets Unlimited** (800–809–8595) packs an incredible gift basket filled with wholesome South Dakota products such as smoked pheasant, honey, cheeses, buffalo and beef sausage, ice cream toppings, taffy, mustard, sunflower seeds, and Native American teas. Other products made in South Dakota include cooking supplies, candles, playing cards, and stationery.

Regional cuisine is at **Minerva's** (yes, it's affiliated with the much-storied original Minerva's in downtown Sioux Falls) in the Best Western Ramkota Hotel

(605–226–2988). Just like its sister restaurants, Minerva's whets the discerning appetite with the finest aged beef, fresh seafood, pastas, fancifully dressed salads, and more. In fact, *USA Today* named the bison ribeye steak as one of the 50 Great Plates of America. I am partial to the 9-inch, handcrafted pizzas. The barbecue chicken pizza (barbecued chicken breast, caramelized onions, cilantro, smoked cheddar, and mozzarella) and the white garlic shrimp pizza (Gulf shrimp with garlic cream sauce, scallions, Roma tomatoes, and basil—and crowned with Parmesan and mozzarella cheeses) are at the top of my list. The restaurant is open for breakfast from 6:30 to 10:30 A.M. Monday through Saturday and 7:00 to 9:00 A.M. Sunday. The Sunday breakfast buffet is served from 9:00 A.M. to noon. Lunch is served from 1:00 to 4:30 P.M. daily; dinner is served 4:30 to 10:00 P.M. daily, except Sunday, when the restaurant closes at 9:00 P.M. Located at 1400 Eighth Avenue Northwest.

Before leaving Aberdeen, check out the **Centennial Village,** located at the Brown County Fairgrounds, near the intersection of Twenty-fourth Avenue Northwest and Brown County 10. The village features nineteenth-century structures, including a post office, a cream-buying station, a Methodist church, a millinery shop, and a funeral parlor. Centennial Village is open from 1:00 to 4:00 P.M. on Sunday. Call (605) 225–2414. Admission is free.

Just west of Aberdeen on US Highway 12 is the cozy burg of Ipswich, which was settled in 1885. One of the more splendid relics of Ipswich's past is the First Baptist Church, which boasts some of the finest fieldstone architecture in the state. The community library, a charming Hansel-and-Gretel-like stone structure, also stands as a testament to the benefits of tender loving care. Outside the library is the mysterious Prayer Rock, a giant boulder with handprints supposedly carved by a Native American medicine man.

The home of **J. W. Parmley,** one of the early movers and shakers in Ipswich, is open to the public. It features family and town memorabilia, as well

TOP ANNUAL EVENTS

Arts in the Park,
Aberdeen, June, (605) 626–3310

Laura Ingalls Wilder Pageant,
De Smet, last weekend in June and
first two weekends in July,
(605) 692–2108

Oz Festival,
Aberdeen, August, (605) 225–2414

Parade of Lights,
Huron, the day after Thanksgiving

South Dakota State Fair,
one week starting Labor Day weekend,
(605) 353–7340,
www.sdstatefair.com

as pioneer and military displays. The two stone fireplaces in the home were constructed from an eccentric array of rocks, shells, and minerals collected during Parmley family travels. An iron fence post, allegedly from a fence around Sitting Bull's grave when his remains were buried at Fort Yates, forms part of one fireplace. Through the efforts of area native Phyllis Herrick, the home became a museum. Herrick's exhaustive research filled in the town's history with tidbits about the benevolent Parmley. Subsequently, J. W. Parmley's descendants took interest in the project and have supported her efforts to this day.

"I was born and raised here and so was Mr. Parmley, and I remember him when I was in high school," Phyllis said. At the time US 12 was called the Yellowstone Trail. Parmley was known as the father of the Yellowstone Trail. Phyllis and her family lived in Minnesota for twenty-five years, and when she returned, she sadly found the home to be empty. "I just thought it should be preserved. So four other people and I purchased it, and we got the consensus of the town," she said. Subsequently the town's one-room museum, which had been located in the basement of the library, was moved to the Parmley home.

"Parmley was a great rock collector, and he collected anything of interest to put in the two fireplaces. He traveled quite a bit, so he was always bringing things home," Phyllis said, and hence the fireplace is laden with quirky pieces such as seashells and screws. Parmley also had a practical mind, and his home was made of concrete—even the floors and the bathtubs. His previous residence had been destroyed in a fire, and most likely Parmley was determined not to be burned twice, so to speak.

For more information call (605) 426–6949. The home is closed from Labor Day to June 1, but doors are open Wednesday, Friday, and Sunday in the summer from 2:00 to 5:00 P.M.

After US 12 was finished (it extends from Plymouth Rock, Massachusetts, to Puget Sound in Seattle), enthusiastic Ipswich folks created a memorial stone arch over their portion of the Yellowstone Trail. When the highway was widened in 1973, the state insisted that the arch be moved. Moving the arch was no small feat since each pillar weighs more than one hundred tons, so the state legislature appropriated money to make sure it wasn't homeless for too long. It now stands in the city park.

Northeast of Aberdeen, the ***Sand Lake National Wildlife Refuge*** boasts 21,451 acres of wildlife and waterfowl in grasslands, forest, lake, and marsh. The area surrounding the refuge was once a vast, rolling grassland interrupted only by the slow-moving James River. Settlers arrived in 1887 and brought sweeping changes to the landscape. Farming and grazing depleted essential wildlife habitat, causing waterfowl to dwindle to alarmingly low numbers by the 1930s.

Congress established Sand Lake in 1935 to preserve critical habitat for nesting and migrating waterfowl. Today, millions of ducks, geese, and other wildlife make Sand Lake their home. In fact, 266 species of birds have been recorded at the refuge since 1935, including white pelicans, snow geese, and Western grebes.

Most people choose to drive through the refuge. A nicely illustrated, self-guided auto-tour guide is available. Along the 15-mile route there are twelve numbered stations, which correspond to symbols and text in the brochure. Station Two, for instance, affords an overlook where two important duck-nesting habitats can be seen. Station Eight is perfect for bird watchers. Great horned owls occasionally roost here, and mallards, pintails, and the smaller blue-winged and green-winged teal also can be seen.

The refuge was designated a Wetland of International Importance under the guidelines developed by the Convention on Wetlands of International Importance. This makes Sand Lake the only such wetland in the Upper Great Plains, and one of only sixteen in the United States.

To reach the refuge from Aberdeen, take US 12 to County Road 16 (Bath Corner, 7 miles east of Aberdeen). Drive 20 miles north, through Columbia, to the refuge entrance. You can visit the refuge seven days a week, from daylight to dark, between early April and late September.

For more information, call (605) 885–6320 or write to Refuge Manager, Sand Lake National Wildlife Refuge, Columbia, SD 57433.

Only an hour's drive from Aberdeen (take State Highway 45 south from Ipswich, then go south on U.S. Highway 212) is the **_Pickler Mansion_** in Faulkton, a friendly town of 810 people. John A. Pickler served four terms as South Dakota's first U.S. representative-at-large, and his wife, Alice W. Alt Pickler, campaigned for the suffrage cause. Fellow suffragette Susan B. Anthony was one of the more famous guests in the home, and some of her original letters found here are on display.

The home, a twenty-room Victorian house on the prairie, is complete with a secret room and a 2,550-book library that features Civil War and congressional sections. Called the Pink Castle (its distinct pink color was chosen by pioneer artist Charles T. Greener in 1894), the mansion is open daily from Memorial Day through

countytrivia

Watertown is located in Codington County, which was named for a Congregational minister and legislator, G. S. D. Codington. The county was formed in 1877, and Watertown was chosen as the county seat in 1878. Interestingly, Watertown is fed by Mineral Spring, which supplies highly mineralized water. It's no surprise that the water's bitter taste quickly repels any geese or ducks lighting on it.

let'splayball

If you continue east on US 12, you'll find the birthplace of American Legion baseball in Milbank, home to 3,879 people on the South Dakota–Minnesota border. American Legion baseball began at a 1925 convention of that organization in Milbank. A historical marker commemorating the birth of American Legion baseball is located near the community baseball field. Former American Legion players include Yogi Berra, Johnny Bench, Jim Palmer, Frank Robinson, Greg Gagne, and Jack Morris.

Labor Day from 1:00 to 4:00 P.M. and at other times by appointment. Call (605) 598–4285 for a guide. Admission is $5.25 for adults and $2.60 for children ten and under.

While you're at the Pickler Mansion, also visit the **Maloney Schoolhouse Museum** (605–598–4285), located 6 blocks south of US 212 and Ninth South Avenue, then turn right into the driveway. This completely restored schoolhouse shows how the three Rs were taught to all grades within one room, certainly unique by today's educational standards but quite common in early plains life. Open by appointment. Admission is free.

Two blocks north of US 212 at 1202 Elm Street is **Wauneta's Gardens,** where master gardener Wauneta Holdren has lovingly tended her plants on the hillside banks of Nixon Creek for the past twenty-nine years. Although this is a private two-and-one-half-acre terraced flower garden, Wauneta kindly shares her botanical wonders and her wealth of knowledge with more than 2,000 visitors each year during the summer months. Be one of the privileged and see more than 250 varieties of iris and 70 to 80 varieties of daylily and peony, as well as poppies, petunias, and other flowers. "My little garden just kept growing," recalled Wauneta. Newspaper stories about her green thumb have appeared in the *Faulkton Record* and, most recently, in the *Aberdeen News.* For years people have been eager to visit Wauneta and her fabled gardens. "My picture just ran in the newspaper last Sunday, and the next day a girl visited my garden, and she had seen my photo. She said, 'You're so famous, you should go to California and run for governor.'" (The young lady was referring to Governor Gray Davis's recall election, which ended in a win for Arnold Schwarzenegger in fall 2003.) "I've done all the work by myself. The Lord willing, I will keep it open as long as I can," Wauneta said. "I just enjoy having people come in." She recently introduced more butterflies into the gardens by growing special plants—including milkweed—that attract the winged beauties. "I'm trying to educate people on the simplicity and the joy of having a garden," Wauneta said. "I have never considered it work." Wauneta told me that the gardens have become so popular that many people are coming in to have their wedding, graduation, or other special occasion photographs taken. "It's not really set up for that, but they always find a spot they like." Visitors are asked to contribute a donation. Reservations are suggested for groups. Call (605) 598–6208.

Faulkton is called the Carousel City because it is home to the state's only electrically operated permanent 1925 Parker carousel. The carousel features nineteen original aluminum-cast horses. Located on Ninth Avenue South, the **Happy Times Carousel** can be enjoyed for free Wednesday evenings and Saturday and Sunday afternoons and evenings during the summer season. Call (605) 598-4285 for hours of operation.

History and High Stakes

The town of Webster, 53 miles east of Aberdeen on US 12, is home to an outlet store that carries home fashions guaranteed to fluff up any interior. Dakotah pillows, comforters, duvets, throws, and table linens are carried in fine department stores nationwide, and their quality and design make **Dakotah Inc.** (605–345–4646) equal to a Ralph Lauren Polo store on the prairie. With the help of VISTA volunteers, the company was founded in 1971 as a cooperative in an effort to revitalize the economically depressed northeast region of the state. People were leaving the state and small family farms, but an incredible wealth of talent remained. Today Dakotah has approximately 700 people working in six very small towns in the region. The outlet store is open from 8:30 A.M. to 4:00 P.M. Monday through Friday.

From Webster take US 12 east to I–29 and go south until you reach the crossroads of I–29 and US 212. It is here that you will find Watertown. Known as the Lake City, Watertown quite naturally lives up to its name; the town is situated along the Big Sioux River and is bordered by Lake Kampeska and Lake

The Legend of Sam Brown

The Dakotas are rich with legends great and small. One such hero is Sam Brown, probably not a household name but a tremendous equalizer in the annals of prairie history nonetheless. In 1866 Sam was chief scout for Fort Wadsworth, now known as Fort Sisseton. He was told of an approaching Sioux Indian war party, and Sam sent a warning message to a fort farther north. Sam mounted his horse and set off to scout a camp 60 miles west. When he arrived, he discovered that the war party was simply several Indians delivering word of a new peace treaty. Sam knew that in order to prevent bloodshed, he must intercept his warning. Struggling through the freezing rain and snow of a ruthless spring blizzard, he managed to reach the fort by morning. But as he slipped from his horse, exhausted and half frozen, he was unable to stand. Sam Brown's heroic 150-mile ride cost him the use of his legs. He never walked again.

Pelican. Originally called Kampeska, the settlement owed its boom to the railroads. The primary industry here is agriculture, which is diversified in small grains, row crops, and livestock. Its enviable location near the crossroads of US 212 and I–29 makes it an important trade center not only for northeast South Dakota but also for west-central Minnesota. Watertown is located 180 miles west of Minneapolis, 100 miles north of Sioux Falls, and 350 miles from Rapid City.

Pioneer and local history through World War II and Native American artifacts are the focal points at the ***Codington County Heritage Museum*** (formerly the Kampeska Heritage Museum) (605–886–7335). Located at 27 First Avenue Southeast, the museum is open afternoons Monday through Saturday. The exhibits change periodically and focus on the homestead era in Codington County. War memorabilia, exhibits on local culture, and Indian beadwork from the early reservation period are among the displays. Admission is free.

If you meander into the residential area on the north side of town, you'll find more history at the ***Mellette House*** (421 Fifth Avenue NW). South Dakota's first governor, Arthur C. Mellette, was the model of honesty and conscience—qualities one almost always dreams of, yet rarely expects, in today's politicians. Mellette was appointed governor of the Dakota Territory by President Benjamin Harrison and later was elected governor of the new state of South Dakota. A drought that lasted well into the 1890s plagued his term, but Mellette used his own personal resources to alleviate the dire circumstances in his state.

Where Everyone Knows Your Name

If your family roots run deep in a rural state like North Dakota or South Dakota, chances are you will bump into people who know your mom, or your grandpa, or your cousin's brother-in-law . . . I think of this fondly when I remember my Uncle Joe, who once coached wrestling and football in Huron and Watertown. He later taught high school in Sioux Falls. As a student at the University of South Dakota, I was surrounded by many of his former students. With a name like McMacken, the connection was easily made.

Uncle Joe was a fine testament to the profession of teaching. He was also an active participant in the Fellowship of Christian Athletes and his church. I would visit him and his family—Aunt Connie Jean, Jodie, and Jennifer—and we would go running. He always emphasized time and not distance, much to my relief. I sometimes felt I could run a marathon alongside Uncle Joe, for his faith and tenacity were quietly infectious.

Our families always had a great time together. I still marvel at the bond between Uncle Joe, the youngest son, and my father, the oldest son. It was a rare, strong, and unspoken brotherhood that you don't often find in today's emotionally or at least geographically fragmented families. I am confident that growing up in the Dakotas nurtured that spirit.

OTHER ATTRACTIONS WORTH SEEING
IN NORTHEASTERN SOUTH DAKOTA

Jerauld County Pioneer Museum,
Wessington Springs

State Agricultural Heritage Museum,
Brookings

Mina State Recreation Area,
Aberdeen

State Fair Speedway,
Huron

The Mellette House, an 1883 Italianate villa, was built on the so-called Mellette Hill. The home was the venue for many extravagant receptions and social gatherings for which guest lists glittered with names of dignitaries, close friends of Mellette, and political associates. When Mellette's close friend W. W. Taylor defaulted on a large amount as state treasurer, Mellette suffered a reversal of fortune as well. As one of the bondsmen, Mellette turned over all of his real estate and other assets, including his own home, to the state as reimbursement. In the process, Mellette went bankrupt. After leaving office, Mellette successfully practiced law until 1895, when he and his family moved to Pittsburg, Kansas. He died one year later. Although the state returned the Watertown home to Mellette's widow, the family never occupied the home again. Over the years the site of once-glamorous galas slowly decayed into a nondescript red brick house. Fortunately, the Mellette Association intervened and restored the home to the luxurious state it had known with the Mellette family. The home is open May through September, Tuesday through Sunday from 1:00 to 5:00 P.M. Call (605) 886–4730. No admission, but donations are welcome.

Twenty-four massive granite columns, visible for miles, lure the visitor to the *Redlin Art Center* at 1200 Thirty-third Street SE. Built by Watertown artist and native Terry Redlin, the center houses 120 of Redlin's original paintings. His works capture the charm of rural life that flourishes just outside the center's door. A high-tech planetarium offers educational entertainment for the entire family. The art center is open 8:00 A.M. to 5:00 P.M. Monday through Friday, 10:00 A.M. to 4:00 P.M. Saturday, and noon to 4:00 P.M. Sunday. Admission is free. The Web site is www.redlinart.com. Call (605) 882–3877 for information.

On State Highway 20 in northwest Watertown, the *Bramble Park Zoo* brings you face to face with more than 400 mammals, reptiles, and birds representing more than one hundred varieties from around the world as well as those native to the Great Plains. See an exotic jaguar or watch the beauty of a pheasant as it struts its stuff in one of the largest waterfowl and pheasant collections in the United States. Education is a primary goal at Bramble Park Zoo, and informational signs, tours, and demonstrations realize that goal. The zoo

Powwow Etiquette

Powwows are a wonderful chance for non–Native Americans to learn about the culture, and most powwows are open to the public. They can last anywhere from a few hours to several days and frequently include craft displays, rodeos, ethnic foods, and cultural exhibits.

To be a courteous guest at a powwow, here are a few tips:

- It's generally acceptable to take photos or videos, but check beforehand.

- Ask permission before taking someone's photo outside of the dance circle.

- Stand at the "Grand Entry" to pay respect to the dancers. Remain standing for the Great Sioux Nation's national anthem.

- The dance area is considered sacred; don't enter it unless invited.

- Many powwows lack seating, so bring along a lawn chair or blanket and make yourself comfortable.

provides for and breeds threatened and endangered species. See deer, arctic foxes, and badgers roam outside. The zoo is open year-round, weather permitting, with hours from 9:00 A.M. to 8:00 P.M. and winter hours from 10:00 A.M. to 4:00 P.M. Admission is charged. Call (605) 882–6269 or visit the Web site at www.brambleparkzoo.com for fees and other information.

The magnificent farming operations of the **Wolf Creek Hutterite Colony,** just forty-five minutes southwest of Sioux Falls, is worth a visit. Here you can see community members make perfectly pleated skirts or fashion rugs. Explore the schoolhouse and communal kitchen, and experience the ways of these gentle people, whose ingenuity allows them to live in a self-sustaining community. Tours can be arranged through Freeman Development Corp. Call Sharon Schamber at (605) 925–4444. There is a fee.

Fifty-seven miles north of Watertown on I–90, **Fort Sisseton State Park** is the home of the annual Fort Sisseton Festival the first weekend in June, as well as Frontier Christmas in June. Another attraction (only 6 miles on Sioux Valley Road) is **Dakota Sioux Casino** (800–658–4717), featuring blackjack with the highest bets in the state ($100.00 maximum, $3.00 minimum). Or take a chance on one of more than 220 reel-slot machines. The casino, with restaurant, lounge, and live entertainment, is owned and operated by the Sisseton–Wahpeton Sioux tribe. The community of Sisseton is located just off I–29 on Highway 10.

The **Joseph N. Nicollet Tower and Interpretive Center** is located 3.5 miles west of Sisseton at the intersection of I–29 and Highway 10. It is dedicated to the French mapmaker who could very well be a sort of real-life

Lieutenant Dunbar from the Academy Award–winning movie *Dances with Wolves*. (The Kevin Costner movie, by the way, was filmed in South Dakota.) Nicollet spent 1838 and 1839 creating the first accurate map of the vast area between the Mississippi and the Missouri Rivers. He was trained as an astronomer in Paris, and he took highly accurate notes in his journals that recorded more than his precise mathematical calculations. Like those of the fictional Dunbar, Nicollet's journals also illuminated a love for the prairies and respect and understanding of native people. He wrote in 1839 of the Coteau des Prairies: "May I not be permitted to introduce a few reflections of the prairies? . . . Their sight never wearies . . . to ascend one of its undulations, moving from wave to wave over alternate swells and depressions; and finally to reach the vast interminable low prairie, that extends itself in front, be it for hours, days or weeks, one never tires; pleasurable and exhilarating sensations are all the time felt. . . . I pity the man whose soul could remain unmoved under such a scene of excitement."

Today, the 75-foot observation tower with three floors affords a breathtaking view of the great valley carved by glaciers some 40,000 years ago.

The "mother map" of the Midwest is displayed at the foot of the tower. Nicollet presented the map to the United States Senate in 1841. The central feature is the Coteau des Prairies, which, at an elevation of more than 2,000 feet, is the highest point between Winnipeg, Manitoba, Canada, and the Gulf of Mexico and the Appalachians and the Black Hills. Original artwork by nationally recog-

Winter Driving Tips in the Dakotas

- Listen to the forecast before departing and postpone travel if inclement weather is occurring or expected.

- Avoid traveling alone. Inform others of your timetable and primary and alternate routes.

- Keep your gas tank near full to avoid ice in the tank and the fuel lines

- Adjust your speed to the conditions and increase following distances.

- Remember that bridges and overpasses are usually more slippery than other parts of the road.

- Always carry a survival kit in your vehicle. Your kit should be equipped with a can of sand or kitty litter; tire chains; flashlight with extra batteries; candles and matches; an empty coffee can (to be used to burn the candles for heat and to melt snow for water); caps, mittens, boots, and sleeping bag or blanket for everyone; nonperishable foods, such as granola bars or dried fruit; booster cables; battery-operated radio with extra batteries; first-aid kit; and cellular phone with fully charged batteries.

nized wildlife artist John S. Wilson is displayed in the Interpretive Center, as are paintings depicting the Dakota Indian people Nicollet described in his journals. Call (605) 698–7672 for hours. Free admission.

Land of Laura Ingalls

If you take I–29 south from Watertown for 44 miles, you'll reach the state's largest university, South Dakota State University, in Brookings. Its varied components contribute much to the town's economy and culture. Open year-round, the **McCrory Gardens and State Arboretum,** at Sixth Street and Twentieth Avenue, features twenty acres of formal display gardens and forty-five acres of arboretum. Called the prettiest quarter section in the state, the gardens include fourteen formal theme gardens and a rose garden with more than thirty varieties, an herb garden, a children's maze, a historic gas station renovated as a garden cottage, and a memorial to the late Governor George S. Mickelson.

The gardens were named in honor of South Dakota State University Professor S. A. McCrory, who headed the horticulture department from 1947 until his death in 1964. McCrory had envisioned a research garden displaying trees, shrubs, grasses, and flowers that were—or could be—a part of South Dakota's landscape. That vision is still the prime directive for all the work done at the gardens. You can view the lovely gardens during a self-guided tour, available from dawn to dusk daily. Admission is free; call (605) 692–6125 or (800) 699–6125 for more information on the gardens.

The university's **Prairie Repertory Theatre** has a slate full of comedies, musicals, and dramas each summer. Call (605) 688–5621 for more information.

The **South Dakota Art Museum** (Medary Avenue and Harvey Dunn Street, named for a well-known artist in the state) has a stylish new look as well as many added features. The museum, which has graciously served the state for more than thirty years, features permanent galleries, changing exhibitions, lectures,

fishingformore

Walleye dominate the fishing scene in northeastern South Dakota, and most are caught trolling over hard gravel or sand bottoms. Other fish found in the area are smallmouth and largemouth bass, white bass, bullheads, yellow perch, and northern pike. More than 120 glacial lakes dot the northeastern landscape of the state. Anglers who travel to this rolling farm and ranch country will find that the lakes range in size from several acres to more than 16,000 acres. There are fourteen state parks and recreation areas and several municipal and private campgrounds in the region. Resorts can be found at most of the larger lakes, but a few of the glacial lakes remain undeveloped and may be surrounded by private land.

workshops, and guided tours—all with the artist, the teacher, the student, and the public in mind. Harvey Dunn once told his students, "If you ever amount to anything at all, it will be because you are true to that deep desire or ideal, which made you seek artistic expression in pictures."

Dunn's artistic desire earned him national recognition and exhibition space in the South Dakota Art Museum and the Smithsonian Institution in Washington, D.C. Now Dunn's work is also featured on a postage stamp. The Society of Illustrators in New York and the United States Postal Service have paid tribute to Dunn by putting his painting, "Something for Supper," on one of twenty stamps honoring America's greatest illustrators. The pane of stamps, unveiled in 2001, features work by members of the Society of Illustrators Hall of Fame, including Robert Fawcett, Arthur Burdett Frost, Rockwell Kent, Frederic Remington, and Norman Rockwell. "Something for Supper" was completed in 1940. The original piece can be seen at the South Dakota Art Museum. Or, for a sneak preview of the stamp version, check out the Postal Service Web site at www.usps.com. Other artists represented at the gallery include Paul Goble and Oscar Howe. The museum is open from 10:00 A.M. to 5:00 P.M. Monday through Friday, from 10:00 A.M. to 4:00 P.M. Saturday, and from noon to 4:00 P.M. Sunday. For more information, call (605) 688–5423. Free admission.

While you're on campus, stop by the university dairy bar, where you can choose from more than seventy-five ice cream flavors or sample the cheeses and butter. It's open weekdays from 8:00 A.M. to 5:00 P.M., and tours are available.

The ***Royal River Casino*** (800–833–8666; www.royalrivercasino.com), located in Flandreau off I–29, is 30 miles north of Sioux Falls. The casino, owned by the Santee Sioux tribe, has rejuvenated the community of 2,311 residents. The town, situated along the Big Sioux River, was first settled in 1869 by twenty-five Christian Santee Sioux families who bravely gave up their tribal rights—and their surnames—so that they could homestead.

Religious themes recur in Flandreau through several historic churches built in the 1800s. Most notable is the First Presbyterian Church, the oldest continuously operating church in South Dakota.

For a historical perspective on the area, the ***Moody County Museum and Complex*** shows antiques and collectibles from the area's pioneer past. You can visit an authentic one-room schoolhouse, a Milwaukee railroad depot built in 1881, and the Riverbend Meeting House, Flandreau's first framed building, built in 1871. During the third week of July each year, the residents don authentic costumes to perform traditional ceremonies during the ***Santee Sioux Powwow***. The complex is open from 9:00 A.M. to 1:00 P.M. Tuesday and Thursday, 1:00 to 4:00 P.M. Friday, and 2:00 to 5:00 P.M. Saturday and Sunday. Call (605) 997–3191 for more information.

For an overnight stay in Flandreau, try the ***Talk of the Town Bed & Breakfast Inn,*** located at 201 West Pipestone Avenue. Hostess Mary Ann Sorensen serves a gourmet breakfast every morning, featuring homemade breads and muffins. Call (605) 997–5170 for more information.

Yes, Virginia, there really is a Little House on the Prairie, and it's located in the heart of Kingsbury County in De Smet, 30 miles west of Oakwood State Park at the intersection of U.S. Highway 14 and State Highway 25. Fresh-faced little girls in crisp gingham bonnets evoke the stories of the town's most famous writer each summer during the ***Laura Ingalls Wilder Pageant*** (605–692–2108), and the saplings that Pa Ingalls planted so long ago are now mature cottonwoods. Laura moved here as a child in 1879, and the prairie town figured prominently in six of her pioneer adventure books. You can see eighteen sites mentioned in the books, including the house Pa built for his family in 1887 and the railroad surveyor's shanty where the family first lived in De Smet. Scenes from *These Happy Golden Years* are re-created during the outdoor pageant, held the last weekend in June and the first two weekends in July. Tours start at the headquarters and gift shop, located 3 blocks east of the city library. Tour hours are from 9:00 A.M. to 6:00 P.M. daily Memorial Day through Labor Day. There is a small admission charge. Call (605) 854–3383 for more information or visit the Web site at www.liwms.com.

The town was named for Pierre Jean De Smet, a Belgian-born Jesuit priest who traveled up the Missouri ministering to the Sioux Indians. A statue of him graces Washington City Park.

Head west on US 14 and enter another county for more intimations of what

Ingalls' homestead site

Gladys Pyle Historic Home

life on the prairie is really like today. Huron is the county seat of Beadle County, and it wears its distinction well. The town is the administrative center for a handful of federal and state agencies, and town promoters claim Huron is the trade and farm-products processing center for a 10,500-square-mile area. Not surprisingly, Huron is the second largest area in the state for livestock sales and among the top in manufactured products.

Huron also has claim to the first elected female U.S. senator, Gladys Pyle, who served in the Senate during the 1930s. This pioneering feminist's home, the ***Gladys Pyle Historic Home*** (376 Idaho Avenue SW), is open to the public. The 1894 Queen Anne–style building features stained glass, ornately carved golden oak woodwork, and Gladys's original furnishings. The home is open January through March on weekends by appointment and on Monday through Friday afternoons the rest of the year. Call (605) 352–2528 for specific times.

Also in the annals of political and state history is Hubert H. Humphrey, the former senator and vice president of the United States. A mid-1930s atmosphere is quaintly preserved in the ***Hubert H. Humphrey Drugstore,*** which was owned by Humphrey until his death and still is owned by the Humphrey family. The vice president worked in the drugstore, which his father owned, during the Great Depression. You don't have to pay a cent to enjoy the nostalgia—and both the era and the man—in the drugstore. It's a refreshing detour from today's ubiquitous big chain stores. Call (605) 352–3386 for more information and store hours.

Memoirs of Humphrey and his wife, Muriel, are found at the ***Centennial Center*** (48 Fourth Street SE). Listed on the National Register of Historic Places, this Gothic-style structure is more commonly known as the Old Stone Church. It

An Angel in South Dakota

South Dakota considers Cheryl Ladd its Hollywood Girl, even though some twenty years have passed since the Huron-born blonde beauty portrayed Kris Munroe in *Charlie's Angels*. The popularity of the series never seems to wane. A big-screen remake of the series—starring Lucy Liu, Drew Barrymore, and Cameron Diaz—was released in the summer of 2000, with a sequel released in 2003.

Ladd was born Cheryl Stoppelmoor in Huron, South Dakota. Her singing—Ladd joined a local band in high school—proved to be her ticket to stardom. After years of acting classes, appearances in commercials, and guest-starring roles on TV, Ladd joined *Charlie's Angels*. She also has recorded two albums, *Cheryl Ladd* and *Dance Fever,* which were big successes in Japan.

Ladd's star continues to shine, as she starred in a remake of the classic children's yarn, *A Dog of Flanders,* with Jon Voight in 1999. She also writes children's books with her husband, Brian.

And watch for Cheryl's daughter, too, on the silver screen. Jordan Ladd is also an actress who was in the hit film *Never Been Kissed.*

was built in 1887 of huge granite boulders from a farm northeast of Huron. The museum also has railroad items, Indian artifacts, and other memorabilia. Call (605) 352–1442 for more information. The center is open from 1:00 to 4:00 P.M. Monday through Friday. Donations are accepted.

For a glimpse into the life of yet another famous native, stop by the **Barn Restaurant,** located just south of Huron on State Highway 37. Literally a big red barn building, the restaurant specializes in juicy hamburgers and down-home cooking at very reasonable prices. Actress Cheryl Ladd once waited tables at this restaurant. Her former place of employment was so proud of her success that it started a fan club and remains the headquarters for the club. Here you can find a wide variety of memorabilia from Ladd's career. Call (605) 352–9238.

Need a compelling reason to visit Huron? Consider the **South Dakota State Fair** (605–353–7348), one of the biggest agriculture fairs in the nation. You haven't experienced true, dyed-in-the-wool Americana without attending a state fair, especially in South Dakota. It is simply a heartwarming occasion, sticky with cotton candy, delirious from roller-coaster rides and rodeos, and full of down-home events. Held during the summer each year, the South Dakota State Fair is the hands-down queen of state fairs. Rodeos, grandstand shows featuring the current stars on the country music charts, 4–H club projects, and a promenade of the newest and fanciest farm equipment and machinery embody all that is sweet to the rural lifestyle. Don't forget the spine-tingling carnival rides (or the carousel for younger or sensitive tummies).

Located 15 miles northeast of Huron, **_Lake Byron_** has consistently been one of the top producers of trophy walleye. Expect to catch perch, crappie, pike, and bullheads as well on this 1,750-acre lake. If you're not into dropping a line, try waterskiing, ski boarding, camping, or picnicking.

Where to Stay in Northeastern South Dakota

ABERDEEN
Best Western Ramkota Inn,
1400 Eighth Avenue NW,
(800) 528–1234

Breeze Inn Motel,
1216 Sixth Avenue SW,
(605) 225–6000

Ramada Inn,
2727 Sixth Avenue SE,
(800) 272–6232

Super 8 Motel,
2405 Sixth Avenue,
(800) 800–8000

BROOKINGS
Comfort Inn,
514 Sunrise Ridge Road,
(800) 228–5150

Fairfield Inn,
at exit 132 off I–29,
(800) 228–2800

The Prairie House Manor Bed and Breakfast,
RR2, Box 61A,
(800) 297–2416

Wayside Motel,
1430 Sixth Street,
(800) 658–4577

FLANDREAU
Talk of the Town Bed & Breakfast Inn,
201 West Pipestone Avenue,
(605) 997–5170

HURON
Bell Motel,
1274 Third Street SW,
(605) 352–6707

The Crossroads Hotel and Convention Center,
Fourth and Wisconsin SW,
(605) 352–3204

WATERTOWN
Best Western Ramkota,
1901 Ninth Avenue SW,
(800) 528–1234,
fax (605) 886–3667

Comfort Inn,
800 Thirty-fifth Street Circle,
(800) 228–5150

Days Inn,
2900 Ninth Avenue,
(800) 329–7466

Traveler's Inn,
920 Fourteenth Street SE,
(800) 568–7074

Where to Eat in Northeastern South Dakota

ABERDEEN
The Flame
(American),
2 South Main Street,
(605) 225–2082

Guadalajara Restaurant
(Mexican),
3015 Sixth Avenue SE,
(605) 229–7555

King House Chinese Restaurant,
311 South Main Street,
(605) 229–2587

Millstone Family Restaurant (American),
2210 Sixth Avenue SE,
(605) 229–4105

Minerva's, in Best Western Ramkota Hotel,
1400 Eighth Avenue NW,
(605) 226–2988

Red Rooster Coffee House,
202 South Main Street,
(605) 225–6603

HURON

Barn Restaurant,
south of Huron on State
Highway 37,
(605) 352–9238

Dakota Style Chicken
(American),
474 Dakota Avenue,
(605) 352–3410

SISSETON

**Dino's Steakhouse &
Lounge** (American),
West Highway 10,
(605) 652–4552

WATERTOWN

Country Kitchen
(American), junction of I–29
and US 212,
(605) 886–9133

**MacGregor's Steakhouse
& Lounge,**
1712 Ninth Avenue SW,
(605) 882–5922

SELECTED CHAMBERS OF COMMERCE

**Aberdeen Convention
& Visitors Bureau,**
514½ South Main Street,
P.O. Box 1179, Aberdeen 57402,
(800) 645–3851,
www.aberdeen-chamber.com

**Brookings Area Chamber of Commerce
and Convention Bureau,**
2308 East Sixth Street,
P.O. Box 431, Brookings 57006,
(605) 692–6125, www.brookingssd.com

Huron Convention & Visitors Bureau,
15 Fourth Street SW, Huron 57350,
(605) 352–8775, (800) HURON SD

Sisseton Chamber of Commerce,
P.O. Box 221, Sisseton 57262-0221,
(605) 698–7261

**Watertown Area Chamber of Commerce
and Convention & Visitors Bureau,**
26 South Broadway, P.O. Box 1113,
Watertown 57201-6113, (605) 886–5814

Southeastern South Dakota

With more than forty museums and galleries, as well as countless parks, the southeastern corner of South Dakota reflects an appreciation for the finer things in life. History abounds in the area, and the people here have showcased both the trying and triumphant times of the area's past with the style and elegance you might find in a much larger cosmopolitan area. The region is easily accessible via Interstate 90, which runs east-west, or Interstate 29, which runs north-south.

Higher learning takes a formidable place in this region as the state's two largest universities—the University of South Dakota and South Dakota State University—are located only a couple of hours apart from each other. Smaller colleges in the area round out the academic pursuits.

As the largest city (few communities in the state can officially be called cities) in the state, Sioux Falls assumes the role of cultural and economic leader. If you live in South Dakota, you have a strong affinity for either Rapid City or Sioux Falls—rarely both. Sioux Falls in particular deftly proves that the prairie can certainly be cosmopolitan if it wants to be.

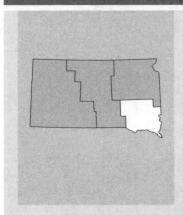

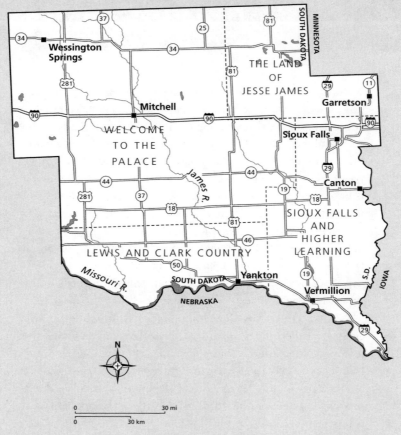

Wessington
Springs

THE LAND
OF
JESSE JAMES

Garretson

Mitchell

WELCOME
TO THE
PALACE

Sioux Falls

Canton

James R.

SIOUX FALLS
AND
HIGHER
LEARNING

LEWIS AND CLARK COUNTRY

Missouri R.

SOUTH DAKOTA

Yankton

Vermillion

NEBRASKA

SOUTH DAKOTA

MINNESOTA

IOWA

S.D.

N

0   30 mi

0   30 km

The Land of Jesse James

Tucked between two lakes, Lake Madison and Lake Herman, the town of Madison is a popular recreation spot. Melting glacial ice formed the 1,350-acre Lake Herman thousands of years ago. More recent history can be seen in the 1870 homestead cabin at Lake Herman State Park.

On Lake Madison the Chautauqua summer program was a pioneer's favorite pastime from 1891 to 1933. People gathered here to hear lectures and concerts, watch plays, and engage in lively debates. The **Smith-Zimmerman State Museum** on Madison's Dakota State University campus is home to the Chautauqua Collection, which is considered one of the most important in the Midwest. While you're here be sure to look at the Civil War memorabilia, covered wagon, period clothing, and 1880s parlor. The museum is open from 1:00 to 4:30 p.m. Tuesday through Friday. Admission is free. Call (605) 256–5308 for more information.

To the west of Madison, **Prairie Village** is a living museum of an authentic pioneer town. Attractions include antique tractors, an 1893 steam carousel, a sod house, and a log cabin. The annual Threshing Jamboree in August embraces an array of pioneer-worthy events that include horse-powered grain threshing, antique tractor pulling, weaving, and quilting. The village is open 10:00 A.M. to 6:00 P.M. daily. For more information call (605) 256–3644.

The annual **Quarry Days** celebration is held the last weekend in June in Dell Rapids, and the event shows the civic pride this small town has for its quartzite quarries. Located north of Sioux Falls, Dell Rapids is just 3 miles east of I–29 and only 15 miles from the intersection of I–29 and I–90. Dell Rapids calls itself "A South Dakota Treasure," and its awe-inspiring landscapes and fascinating

SOUTHEASTERN SOUTH DAKOTA'S TOP HITS

Corn Palace	Minerva's
Devil's Gulch	National Music Museum
Falls Park	Old Courthouse Museum
Great Plains Zoo and Delbridge Museum	Prairie Village
Heartland Arabians	Rose Stone Inn
Middle Border Museum– Oscar Howe Art Center	Zanbroz Variety

buildings make it a stunning piece in the state's ever-growing patchwork quilt of experience.

The bounty of the Dell Rapids quartzite quarries is handsomely displayed as building stone in walls and foundations throughout the downtown district. Many of the buildings, which showcase Victorian, Romanesque Revival, and Neo-classical Revival architectural styles, are listed on the National Register of Historic Places. The dells were formed more than 12,000 years ago by strong currents of water passing over exposed Sioux quartzite fissures. Native Americans called it *imnizeusteca,* or "canyon."

Winston Churchill once said, "We build buildings, and then they shape us," and Dell Rapids' architecture has magnificently primed the community's cultural scene, no doubt. Art deco glamour oozes from the facade of the 1938 **Dells Theatre,** which still has its original paint, seats, stage curtain, and light fixtures. The theater recalls a time when going to the movies was an important social occasion, well before the era of television and videotapes.

Stay the night in the 1908 **Rose Stone Inn** for another experience of small-town intimacy and the bewitching iridescence of quartzite, which is the inn's main building material. According to owners and operators Rick and Sharon Skinner, the bed-and-breakfast features four themed rooms—the Ivy and Violets Room, the Old Friends Room, the Garden Room, and the Country Garden Room—plus a smaller room, the Peach Blossom Room, if additional beds are needed. This beautifully renovated hotel, which is on the National Register of Historic Places, is furnished with loving care and fashionable pieces from the late nineteenth/early twentieth centuries. Room rates range from $80 to $115 per night for two people, including breakfast. Open year-round. For more information write to 504 East Fourth Street, Dell Rapids, SD 57022 or call (605) 428–3698. Reach the Skinners via email at rostoninnbb@aol.com, or visit the Web site at www.bbonline.com/sd/rosestone.

A perfect souvenir of your trip to this region is the 100 percent cotton cov-

ROBIN'S FAVORITES

Corn Palace,
Mitchell, (605) 996–7311

**Earth Resources Observation
Systems (EROS),**
Sioux Falls, (605) 594–6511

Great Plains Zoo,
Sioux Falls, (605) 367–7003

**Lewis and Clark Lake/
Gavins Point Dam,**
Yankton, (605) 667–7873

National Music Museum,
Vermillion, (605) 677–5306

Devil's Gulch

erlet that the Dell Rapids Society for Historical Preservation sells. This tastefully designed throw features historical sites from the state, including the Dells of Big Sioux River, St. Joseph Cathedral in Sioux Falls, Gavins Point Dam, and, of course, the omnipresent Mount Rushmore. South Dakota trivia is also woven into the scenic scheme, such as the state bird (pheasant), state animal (coyote), state flower (the pasque flower), and state tree (Black Hills spruce). The color choices are eye-pleasing, too: hunter green, cranberry red, and cream. You can order a coverlet through the society—for $49.50 plus tax and shipping—by writing to Box 143, Dell Rapids, SD 57022, or by calling (605) 428–3251.

Drive southeast of Dell Rapids and walk in the footsteps of the legendary outlaw Jesse James near Garretson. At *Devil's Gulch,* a rocky chasm at least 20 feet across and 50 feet deep, the notorious outlaw stymied a posse trying to catch him after a failed bank robbery in Minnesota. The story goes like this: The James brothers were chased into eastern South Dakota. When he reached Devil's Gulch, Jesse reined in his horse and stared into the forbidding chasm. Jesse turned, retraced his steps to get a running start, let out a whooping battle cry, and dug his spurs into his horse. The horse bounded forward. Time stood still; then the bandit lurched forward as his mount landed. He had made it. The posse, too dumbfounded by Jesse's daring jump to follow, simply milled about as the outlaw rode off. Today you can stand on a footbridge that spans Devil's Gulch and picture yourself visiting the site in 1876, just like Jesse James.

Each June, the escapades of the James brothers are celebrated during the *Jesse James Roundup Days* at Split Rock Park, just north of Garretson off State

Highway 11. A Dutch oven cook-off, craft fair, chuck-wagon feed, and theater production commemorate the nefarious, although exciting, James brothers' connection to South Dakota. The park is a perfect place for camping, hiking, and other outdoor sports. Don't forget to see quartzite rock formations along Split Rock Creek.

Spectacular quartzite chasms are a drawing card, too, in *Palisades Park,* southwest of Garretson. The view is breathtaking, and the waters here are an inviting and dreamy blue. Colorful red quartzite pinnacles and formations with 50-foot vertical cliffs line Split Rock River, which travels through the park. Notice too the unique architecture of the WPA (Works Progress Administration) of the 1930s, which features a dam with a waterfall, a bathhouse, bridges, and a rock wall with a flower garden. You can camp at the park or stay in the cabins. For reservations, call (800) 710–2267.

In Garretson (take State Highway 115 southwest to Garretson) the past and the present meet amicably at *Christmas in the Attic* (505 Third Street), where you can enjoy an old-fashioned ice cream soda (made from real homemade vanilla ice cream) and savor the colors and nostalgia of Christmas. Bruce and Karen Rekstad have preserved an enchanted piece of the past with newfound treasures in the shop, located in an old hatchery building. The store is a favorite for its Christmas collectibles and genuinely relaxed spirit. Store hours are from 9:00 A.M. to 5:30 P.M. Monday through Saturday and from noon to 5:30 P.M. Sunday. For more information call (605) 594–2225.

Enjoy the 1920s setting of *Dakota Good Times Corner* (605–594–3404) and view the delightful watercolors of artist Nancy Kentfield in the art gallery. She's especially praised for her landscapes and florals. The corner also serves homemade soup and sandwiches, and South Dakota–made products are available. Guide services to Devil's Gulch also are offered. The store, located at the corner of Third and Main Streets, is open from 7:00 A.M. to 4:00 P.M. Monday through Friday, and 7:00 A.M. to 4:00 P.M. Saturday.

Heartland Arabians, just 11 miles north of Sioux Falls, is a showplace for internationally famous horses. Nestled in the rolling hills of the Big Sioux River Valley, this all-weather facility also is home to exotic animals like llamas, angora

Art and Science Mix

Located at the corner of Eleventh and Main Streets, the Washington Pavilion of Arts and Science is a place where visitors can be touched by extraordinary artwork—or actually touch interactive science displays.

The Pavilion's Visual Arts Center features seven galleries of changing exhibits, including Native American artists, regional and national contemporary visual arts exhibitions, and a hands-on children's gallery. The Visual Arts Center presently has a collection of 300 works, including pieces by noted South Dakota artists Oscar Howe, Lova Jones, and Charles Greener. Other artists represented include Signe Stuart and Robert Aldern.

The 300-seat Small Theater is available for performances requiring more intimate space such as musical ensembles, lectures, poetry readings, experimental theater, and dance and piano recitals. It is also used for meetings, conferences, seminars, and other private functions.

The Husby Performing Arts Center brings the best in music, dance, and theater from around the world. The 1,800-seat Great Hall is home to local community groups, as well as the South Dakota Symphony.

If science is more your style, check out the three-story Kirby Science Discovery Center, where you can fly a space shuttle, dig up a dinosaur, or touch a tornado. The Kirby Science Discovery Center occupies about 45,000 square feet along the Twelfth Street side of the Pavilion.

Science adventure films are shown hourly on the four-story dome screen at the Wells Fargo CineDome Theater.

The stunning building is a history lesson in itself. It was formerly Washington High School, and it reopened as the new Washington Pavilion of Arts and Science in the summer of 1999. It was built in 1906 and has been expanded twice.

The visually distinctive, 255,000-square-foot building is constructed of native Sioux quartzite. The roof balustrade and dentiled cornices are visible from many downtown Sioux Falls locations.

The center is open from 10:00 A.M. to 5:00 P.M. Monday through Thursday, from 10:00 A.M. to 8:00 P.M. Friday, from 10:00 A.M. to 5:00 P.M. Saturday, and from noon to 5:00 P.M. Sunday.

For a schedule of events, tickets, or membership information, call (877) WASHPAV or visit the Web site at www.washingtonpavilion.com. Open daily.

goats, peacocks, and donkeys. You also can see equine art and clothing in Heartland's shop, or take an antique sleigh or buggy ride around the historically authentic one-hundred-acre farm. Heartland is open by appointment at no charge to the public. For more information call (605) 543–5900.

Also near Baltic (10 miles north of exit 402 on I–90) is the **_Earth Resources Observation Systems (EROS) Data Center_** (605–594–6511), which houses the government's central archives for nonmilitary satellite images and aerial photography. The center operates an archive with more than eight million photographs of the United States taken from aircraft and more than three million worldwide images acquired by sensors aboard several satellites. The complex center reproduces and disseminates data to scientists throughout the world and assists users in the application of such photographs. Audiovisuals in the lobby will take you on an engrossing thirty- to forty-five-minute self-guided tour. Guided tours are offered at 10:00 A.M. and 2:00 P.M. Open Monday through Friday from 8:00 A.M. to 4:00 P.M. Free admission.

Sioux Falls and Higher Learning

Unlike the semiarid clime of western South Dakota, the atmosphere of the southeastern region around Sioux Falls gets downright muggy in the summer. That fact doesn't detract from the city's great reputation.

With a population of more than 131,000, Sioux Falls is the largest city in the state. Established in 1865 at the falls of the Sioux River, the town has been like the Energizer Bunny: It keeps going and going and going. Its résumé reads like one of a proud college graduate. The city is consistently listed as one of the Top Ten Best Places to Live in America. A remarkably low crime rate, an abundance of jobs, clean air, and a cordial atmosphere make it a wonderful place to live or visit. The growth of Sioux Falls has been buoyed by its diversified industry and farming as well as by its citizens, who eagerly embrace change and the cultural and economic promises a larger city can bring. Today Sioux Falls is called a mini-Minneapolis, which is called, in turn, a mini-Big Apple. In Sioux Falls it's obvious the apple doesn't fall too far from the tree in terms of shopping, cultural activities, and entertainment. Moreover, the city is within reasonable driving distance from other urban centers, such as Des Moines, Omaha, Minneapolis, and Kansas City.

The downtown district is especially appealing. As America becomes "mallified," downtown areas must draw on unique services, products, and history to recapture shoppers, and Sioux Falls has done that commendably. The

Divorce Prairie-style

At the turn of the century, Sioux Falls and South Dakota earned the less-than-flattering moniker of "divorce colony" because of the great ease with which unhappily married couples could obtain a divorce in the state. At that time, law required that residents live in the state only six months before they could obtain a divorce. Sioux Falls in the early 1900s rivaled Reno, Nevada, of today with as many as 145 divorces in a year. The law changed in 1908, extending the residency requirement to one year.

TOP ANNUAL EVENTS

Christmas Downtown,
Sioux Falls, November through
December, (605) 338–4009

Great Plains Powwow,
Sioux Falls, second weekend
in October (in conjunction with
Native American Day),
(605) 339–7039

Riverboat Days,
Yankton, third weekend in August,
(605) 665–3636

Sidewalk Arts Festival,
Sioux Falls, September, (605) 336–1176

Sioux Empire Fair,
Sioux Falls, early August, (605) 367–7178

district extends from Fourth to Fourteenth Streets and includes Dakota, Main, and Phillips Avenues.

One thing Sioux Falls has learned is that the way to shoppers' hearts is through their stomachs. Gastronomical delights are easily found in elegant restaurants or quirky bistros. *Minerva's*, at 301 South Phillips Avenue, is one of the best restaurants in the city. A classy establishment, the restaurant is perfect for special occasions, dates, or any time you just want excellent food and impeccable service. Appetizers such as pheasant ravioli, almond duck strips, crispy fried oysters, Pandang peanut chicken, coconut shrimp, sweet-and-sour oriental green beans, and crabmeat artichoke pique the taste buds. There is more to come at Minerva's in tantalizing main courses such as pasta dishes and aged steaks. Cajun chicken linguine, and pepper steak and pasta are must tastes for carbohydrate lovers or just plain hungry appetites. Meat-and-potato enthusiasts will find a mouth-watering selection of top sirloin, roast prime rib of beef, rib eye, occasionally filet mignon, and New York strip-sirloin steaks. The specialty salad bar at Minerva's is exceptionally well done—and visually satisfying as well—with fresh cheeses, fruits, cold cuts, homemade soups, and breads. Minerva's is open from 11:00 A.M. to 2:30 P.M. Monday through Saturday, from 5:30 to 10:00 P.M. Monday through Thursday, and from 5:00 to 10:00 P.M. Friday and Saturday. Lunches average about $7.95 and dinners range from $10.95 to $34.95. (Dinner reservations are suggested.) A children's menu is available. Call (605) 334–0386 for more information.

The Book Shop in Sioux Falls (223 South Phillips Avenue) buys and sells used and collectible books in a refreshingly well-organized manner. You'll find paperback and hardcover, fiction and nonfiction, old favorites, and recently published books on a wide variety of topics. The store is located mid-block in the old Carpenter Hotel. Open Monday through Saturday from 10:00 A.M. to 5:30 P.M. For information call (605) 336–8384.

Both serious and casual cooks will enjoy **Kitchen Cordial** (605–334–4405), located at 218 South Phillips Avenue. The store is open from 10:00 A.M. to 8:00 P.M. Monday through Saturday. Service is a top priority in this shop; the staff will gladly ship anywhere, and, if you're pressed for time, gift wrapping is free. For the Christmas holiday, Kitchen Cordial puts on all the right bells and whistles with custom baskets full of delectables or festive platters, teapots, collectibles, ornaments, and homemade fudge.

At the corner of Sixth and Phillips Streets, the **Northern Plains Gallery,** housed within Rehfeld's Dakota Galleries, specializes in the authentic work of the Plains Indians. Traditional crafts include bead- and quillwork; contemporary works include lithographs, monotypes, acrylics, and bronzes. The gallery is host of the impressive and well-regarded Northern Plains Juried Art Shows and Market, held the last full weekend in September. More important, the gallery is operated by American Indian Services, Inc., a nonprofit relief and economic and cultural development agency. The gallery is open from 10:00 A.M. to 6:00 P.M. Monday through Friday and from 10:00 A.M. to 5:00 P.M. Saturday. For more information call (605) 334–4060 or (800) 658–4797, or visit the Web site at www.aistribalarts.com.

Nostalgic in a happy, New Wave sort of way describes **Zanbroz Variety** (605–331–5137). Located in the heart of downtown Sioux Falls at 209 South Phillips Avenue, the place oozes with a "happening granola" attitude, but it has a universal appeal that even Grandma would like. Candles, books, cards, baskets, jewelry, gourmet foods, and other nifty things for giving (or keeping for yourself) make this shop a heavenly expedition. The real bonanza, however, is located at the back of the store, where the **Soda Falls Fountain & Coffee Bar** is located. It has all the perks: cute, bubbly waitresses; an extensive menu of iced and gourmet coffees; and plenty of mental room for talking. Other treats are the malts, shakes, and old-fashioned sodas. Authenticity is the name of the game here, and even the whipping cream is 100 percent real dairy. (Don't be put off by the aerosol can; the staff says it helps them deliver a consistent whipped cream.) Since life is uncertain, eat dessert first, and make it the tiramisu cake or caramel apple tart, both worth every calorie. The Back Room features authors, poets, musicians, and other entertainment.

Several classic structures have been grandly maintained by families and preservationists in the **St. Joseph's Cathedral Historic District,** located between Fourth and Tenth Streets and bordered by Prairie and Spring Streets.

One of the most magnificent is the **Pettigrew Home and Museum,** located at 131 North Duluth Avenue. The museum was the home of South Dakota's first full-term U.S. senator. A seasoned traveler, Richard F. Pettigrew collected artifacts from all over the world and displayed them in his home.

These items are shown with natural history and cultural artifacts from the Siouxland area, which include Native American objects and the home's 5,000-volume research library that contains Pettigrew's personal papers. Trained tour guides will take you through the 1889 home and share Pettigrew's many contributions to South Dakota. The site is open from 9:00 A.M. to 5:00 P.M. Monday through Saturday, and from noon to 5:00 P.M. Sunday. Admission is free. For more information call (605) 367–7097.

Whet your appetite for history and discover the heritage of Siouxland in the *Old Courthouse Museum* (200 North Sixth Street), a recently restored structure listed on the National Register of Historic Places. The massive stone building served as the county courthouse from 1890 to 1962. The first-floor exhibits bring to life the history of early settlers and the Plains Indians, along with the art and cultural significance of Siouxland. On the second floor see the restored circuit courtroom and law library. A handsomely laid-out building, the Old Courthouse is decorated with sixteen murals of different sizes, created by the Norwegian artist Ole Running in 1915. The building also houses the Minnehaha County Historical Library and the Sioux Valley Genealogical Society Library, both listed as landmarks on the National Register of Historic Places. The Old Courthouse Museum is open from 9:00 A.M. to 5:00 P.M. Monday through Wednesday, from 9:00 A.M. to 9:00 P.M. Thursday, from 9:00 A.M. to 5:00 P.M. Friday and Saturday, and from 1:00 to 5:00 P.M. on Sunday. There is no admission charge. Call (605) 367–4210 or visit the Web site at www.siouxland museums.com for more information.

You also can find the Queen City Mercantile at the museum, where local and regional books, crafts, old-fashioned toys, holiday collectibles, souvenirs, and exhibit-related items are for sale.

Following America's interest in "handcrafted" beer, the *Sioux Falls Brewing Co.* picks up on the craze with style and incredible grace. Located at 431 North Phillips Avenue, the brewery makes its home on the main and lower floors of the restored Jewett Brothers Warehouse. (The building was constructed in 1899, with an addition in 1909, by the Jewett Brothers to house their wholesale food business. In 1983 the building was placed on the National Register of Historic Places as part of the Old Courthouse and Warehouse Historic District.) Six beers are on tap for the thirsty traveler: Midnight Star Signature Ale, Prairie Wheat Ale, Phillips Avenue Pale Ale, Ringneck Red Ale, Buffalo Stout, and a Revolving Specialty Beer, which changes according to the season. The selections from the restaurant menu will hit the spot, too. Dinner entrees include scallop and shrimp scampi, crisp duck topped with a mild vegetable salsa, pork tenderloin tips Dusseldorf, and top sirloin, char-grilled to your liking. For lighter appetites, sandwiches and salads also are offered, but whatever you choose, save room for dessert. The Buffalo Pie—a cheesecake made with stout (dark ale) and dark chocolate—has become a classic.

Live jazz and blues entertainment makes the brewery a hot spot on weekends. The textures of quartzite rock and brick that make up the foundation and walls of the Jewett Building make it a touchy-feely place. (Quartzite, a pink, hard rock, is common throughout the region.) Sioux Falls Brewing Co. is open from 11:30 A.M. to 2:00 A.M. Monday through Saturday. (The brewery is not open on Sunday during the off-season.) For more information call (605) 332–4847 or visit the Web site at www.sfbrewco.com.

The annual *Sidewalk Arts Festival* entertains more than 60,000 visitors each year. The downtown festival fills Phillips Avenue from Ninth to Fourteenth Streets and showcases artists and vendors from fifteen states. Art Rocks! is the free entertainment stage. The event, which is held the first Saturday after Labor Day, is the annual fund-raiser for the Visual Arts Center at the Washington Pavilion of Arts and Science. For more information call (605) 367–7397, extension 2353, or visit the Web site at www.sidewalkartsfestival.com.

Sioux Falls' namesake is located 1 mile east of the downtown district. See the waterfalls of the Big Sioux River at *Falls Park.* Walkways give the visitor a magnificent view of the thundering falls. The outdoor museum was the setting for the Queen Bee Mill, built in the late 1800s, which was an effort to harness the power of the falls. R. F. Pettigrew convinced an eastern investor to finance the construction of this huge, seven-story 1,200-barrels-per-day flour mill. The remains of the mill help paint a nostalgic picture of what industry was like in Sioux Falls in its early days. Enjoy the picnic shelter on the grounds. And there's more: The Falls Park Visitor Information Center offers information on Falls Park and other Sioux Falls attractions, and includes a five-story observation tower and elevator. The Horse Barn Arts Center adds an artsy touch with gallery shows and other arts-oriented activities. The Wells Fargo Park Sound and Light show spectacularly outlines the history of Sioux Falls. You can watch the show nightly during the summer months after sunset.

Sioux Falls has more than sixty parks, and if you visit any, be sure to check out *Terrace Park,* at Sixth Street. The Shoto-Teien Japanese Gardens are located here, next to Covell Lake. The Gardens were built from 1928 to 1936 and feature a lush array of flowering trees and shrubs, pagodas, and lanterns. The Terrace Park Aquatic Center is a perfect jumping-off point, too, with swimming pools and water slides.

The full-scale cast of Michelangelo's David stands in the heart of Sioux Falls at *Fawick Park* (located on Second Avenue between Tenth and Eleventh Streets). Thomas Fawick, a Sioux Falls philanthropist and industrialist who made a fortune as an inventor, gave the city the statue in 1972. The statue of

David, fully in the buff, created enormous controversy when it first arrived. To mollify public opinion, the statue was placed facing away from traffic, and trees were planted to screen it from the street. (Fawick later gave the city the sculptor's statue of Moses, which was placed on the Augustana College campus.)

Augustana College is the home of the **Center for Western Studies** (located on South Summit in the lower level of the Mikkelson Library). The center is dedicated to preserving and interpreting the history and cultures of both native and immigrant people in the area. It's open Monday through Friday 8:00 A.M. to 5:00 P.M. For information call (605) 247–4007.

At Twelfth and Kiwanis Streets, the *USS* **South Dakota** *Battleship Memorial* is a patriotic sample of World War II naval history. The battleship, which participated in every major battle in the Pacific from 1942 to 1945, was the most decorated of World War II. Visitors can walk through the concrete configuration and pay tribute to the military personnel who gave their lives while serving on the vessel. Open daily 10:00 A.M. to 5:00 P.M. Memorial Day through Labor Day. For information call (605) 397–7060.

The *Great Plains Zoo and Delbridge Museum* combines the rugged expanse of a North American plain, the wild recesses of an African veldt, and the quiet beauty of the Australian Outback. Located at 805 South Kiwanis Avenue (0.5 mile east off I–29, exit 79 to Twelfth Street), the Delbridge Museum of Natural History houses one of the largest collections of mounted animals in the world. The Asian Cat Habitat is fascinating. The spacious environment for all creatures great and small was modeled after the San Diego Zoo. Open daily year-round. Zoo hours are from 9:00 A.M. to 7:00 P.M., with the last group accepted at 6:00 P.M. Tickets are $6.75 for adults, $6.00 for senior citizens, $3.75 for children ages three to twelve; and admission is free for children two years of age and younger. Call (605) 367–7059 for more information or visit the Web site at www.gpzoo.org.

The *Empire Mall* (605–361–3300) boasts that it has the best shopping between Denver and Minneapolis, and, judging from the traffic here, it's not an exaggeration of an eager marketing department. The Empire Mall is definitely the largest in South Dakota, and with anchor stores such as Younkers and Dayton's and more than 180 restaurants and specialty stores, shoppers feel as though they're in a metropolitan mall. The mall hours are 10:00 A.M. to 9:00 P.M. Monday through Saturday and 11:00 A.M. to 6:00 P.M. Sunday. To break the national retail chain monotony, visit *Dakota Zone,* which appropriately stocks a large selection of products made in South Dakota: Cheese, honey, taffy, and Dakota Style Potato Chips are just a few of the foodstuffs you can bite into. There are many gift basket items, too, from artwork, jewelry, and pottery to books and Native American dream catchers. Call (800) 446–8166 for more information or visit the Web site at www.TheEmpireMall.com. To find the Empire Mall, take exit 77 off I–29 at Forty-first Street; also located at exit 1C off I–229 at Louise Avenue. There may not be a factory outlet mall in South Dakota, but the state does have a T. J. Maxx store, which at least qualifies as an outlet store. It's located in the same block as the Empire Mall.

Several chain restaurants are located near the mall. For overnight shoppers the **Radisson Encore Inn** (4300 Empire Place) offers both convenience and away-from-home elegance. Call (800) 333–3333 for reservations or visit the Web site at www.radisson.com.

For shoppers in the holiday spirit, the **Cliff Avenue Year-Round Christmas Store** is just that—365 days a year of Christmas collectibles from traditional folk art to contemporary designs. You also can find a variety of Christmas theme ornaments, such as snowmen and crystal, and the whimsical patterns of Mary Engelbreit. The store is located at 7000 West Forty-first Street. Store hours are Monday through Friday 9:00 A.M. to 6:00 P.M., Saturday 9:00 A.M. to 5:30 P.M., and Sunday noon to 5:00 P.M. For more information call (605) 362–9727.

Tired of doing the big-mall crawl? Check out a small yet enormously charming strip mall on South Western Avenue. The **Park Ridge Shopping Mall** shows the personal care that local shop owners take in their stores. Twelve specialty stores offer something for everyone. Mall hours are 10:00 A.M. to 6:00 P.M. Monday through Saturday and 10:00 A.M. to 8:00 P.M. Thursday.

The Patina could easily be called Antiques R Us because the shop offers an ever-changing panoply of vintage items and unique furniture. Owner Joni Persing also stocks armoires from Europe, where, once, they were considerably vogue items since closets were taxed as extra rooms. Joni also carries

Local Writer

The term "Siouxland" is used to describe the Sioux Falls area, and its ubiquity can be seen and heard everywhere—from TV news broadcasts to business names. The term actually was coined by writer Frederick Manfred, who was my creative writing teacher at the University of South Dakota in Vermillion during the 1980s. "Writing is like farming," Fred once said. "You cultivate a manuscript, and, like a farmer, you need discipline. A farmer farms soil, writers farm brain cells."

Fred was one of the great novelists of America's heartland, and he first achieved recognition for the five novels known as the Buckskin Man Tales: *Conquering Horse, Lord Grizzly, Scarlet Plume, King of Spades,* and *Riders of Judgment.* Fred was a prolific writer, and his tales often were wrought with dark, ancestral sufferings of the mind, heart, and body. In describing romantic underpinnings, he often woefully observed, "You can't legislate love."

antique-reproduction mirrors, vintage costume jewelry, lamps, and clocks. She also has a gift-book section, and like the expert collector she is, Joni can find books of almost any genre—specialty, regional, inspirational, and more. South Dakota–made cards also are featured in the store. You can reach Joni at (605) 357–8884. Hours are 10:00 A.M. to 6:00 P.M. Monday through Friday and 10:00 A.M. to 5:00 P.M. Saturday. If you have children in tow, take them to *Toys and Treasures International* (605–339–2226). In addition to stuffed animals, toys, and collectible dolls, the store carries stylish yet practical clothes for kids.

Hungry after shopping this easy-for-Sunday-strolling mall? *Spezia* (it's affiliated with the dressier Minerva's downtown) is next door to lend comfort and sustenance. Menu items include focaccia flatbread pizza, or what the staff likes to call the "adult pizza," chicken breast Alfredo, and rotisserie pork dishes, all of which reflect the restaurant's Italian theme. A wood-burning oven enables the staff to create salmon pizzas and savory Mediterranean appetizers like crostini and bruschetta. Pasta and veal dishes are prominent on the menu as well. The restaurant, which is famous for its Sunday brunch, is open 11:30 A.M. to 2:30 P.M. and 5:00 to 10:00 P.M. Monday through Thursday, until 11:00 P.M. Friday, 11:00 A.M. to 11:00 P.M. Saturday, and 9:00 A.M. to 1:30 P.M. and 5:00 to 8:00 P.M. Sunday. Spezia is located at 1716 South Western Avenue (605–334–7491). For more information, visit the Web site at www.ciaodown.com.

At *Country Corner Orchard,* 4 miles south of Sioux Falls on Minnesota Avenue, apple seekers can buy bagged red, shiny apples or pick their own during one of the most treasured rites of autumn. You can hop on a tractor-pulled wagon and jump off when you reach the spot where your favorite variety of apple is grown. Just pluck the ripe apples from tree branches already straining from the weight of fragrant fruit. For information call (605) 743–2424.

When people think of downhill skiing in South Dakota, they usually think of the Black Hills. *Great Bear Ski Valley,* however, is a natural for schussing a la East River, with eleven runs nearly 1,500 feet long, a 250-foot vertical drop, chairlifts, and a chalet. A tubing hill and outdoor skating are also offered at the resort. Great Bear (605–367–4309, www.greatbearpark.com) is located 2 miles east of Sioux Falls on Rice Street. Ski instruction and rentals for both downhill and cross-country skiing are available. The park is also open for hiking during the summer.

Just 5 miles east of Sioux Falls on I–90 at exit 406 is Brandon, one of the state's fastest-growing communities. The two city-owned parks, *Aspen Park* and *Pioneer Park,* offer tennis courts, swimming, ice skating, sledding, walking paths, and soccer fields. Two state parks also are located near Brandon: the *Beaver Creek Nature Area* and the *Big Sioux Recreation Area.*

One of the many treasures at Big Sioux Recreation Area is the *Bergeson's Homestead*—the park's very own little house on the prairie—which was built in 1869 by Ole and Soren Bergeson. Ole was one of the first settlers in Split Rock Township. The log frame, which is constructed of hand-hewn cotton-wood, was inadvertently discovered in the twentieth century during the process of razing the entire old Bergeson homestead. Notice the fine dove-tailed notchwork. Nature trails and an archery range are also found at the Big Sioux Recreation Area.

The *Brandon Arts & Crafts Festival* is held annually in McHardy Park, a county-operated park, in July. The two-day event attracts a wide variety of artists and food vendors.

As you drive outside Sioux Falls, you can see firsthand the crops that have been so vital to the area's economy. As George Washington once said, "No pur-suit is more congenial with my nature and gratification than that of agriculture; nor none I so pant after as again to become a tiller of the earth." As you drive along the country roads, you'll see a checkerboard of grasses and crops. Freshly tilled plots of land, like giant quilts, hint of fertility.

South Dakota crops include alfalfa, barley, corn, flaxseed (which contains linseed oil, an extract used in paints and varnishes), rye, and sorghum. Sunflowers, unmistakably bright yellow with dark brown centers, put South Dakota second in the nation in the production of sunflower seeds. And who can forget the golden-brown beauty of wheat, which is a major cash crop for the state? That is not to say farming is an easy life. A story passed down through generations illustrates the faith and tenacity of those who till the land: In 1874 swarms of grasshoppers plagued the fields of eastern South Dakota. They tormented cattle and ate the plants. Pierre Boucher, a local pastor, finally appealed to a higher power. The priest led his parishioners in an 11-mile trek from field to field. In each field, the people prayed and erected a giant cross to ward off the grasshoppers and save the crops. Miraculously, the pests dis-appeared that very day.

The annual *Homesteader Day Harvest Festival* at Beaver Creek Nature Area (south of Brandon off I–90) offers a glimpse into what life on the prairie was like for the pioneers. First of all, turn back the clock to the year 1869: John and Anna Samuelson, both Swedish immigrants, were newlyweds, and John bought his bride a 160-acre homestead east of present-day Sioux Falls. For the first three years, they made their home in a dugout carved from a nearby hill. They later moved to a log cabin, which is now the centerpiece of the Homesteader Day Harvest Festival. At present Arlene and Eleanor Erickson, John and Anna's twin granddaughters (who married twins), welcome visitors into their grandparents' log home. As part of the celebration, volunteers demonstrate candle making, sheepshearing, tatting, butter churning, wheat grinding, and more. Visitors can try their hand at rope making and can sample fresh-squeezed apple juice made in a sixty-year-old apple press. The festival is held in autumn. For more information call (605) 594–3824.

While you're enjoying the fruits of your labor at the festival, explore Beaver Creek Nature Area, an ideal place for hiking, picnicking, fishing, cross-country skiing, and snowmobiling.

As you drive in the country outside Sioux Falls, you get a distinct flavor of what farm life is like. Big clapboard farmhouses built by past generations are surrounded by state-of-the-art machinery. This familiar sight symbolizes how agriculture has survived and progressed through the years.

Those who work the land in this area have seen the best and the worst of times. On a fragrant summer day, the prairie here seems placid and inviting, which belies the truth that drought is a stern possibility of summer. Winters also can be brutally harsh.

Vermillion, 56 miles south of Sioux Falls on I–29, best fits the old description of a place where the college is the community. The economy of this town of 10,276 people thrives on the presence of the University of South Dakota (USD), the state's second-largest university, founded in 1862. Vermillion, the seat of Clay County, originally was settled below the bluffs of the Mighty Mo until the flood of 1881 changed the river's course, forcing residents to higher ground. Now it's located in a part of the state that was twice claimed by France and once by Spain before it was sold to the United States. As in any college community, there is a vibrant energy that students and higher education bring. Then there is the cultural life, which is manifested in the university's impressive fine arts college and three distinctly unique museums.

Named for one of its early directors, The **W. H. Over State Museum** (1110 Ratingen Street) is a tribute to state and natural history. Exhibits include a life-size diorama of a Teton Dakota village. The museum's Clark Memorial Collection includes pre-reservation and reservation Lakota art, as well as pioneer artifacts, costumes, firearms, and the Stanley J. Morrow collection of historic photographs. The Lewis and Clark/Spirit Mound Learning Center sheds light on the explorers' famous journey, especially through the region. The artifacts include a map drawn in 1806 from Lewis's notations and journal entries. The gift shop features Native American and Scandinavian crafts, as well as Oscar Howe and Robert Penn prints and note cards and lithographs by other regional artists. Best of all, there is no admission charge, and the museum is open daily. Hours are 9:00 A.M. to 5:00 P.M. Monday through Friday, 9:30 A.M. to 4:30 P.M. Saturday, and 1:00 to 4:30 P.M. Sunday. For more information call (605) 677–5277.

On the University of South Dakota campus, you will find more than 10,000 musical instruments from all over the world in the ***National Music Museum*** (located at Clark and Yale Streets). Exhibits include a 1693 Stradivarius violin, a 9-foot-tall slit drum from the South Pacific, Civil War band instruments, Elizabethan ivory lutes, and a 1785 French harpsichord. A B. B. King auto- graphed guitar is displayed here as well. This one-of-a-kind facility is open daily, and there is no admission charge. Call (605) 677–5306. (Give advance notice for group tours.)

The last building in Vermillion's museum trio is the **Austin-Whittemore House,** an impressive Italian villa–style structure that also houses the **Clay County Historical Society Museum.** The museum, built in 1882 on a river- side bluff overlooking Vermillion, is best known for its Victorian displays and settings. The museum is open June through August on Friday, Saturday, and Sunday afternoons. Call (605) 624–8266 for more information.

The campus of the University of South Dakota is a stately one, with his- toric buildings and grand shade trees. The Dakota Dome sports facility includes an indoor football stadium, where the USD Coyotes meet other col- leges for competition. The school's strongest rival is the South Dakota State University's campus Jackrabbits. Sportsmanlike conduct takes a back seat dur- ing basketball season when USD students have, on occasion, tossed a frozen jackrabbit onto the court. Parties afterward are equally wild. Just so you know that the school has its more civilized moments, I should mention that USD, my alma mater, is considered one of the best liberal arts colleges in the state. (Tom Brokaw is an alumnus.) Accordingly, there are fine productions to see on cam- pus, including dance, theater, and fine arts. Slagle Auditorium is often home to concerts by the USD Chamber Singers and Chamber Orchestra and the USD Men's and Women's Chorus Concert. You also can see a play at the Fine Arts Building theater, or enjoy a piano concert at the Colton Recital Hall.

Not too far from downtown and the National Music Museum is the quaint **Goebel House,** a traditional bed-and-breakfast filled with antiques. Located at 102 Franklin Street, this charming inn—built in 1916 in the Queen Anne style— has four bedrooms, with either private or shared baths, and offers a home- cooked, candlelight breakfast each morning. Rates are $65 a night. Call (605) 624–6691 for more information.

Once you get your nose out of the books or museums, stop by the **Silver Dollar Saloon** and enjoy a prime rib dinner amid an early-Western gambling hall atmosphere. Located at 1216 East Cherry Street, the restaurant is open from 11:00 A.M. to 10:00 P.M. Monday through Sunday. Call (605) 624–4830 for reservations.

When explorers Lewis and Clark visited the Vermillion area, they were intrigued by a cone-shaped mound of land the Sioux claimed was bewitched. Undaunted by such stories, the pair traveled to **Spirit Mound,** the highest point in the county, where they found the beautiful landscape and "sea of bufalow" most intriguing. The mound itself was built sometime between A.D. 500 and 1000 by the Mound Builders, who lived in the Midwest before the Indian tribes of recent times moved in. The builders buried their dead in the mounds with as much precise care as the Egyptians used in their pyramids. The Mound Builders' fate remains a mystery, but they left clues to their existence in many mounds throughout eastern South Dakota. Spirit Mound is 8 miles north of Vermillion on Route 19.

The **Union County State Park** in Beresford (11 miles north off I–29) offers hiking and bridle trails, picnicking, camping, and a playground, as well as an arboretum, on 500 beautiful acres. (Historical fact: Union County was the first county in South Dakota that Lewis and Clark crossed on their expedition.) For more information call (605) 987–2263.

Newton Hills State Park, just south of Canton on Route 11, is a wooded oasis where plants and animals thrive. This southern tip of the Coteau des Prairies (Hill of the Prairies) was spared the plow, and its grassy knolls and wooded ravines today shelter deer, wild turkey, and more than 200 species of birds. Explorers can make their way along several hiking trails, while horse riders and all-terrain bikers can enjoy a 6-mile multiuse trail. The annual Sioux River Folk Festival attracts music aficionados from all over.

History runs deep in North Sioux City, which is located at the farthest tip of southeastern South Dakota on State Highway 29 and pokes into Iowa and

An Excellent Adventure

Like North Dakota, South Dakota takes great pride in its close relation to explorers Meriwether Lewis and William Clark, who set out to explore America's newest land acquisition—the Louisiana Purchase—in 1804.

The Lewis and Clark National Historic Trail follows Highways 1804 and 1806, which hug the Missouri River and trace the route that Lewis and Clark traveled. Indeed, some parts of the vast Missouri shoreline remain as wild and breathtaking as they were in the explorers' days.

On August 25, 1804, Lewis and Clark visited Spirit Mound near Vermillion. They wrote: "From the top of the mound, we beheld a most beautiful landscape. Numerous herds of buffalo were seen feeding in various directions. The plain to the north, northwest, and northeast extends without interruption as far as can be seen."

The South Dakota Tourism Department has put together a helpful brochure—aptly named *Lewis and Clark's Excellent Adventure*—that includes a map of the explorers' journey, excerpts from their journal, and a complete list of campgrounds and other accommodations along the way.

Nebraska. Charles Lindbergh chose North Sioux City as his landing site for the *Spirit of St. Louis* in 1927.

Known as the Las Vegas of the Heartland, **North Sioux City's strip, Military Road,** features more than thirteen casinos that buzz with the sounds and flash of video games and entertainment. Here you can test your luck at a variety of games: keno, bingo, blackjack, draw poker, and joker poker. The Video Lottery Capital of South Dakota has the largest concentration of machines in a 2½-block area.

If bright lights and the sound of gambling machines aren't your style, head for peace and solitude at the 1,500-acre **Adams Homestead and Nature Preserve,** located in nearby McCook, 1 mile west of I–29 at McCook Lake. This land was the property of three generations of Adamses. The family donated the land to the Department of Game, Fish, and Parks so that others could visit it for inner renewal. The town of McCook was the first homesteaders' settlement in the state, and the McCook Cemetery, platted and registered in 1869, is regarded as the first homesteaders' cemetery. The visitor center is open from 8:00 A.M. to 4:30 P.M. Monday through Friday and from 10:00 A.M. to 6:00 P.M. Saturday and Sunday. For more information, call (605) 232–0873.

Lewis and Clark Country

Less than 30 miles west of Vermillion, Yankton (population: 13,528) today is a small town. Yet it once bustled as the capital of the Dakota Territory in the 1860s. In 1889 it was passed over as the state capital. That honor went to the more centrally located town of Pierre.

The **Dakota Territorial Capitol Replica** in Yankton's Riverside Park stands as a reminder of the glory days when Yankton served as the capital, from 1861 to 1883. The simple white structure is located on the banks of the Missouri River.

While in Riverside Park, learn about the area's history and contributions at the **Dakota Territorial Museum** (610 Summit Avenue). The Yankton County Historical Society has lovingly preserved and displayed rare memorabilia from

Yankton Daily Press & Dakotan

The *Yankton Daily Press & Dakotan* is the oldest daily newspaper in South Dakota. It was the first in Dakota Territory—founded in 1861 as a weekly and then as a daily in 1875. The paper's annual *Lake Guide* is a wonderful resource for summer travelers. The free *Yankton Magazine,* too, is published by the Daily Press & Dakotan. For more information call (605) 665–7811.

early Yankton and Dakota Territory days, including a rural schoolhouse, a blacksmith shop, a Burlington Northern caboose, and an American LaFrance fire engine. Call (605) 665–3898 for hours. Admission is $2.00 for adults and free for kids.

Yankton boasts some of the finest historical homes in the Midwest. The Architectural Walking and Auto Tour of Historic Yankton Homes offers visitors at least a curbside glimpse at the exteriors of some homes, most of which are clustered on Douglas, Capital, Pine, and Mulberry Streets, between Fifth and Sixth Streets.

The *Cramer Kenyon Heritage Home and Dorothy Jencks Memorial Garden,* for instance, at 509 Pine Street is an outstanding example of Queen Anne architecture. The home, erected in 1886, is open to the public from Memorial Day to Labor Day from 1:00 to 5:00 P.M. Tuesday through Saturday and by appointment year-round. There is a $2.00 fee. Call (605) 665–7470 for more information.

Another historic building is the 1800s *Charles Gurney Hotel* (corner of Third and Capital Streets). Formerly the courthouse, it was here that Jack McCall was tried a second time for the murder of Wild Bill Hickok in Deadwood. McCall was found guilty and hanged; he was buried in an unmarked grave.

For more information on the walking/car tour, visit the Yankton Area Chamber of Commerce office at 218 West Fourth Street, or call (605) 665–3636.

After your tour, stop in at *The Pantry* (605–665–4480) for an espresso or cappuccino. Pastries and chocolate wafers are also available, the perfect companion to a steaming cup of java. The store is located at 215 West Third Street.

Not too far from The Pantry at 221 West Third Street is *Lewis & Clark Gallery,* which carries the artwork of popular regional artists such as Terry Redlin and Jon Crane. Jewelry and collectibles also are sold here. Call (605) 665–0129 for more information.

Yankton's *Riverboat Days and Summer Arts Festival* is the perfect event to witness firsthand the strong community pride and cooperation of small towns, especially those in the Dakotas. The citywide event is held annually the third full weekend in August. The schedule is packed with activities to appeal to almost any age group or appetite. A fireworks display and dance mark Friday evening. A parade kicks off the Saturday activities, which include an antique tractor pull, a 5K walk/run, an arm wrestling competition, an outdoor dance, and children's programs. Sunday is celebrated with a pancake feed, a kids' tractor pull, a classic car show, and a golf tournament. More than 150 artists and craftspeople, too, peddle their wares during Riverboat Days. Foodies will enjoy fajitas, chili dogs, lefse (yes, that is the Norwegian

theLawrenceWelk legend

In 1928 a young accordionist and his novelty band from Strasburg, North Dakota, arrived in Yankton and asked a new radio station, WNAX, if they could perform. Audience reaction was so tremendous that the manager offered to add the band to the station's roster of entertainers.

That brief stop lasted almost nine years and began the career of the great Lawrence Welk.

flatbread), burritos, homemade ice cream, funnel cakes, and teriyaki sticks.

For more information, call the Yankton Area Arts Association at (605) 665–1657, or visit the Web site at www.riverboatdays.com.

Straddling the South Dakota–Nebraska border, *Lewis and Clark Lake* brims with large- and small-mouth bass and offers postcard-perfect opportunities for sailing. Situated 5 miles west of Yankton on Highway 52, the lake is actually a man-made reservoir above Gavins Point Dam on the Missouri River, and it covers more than 30 square miles.

And if you have a penchant for dams, by all means stop by the *Gavins Point Power Plant.* The Gavins Point Dam, part of the 1944 Pick-Sloan Plan, is vital to the successful operation of six main stem dams and reservoirs on the Upper Missouri River Basin. The dam was completed in 1957 at the cost of $51 million.

Tours are given daily Memorial Day through Labor Day. During the thirty-minute tour, visitors can examine such areas as the control room, generator housing, and high-voltage cable areas. Free tours are offered every hour during weekends and holidays, and at 11:00 A.M., 1:00 P.M., and 3:00 P.M. Monday through Thursday. For more information call (402) 667–7873.

Anchoring the area's water sports is Lewis and Clark Marina, on the lake's northeast corner. The marina is home to hundreds of boats from April to October. Slips are available by the night, week, or season, and boats and personal watercraft can be rented. A boat-up gas dock, convenience store, and full-service dealer will keep you well provisioned. For more information call (605) 665–3111.

Enjoy the view and a leisurely meal on the waterfront at the *Marina Grille* restaurant (Lewis and Clark Marina; 605–665–3111). Free boat rides are offered with dinner Monday through Friday during the summer months. *Lewis and Clark Resort* (605–665–2680), located near the marina and restaurant, offers moderately priced motel rooms and two- and three-bedroom cabins. There's also an outdoor pool.

If you're more in the mood for roughing it, the *Lewis and Clark State*

Recreation Area—one of the top three most-visited major attractions in the state—has more than 370 campsites and cabins, all available by reservation. You'll find all the amenities here—from hot showers and electric hookups to paved pads. Call (800) 710–2267 for more information or visit the Web site at www.lewisandclarkpark.com.

The lake, restaurant, resort, and campgrounds are all located in the Lewis and Clark State Recreation Area, 4 miles west of Yankton on Highway 52.

Welcome to the Palace

Located 60 miles west of Sioux Falls on I–90, Mitchell is home to 14,558 people and the world's only ***Corn Palace*** (866–273–2676; www.cornpalace.com). Every year thousands of bushels of native, naturally colored corn, wheat, grain, and grasses are used to create beautifully decorated mosaics on the outside of the building. The look is the Taj Mahal of the Great Plains—an ode to agriculture, as was first intended by city founders. Mitchell's first Corn Belt Exposition was opened to the public in 1892. Nowadays more than 750,000 people visit annually. Every year by late September, old decorations have been removed and new corn and grain have been applied. Throughout the summer crews are busy applying the corn; they must follow precise instructions, which are printed on roofing paper that is attached to wood panels on the exterior of the

Mitchell Corn Palace

building. The Corn Palace is open year-round daily 8:00 A.M. to 9:00 P.M. Memorial Day through Labor Day, daily 8:00 A.M. to 5:00 P.M. in May and September, and Monday through Friday 8:00 A.M. to 5:00 P.M. October through April. Free admission.

The Corn Palace serves as a multiuse center for the community and region. The facility hosts stage shows as well as sports events in its arena. Every third weekend in July, thousands of people gather here to attend the nightly PRCA rodeo performances, as well as the many other activities that are provided throughout Rodeo Week.

The corn craze peaks in late August with the Corn Palace Festival, a week-long celebration with marching bands, country music concerts, a polka fest, and carnival rides. The highlight comes when the new mural is officially presented. Most years, themes are agricultural or nature related, although previous designs have celebrated the space race, the youth of America, and the Internet.

Not surprisingly, the Corn Palace makes a mighty fine bird feeder. After Corn Palace Week ends and winter arrives, local pigeons and squirrels devour the murals.

In 2002 Mitchell celebrated the 110th anniversary of the beginning of the Corn Palace ritual.

The downtown area isn't all about kernels and husks, however. The **Enchanted World Doll Museum** (615 North Main Street) features more than 438 displays, with more than 4,800 antique and modern dolls from about 127 countries. The museum is open daily April through November. For more information call (605) 996–9896.

The area around the Corn Palace is touristy, but farther away you'll find some interesting, and less visited, attractions.

One block north of the Corn Palace, at 700 North Main Street, is the **Soukup & Thomas International Balloon and Airship Museum.** More than 200 years of ballooning and airship history are detailed in this lighter-than-air collection. Here you can see one of the world's best collections of artwork, baskets, videos, and collectibles and learn about the history of gas and hot-air ballooning. Find out how hot air rises, experience the excitement of ballooning, and relive events such as the fiery crash of the *Hindenburg*. Open daily from 8:00 A.M. to 8:00 P.M. during the summer and 9:00 A.M. to 5:00 P.M. Monday through Saturday and 1:00 to 5:00 P.M. Sunday during

theberrybest

If you want to pick your own berries in South Dakota, head for Garritys' Prairie Gardens, an orchard/berry farm just 7.5 miles east of Yankton near Mission Hill. Pluck strawberries or raspberries. Hayrides are offered too. Call (605) 665–2806 for more information. The Web site is www.garritys.com.

OTHER ATTRACTIONS WORTH SEEING
IN SOUTHEASTERN SOUTH DAKOTA

Bede Art Gallery,
Yankton

Majic Kastle Family
Entertainment Center,
Sioux Falls

Shoto-teien Japanese Gardens,
Sioux Falls

Sioux River Amusement Park,
Sioux Falls

Warren M. Lee Changing Gallery,
Vermillion

Wild Water West Family
Amusement Park,
Sioux Falls

the off-season. The museum is open May through December. Donations are accepted. For more information call (605) 996–5533.

Mitchell's **Dakota Wesleyan University** campus (which proudly claims Oscar Howe, a Native American artist, as one of its alumni) houses the state's largest museum, the **Middle Border Museum–Oscar Howe Art Center** (1300 East University Street). More than 100,000 Native American and pioneer artifacts are displayed in the building complex. Sites include a restored 1886 Italianate home, built for the co-founder of the Corn Palace; the 1909 Farwell Methodist Church; the Sheldon School, an 1885 one-room territorial school; and a 1900 railroad depot. The **Case Art Gallery** is best known for its display of the oil painting *Dakota Woman,* by Harvey Dunn. Over the years this classic of Plains art has become synonymous with prairie life and prairie people. It depicts a young woman basking in the sunshine in an open field, while her baby rests under a parasol. (The Middle Border Museum takes its name from The Middle Border, author Hamlin Garland's name for America's last frontier, the Missouri River, where immigrants and homesteaders moving west met the prospectors and cattlemen returning east.)

Three other art galleries (Oscar Howe, Charles Hargens, and one for changing exhibits) feature original works by Howe, Dunn, and Hargens, James Earle Fraser, Gutzon Borglum, and others. The changing exhibits gallery features one-person shows, emphasizing American Indian artists of the Northern Plains.

A great source of pride and cultural identity for the community, the **Oscar Howe Gallery** features a permanent collection of original paintings by one of South Dakota's most revered artists. Howe was born on the Crow Creek Indian Reservation in South Dakota. As an artist and a teacher, his influence and inspiration provided a living legacy. In 1940 the painter was commissioned to create the dome mural, *Sun and Rain Clouds Over Hills,* for the Mitchell Public

Library as a WPA project. In 1972 Howe was widely recognized as one of America's preeminent Native American artists. When a building was rededicated to house the Mitchell Area Arts Council, the decision was made to recognize him.

The Howe Gallery boasts a collection of drawings and paintings that traces the history of Howe's development as an artist from when he was a student of the Santa Fe Indian School. His later work reflects a highly stylized interpretation of his heritage, using the formal elements of line, color, and space to create vivid, abstract designs.

The gallery's gift shop features the work of area artists and artisans, including original works on canvas and paper, sculpture, pottery and ceramics, quilts, jewelry, and reproductions.

The museum is open May and September Monday through Friday from 9:00 A.M. to 6:00 P.M. and Saturday and Sunday 1:00 to 4:00 P.M.; during June through August the center is open Monday through Friday 8:00 A.M. to 6:00 P.M. and Saturday and Sunday 10:00 A.M. to 6:00 P.M.; other months by appointment. Admission is $5.00 for adults, $4.00 for senior citizens, $2.00 for teens thirteen to eighteen, and free for children twelve and under. There are discounts for group and bus tours. For more information call (605) 996–2122.

Just north of town on the shores of Lake Mitchell is the state's only National Archaeological Landmark. The ***Mitchell Prehistoric Indian Village,*** which dates to about 900 B.C., reveals the lives of prehistoric people who vanished from the Great Plains in the thirteenth century, most likely after a great drought. Here as many as 800 seminomadic hunters and gatherers stalked buffalo, built lodges, and dwelled within a protective community. Highlights include a swinging bridge, walk-through lodge, and complete buffalo skeleton. The site is open daily from 8:00 A.M. to 6:00 P.M. May 1 through Labor Day. Call (605) 996–5473 for more information.

A drive through the hinterlands of South Dakota may seem lonely at first, but it can be the best way to see a generous slice of Americana. That's why it's worth a trek up to State Highway 34 from Mitchell to Forestburg. Along the way you'll drive through the lovely James River Valley. If you happen to be in the area from mid-August through the end of October, you'll see the old-fashioned produce stands that display a colorful harvest bonanza. There's a plethora of watermelon, pumpkins, squash, Indian corn, sweet corn, and gourds. Apparently the local melon rage began in the grim 1930s, when Ernie Schwemle and Harold Smith planted a few seeds in the sandy soil west of the James River. The fruits of their labor soon appeared, and the melon harvest has been an autumnal tradition ever since. There are several stands in the area, which are usually open every day, so the out-of-towner may savor the bounty.

From Forestburg travel west on State Highway 34 to Wessington Springs and step back in time to the Renaissance. For instance, the **Shakespeare Garden and Anne Hathaway Cottage** in Wessington Springs is open to the public during daylight hours. Admission is free, and you can arrange a tour of the cottage or make reservations for English tea by calling The Gazebo and Garden at (605) 539–9161. The high tea is $5.00 per person and includes a lovely arrangement of scones, finger sandwiches, and salad.

Wessington Springs also is fabled for its excellent pheasant hunting in the fall. The town is located in the draws of the Wessington Hills, surrounded by wooded gulches, fertile farmland, and rolling prairie. Two large springs that still provide water for the town first attracted native tribes, French fur traders, and settlers.

SELECTED CHAMBERS OF COMMERCE

Mitchell Area Chamber of Commerce,
P.O. Box 1026, Mitchell 57301,
(866) 273–CORN (2676)

**Sioux Falls Convention
and Visitors Bureau,**
200 North Phillips Avenue, Suite 102,
Sioux Falls 57102,
(605) 336–1620,
www.siouxfallscvb.com

**Vermillion Area Chamber of
Commerce,**
906 East Cherry Street,
Vermillion 57069, (800) 809–2071

Yankton Area Chamber of Commerce,
218 Fourth Street, P.O. Box 588,
Yankton 57078,
(800) 888–1460, www.yanktonsd.com

Where to Stay in Southeastern South Dakota

DELL RAPIDS

Rose Stone Inn,
504 East Fourth Street,
(605) 428–3698

SIOUX FALLS

Country Inn & Suites,
200 East Eighth Street,
(605) 373–0153,
(800) 456–4000

Days Inn–Empire,
3401 Gateway Boulevard,
(605) 361–9240,
(800) DAYS–INN

Oaks Hotel,
I–29 at exit 81, (605)
336–9000

Kelly Inn,
I–299 at exit 81,
(605) 338–6242,
(800) 635–3559

Radisson Encore Inn,
4300 Empire Place,
(800) 333–3333

VERMILLION

Comfort Inn,
located just west of I–29
on Highway 50,
(605) 624–8333

YANKTON

Best Western Kelly Inn,
1607 East Highway 50,
(605) 665–2906,
(800) 528–1234

Lewis and Clark Resort,
Lewis and Clark Marina,
(605) 665–2680

Where to Eat in Southeastern South Dakota

MITCHELL

Chef Louie's
(American),
601 East Havens Street,
(605) 996–7565

The Depot
(American),
210 South Main Street,
(605) 996–9417

SIOUX FALLS

Chi-Chi's
(Mexican),
4301 West Forty-first
Street,
(605) 361–9900

Minerva's,
301 South Phillips,
(605) 334–0386

Spezia
(Italian/American),
1716 South Western
Avenue at the
Park Ridge Mall,
(605) 334–7491

Tea Steak House,
on Main Street in Tea, SD
(5 miles north of Sioux
Falls on I–29),
(605) 368–9667
(voted best steak house in
South Dakota by *Midwest
Living* magazine)

Touch of Europe
(Eastern European),
337 South Phillips Avenue,
(605) 336–3066

VERMILLION

Silver Dollar Saloon,
1216 East Cherry Street,
(605) 624–4830

YANKTON

Marina Grille,
Lewis and Clark Marina,
(605) 665–3111

JoDean's
(American),
2809 Broadway,
(605) 665–9884,
jodeans.com

Western South Dakota

Topography, history, and the attitude of its residents set this region apart from the rest of South Dakota, so much, in fact, that people here like to think it could be a separate state. As long ago as 1877, residents wanted to separate the Black Hills from Dakota Territory and form their own Lincoln Territory.

The Missouri River divides the state into two distinct regions: West River and East River, and that's how residents define themselves as well. West River people gladly will tell you they would live nowhere else; they don't care much for the eastern lifestyle—coastal or within the boundaries of their own state. The Black Hills especially seem to be where individualism is most valued, as seen in the cowboy lifestyle and in the traditions of the Plains Indians.

Regional pride is understandable. It's almost dizzying how quickly the landscape can change in just a short drive. If you leave the eerie moonscape beauty of Badlands National Park, you're soon traveling over rolling grasslands, but then an hour later, you're breathing the heady scent of fresh pine in the verdant Black Hills National Forest. Western South Dakota, left untouched by the glaciers that shaped the eastern half of the state, pleases the soul with its smooth hills, isolated buttes, and

WESTERN SOUTH DAKOTA

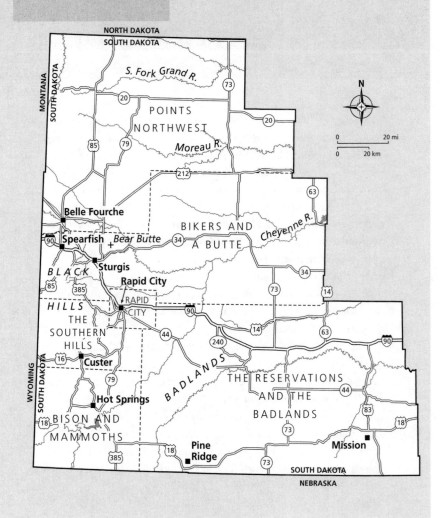

castellated Badlands. Agreeable, with occasional extremes of hot or cold, defines the climate. Warm summer days are almost always followed by cool evenings. The summer months are considered tourist season. From Memorial Day to Labor Day each year, the Hills' unaffected rhythm picks up as seasonal shops open and visitors stream in from all over the world.

Black Hills residents realize that tourism is the lifeblood of the area, and the traveler will find Western hospitality is more than just a catchphrase.

While the Black Hills/Badlands area has its share of big-ticket attractions, a little investigation will reveal some picturesque, sometimes eccentric, but assuredly off-the-beaten-path places.

The Reservations and the Badlands

The Lakota Indian culture and history present rich tableaux in the area. The Pine Ridge and Rosebud Indian reservations are located here. The term Sioux, short for *nadouessioux,* or "little snakes," actually came from the Chippewa, a longtime foe. Over the years the word has been widely adopted. The people of the Great Sioux Nation, however, prefer to be called Dakota, Nakota, or Lakota, according to their language group. (Dakota means "friends" or "allies.")

Buechel Memorial Lakota Museum, located in St. Francis on the Rosebud Indian Reservation in south-central South Dakota, is far away from the noise of more prominent attractions in the state, but the trip itself reveals another world. The museum displays many Lakota items, ranging from traditional dress to hunting tools as well as historic photographs of Sicangu Sioux Chief Spotted Tail, who strove for peace between Native Americans and the

WESTERN SOUTH DAKOTA'S TOP HITS

Badlands National Park	Mammoth Site
Black Hills National Forest	Mount Rushmore National Memorial
Crazy Horse Memorial	Museum of Geology
Custer State Park	Sturgis Rally & Races
Dahl Fine Arts Center	Wall Drug Store
Jewel Cave National Monument	Wounded Knee Historical Site
The Journey	

white settlers during the turbulent 1800s. Spotted Tail selected this land for his people in 1877.

The museum was named for another spiritual leader of the times, although he was not a Sioux. Father Buechel was a Jesuit priest assigned to the St. Francis Mission. Intrigued by the native culture, he collected photographs and artifacts and wrote several books in Lakota. His collection is the heart of the museum. Located on the grounds of the St. Francis Mission, the museum is open seven days a week from 8:00 A.M. to 4:30 P.M. Admission is free. Call (605) 747–2745 for more information.

Twelve miles east of Rosebud, on U.S. Highway 18 in Mission, is the Sinte Gleska University, a tribally chartered school that was founded in 1971. It is the state's only college on a reservation.

To borrow from Robert Frost, there is always the chance to take the road less traveled in South Dakota, and a fine opportunity is to venture southwest into the **Pine Ridge Indian Reservation** and its portion of the Badlands. Certain parts of the reservation, 120,000 acres to be exact, lie in Badlands National Park. The South Unit was added to the park in 1976, and the White River Visitor Center (605–455–2878) houses cultural exhibits and a videotape program on Oglala history. The center is open daily from 9:00 A.M. to 5:00 P.M. during the summer and from 8:00 A.M. to 5:00 P.M. Monday through Friday the rest of the year.

The **Red Cloud Heritage Center** (605–867–5491), at Red Cloud Indian School in Pine Ridge, features a collection of Native American art that is regarded as one of the finest in the Northern Plains. This collection includes graphics, paintings, and sculptures from the annual Red Cloud Indian Arts show, a large national competition for native artists from all over North America. The newly renovated Heritage Center is located in the historic old school building, constructed in 1888 by Jesuit priests and brothers, who have operated the school with the Franciscan sisters since that time. The great Oglala chief and statesman Red Cloud asked the Jesuit "Black Robes" to start the school, and it later was named in his honor. Red Cloud's grave can be seen in the cemetery that overlooks the school. (Red Cloud also led the successful fight to close off the Bozeman Trail, a pass that led to the gold mines of Montana. The trail crossed over the traditional hunting grounds of the Teton.) Notice the Holy Rosary Mission church, which features a Gothic interior decorated with a profusion of traditional designs by Sioux artist Felix Walking.

The people here are proud of their ancestors, yet today's world also includes Lakota people who have reached great heights in other areas, such as athletics. Runner Billy Mills, an Oglala Lakota, is one of the more famous native sons of Pine Ridge. He won the gold medal for the 10,000-meter race during the

1964 Summer Olympics in Tokyo. He was the first American to win that race, and he did it in record time.

It would be naive to think of Native American history only as moments of grand celebration or artistic endeavor. The cries of Wounded Knee can still be heard when you look at historic photographs of that bloody battle in the dead of winter. Following the death of spiritual leader Sitting Bull on December 15, 1890, Chief Big Foot and his Minniconjou band set out for Pine Ridge. They were intercepted by the Seventh Cavalry and were brought, under a white flag of truce, to Wounded Knee. On the morning of December 29, soldiers prepared to search the band for weapons. A rifle was fired, setting off intense shooting that killed more than 250 natives, most of them unarmed. Bodies of women and children were found as far as 3 miles from the site, apparently shot as they fled into the plains.

The ***Wounded Knee Historical Site*** is located 8 miles east of Pine Ridge on US 18, then 7 miles north on an unnumbered paved road to Wounded Knee. A solitary stone monument stands on the mass grave site. The Native American community, the National Park Service, and the state of South Dakota are working to create a national memorial park in honor of the victims of the Wounded Knee massacre. In 1973, as a way of drawing attention to grievances, some 200 armed Native Americans occupied Wounded Knee for seventy days. These stories bear retelling for the simple hope that, someday, cultural and racial differences will be genuinely embraced rather than mindlessly condemned. *Bury My Heart at Wounded Knee,* by Dee Brown, is an excellent book on what is often called the last major conflict between the U.S. Army and the Great Sioux Nation. For South Dakotans, the image of Wounded Knee is hauntingly stark and familiar. The photograph of Big Foot's body, partially clothed and stiff on the snow-covered land, is often used in newspapers and books when recounting the massacre. A reporter who witnessed the aftermath described it this way: "Big Foot lay in sort of a solitary dignity."

ROBIN'S FAVORITES

Badlands National Park,
62 miles east of Rapid City on I-90,
(605) 433–5361

Black Hills National Forest,
(605) 673–9200

Crazy Horse Memorial,
5 miles north of Custer, (605) 673–4681

Jewel Cave National Monument,
14 miles west of Custer on
U.S. Highway 16, (605) 673–2288

Mount Rushmore National Memorial,
25 miles southwest of Rapid City,
(605) 574–2523

At the east entrance of Badlands National Park, the **Prairie Homestead Historic Site** is the only original sod building on public display in South Dakota. Located 0.5 mile from the east entrance of the park on State Highway 240, it is furnished in the style of the original homesteaders, and letters and photographs of the original homesteader's family and neighbors offer riveting insight into the hardships they endured. Many of the early homes on the plains and prairies of the Dakotas were built of sod. The homes were efficient—cool in the summer and warm in the winter—but also dark, dirty, and often infested with mice, bedbugs, and other unsavory houseguests. It is open daily from May through September. For more information call (605) 433–5400. The Web site is www.prairiehomestead.com.

Badlands National Park (605–433–5361) is as otherworldly as land can be. Soft clays and sandstones deposited as sediments twenty-six to thirty-seven million years ago by streams from the Black Hills left vast plains, which attracted a community of creatures. Saber-toothed cats and ancestors of today's camels and horses lived in this area, and their fossilized bones make a giant prehistoric graveyard.

Famous Sons

The traditional language on Rosebud reservation is Lakota, and the band of Sioux is Sicangu (also known as Brule or Burnt Thigh). Rosebud, which covers 882,416 acres, is the most populated of the state's reservations, but it's still a community with few towns and lots of space in between. Tribal headquarters are located in the town of Rosebud.

Little-known facts: The late Ben Reifel, a five-term U.S. congressman, was born near Parmelee on the reservation in 1906. During his lifetime he worked for the Bureau of Indian Affairs, served in the U.S. Army, and received a doctoral degree from Harvard University. Reifel ran for office in 1960 and served until his retirement in 1971. He died in 1990. White Eagle, a member of the Rosebud Sioux Tribe, was the first Native American to sing leading tenor roles in American musical theater and opera. He graduated from the prestigious Merola Opera program at the San Francisco Opera and performed with the Pennsylvania Opera Theatre, Florentine Opera, and Cleveland Opera, among others.

You can explore the area's backcountry on a scenic drive through **Crazy Horse Canyon,** southwest of Rosebud. This canyon entices visitors with 50,000 acres of magnificent views. Guides are available to lead travelers through the canyon or any other area of the reservation. Call ahead for guide service, which I strongly recommend, as this area is remote and has no developed roads. Call the Rosebud Sioux Tribe at (605) 747–2381.

About 2 miles west of Rosebud on BIA 7, you can enjoy a picnic along the Little White River, which flows through Ghost Hawk Park, 50,000 acres of raw beauty.

Eventually humans stumbled upon this seemingly hostile land. Upon arriving in the Badlands, native tribes called it *mako sica,* meaning "land bad," and the French Canadian trappers who later traveled across its rugged terrain in the early 1800s dubbed it *les mauvaises terres à traverser,* or "bad lands to travel across." At present, antelope, mule deer, prairie dogs, and Rocky Mountain bighorn sheep inhabit the Badlands. To get an up close and personal view of all creatures great and small, take the **Badlands Loop,** which begins at exit 131 off Interstate 90. This 32-mile loop through the Badlands includes numerous scenic points. Don't forget to step out of the car and smell the flowers; although the Badlands look barren from the highway, they are actually blooming with more than 200 kinds of wildflowers and 50 grasses.

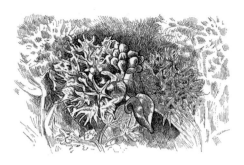

Wildflowers in Badlands National Park

As you wind down the road, you'll pass the **Ben Reifel Visitor Center,** which is open from 8:00 A.M. to 9:00 P.M. daily, with extended hours during the summer. This is park headquarters, and the center offers information, an audio-visual center, a small museum, and a "touch room," where you can pick up various fossils and natural history specimens.

If camping's not your thing, check into **Cedar Pass Lodge** (605–433–5460), which features full accommodations, a dining room, and souvenir shops—all under one roof. Located near the national park headquarters on State Highway 240, the lodge is operated by the Oglala Sioux tribe under contract with the U.S. National Park Service. Open from April through October, the lodge's rates are moderate: $57.75 for two people.

TOP ANNUAL EVENTS

Black Hills Powwow and Art Expo,
Rapid City, early July

Central States Fair,
Rapid City, every August

Days of '76 (rodeo and parade),
Deadwood, first full weekend in August,
(605) 578–1876

Gold Discovery Days,
Custer, late July,
(605) 673–2244

Sturgis Rally & Races,
Sturgis, every August,
www.sturgisrallynews.com

Back on the road, it's easy to imagine how the early wayfarer might have been stymied by the craggy buttes of this area. Fortunately, the Badlands are more hospitable for the modern traveler, with the paved highway, nine scenic overlooks, developed nature trails, and the air-conditioned visitor center at Cedar Pass. Like a fine wine, the Badlands are improving with time. Every rainstorm and windstorm gnaws at the sediments, accentuating every ravine and ragged pinnacle.

As you leave the Badlands at exit 110, you might be a bit parched if you are traveling in the summer heat. Respite is close by at **Wall Drug Store** (605–279–2175; www.walldrug.com), where the Hustead family still promises free ice water, as it did during the Great Depression. Once listed as one of the corniest places in the country by *USA Today,* Wall Drug Store nonetheless attracts thousands of visitors each year with its campy cowboy theme. The Hustead family has taken the designation in stride, pointing out that even sarcastic comments are better than no publicity at all. First of all, there's the 6-foot jackalope. City slickers take note: Jackalopes, a cross between an antelope and a jackrabbit, do not exist. Someone long ago had a good time—and probably a good laugh—making up this peculiar creature. There's also a life-size animated cowboy quartet and orchestra. And you can see it for yourself at Wall Drug Store. On the authentic side, the walls are decorated with more than 600 cattle brands, hundreds of historical pictures, and a collection of Native American artifacts. The food in the cafeteria is darn good, too, and a hot cup of coffee is still just 5 cents. Wall Drug Store is open year-round, with summer hours from 6:30 A.M. to 9:00 P.M. Two blocks south of Wall Drug Store is the National Grasslands Visitor Center, where you can explore the four main ecosystems of the High Plains.

Get back on I–90 west, and as you leave behind the dusty Badlands, you'll traverse a short stretch of prairie. In just an hour you'll be in Rapid City, located at the foothills of the Black Hills National Forest. The **South Dakota Air & Space Museum** (605–385–5188) is located on exit 66 outside the main gate of Ellsworth Air Force Base, 7 miles east of Rapid City. See historic bombers, fighters, and utility aircraft, as well as many indoor exhibits of aviation memorabilia for a nominal fee mid-May through mid-September. Here you can see a three-

fifteenminutes offame

Scenes from *Starship Troopers,* the Paul Verhoeven movie based on Robert A. Heinlein's classic 1959 science-fiction novel, were filmed in the Badlands. Although the movie didn't win an Oscar for best acting or script writing, it definitely gets two thumbs-up for best natural location that is as otherworldly as it gets.

fifth scale model of the Honda Stealth Bomber and General Eisenhower's personal Mitchell B-25 bomber. Ellsworth is home to the second-largest fleet of B-1 bombers in the nation, and it's not uncommon to see the sleek, low-level bomber graze the skyline. The museum is open seven days a week from 8:30 A.M. to 4:30 P.M., with expanded hours until 6:00 P.M. from mid-May to mid-September. Free admission. You can take an official base tour, which includes a Minuteman Missile silo, for a nominal fee.

One of the latest perks for tourists (and locals, if the truth be told) is the **Black Hills Visitor Information Center.** The $3.2-million center offers many free services, including brochures, maps, and onsite trip counseling. Exhibits and displays also preview national parks, state parks, and every community in the Black Hills and Badlands region. To reach the center, take exit 61 (Elk Vale Road) north off I-90. Open year-round from 8:00 A.M. to 6:00 P.M. daily, with extended hours from May through September. Call (605) 355-3700 for more information.

Head west again on I-90 and you'll reach Rapid City. With a population of 61,000, it's the state's second-largest city.

Rapid City

To "lay out a Denver" was what the city founders—a group of unlucky miners—had in mind for Rapid City more than one hundred years ago. The city hasn't reached the population base of Denver, Colorado, but that's okay with its residents today. Growth here is steady and managed. With no state income tax or corporate income tax, the city attracts a variety of businesses. People in Rapid City are fiercely loyal. If you even utter the words "Sioux Falls," you might as well be prepared to listen to a lengthy discourse on why Rapid City is a far better place.

The **Rushmore Mall** (take exit 58 off I-90) offers one-stop shopping for the busy person. It hosts anchor stores such as Sears and JCPenney, but a few boutiques and occasional craft shows lend a personal touch to the mall. Two movie theater complexes close by and a host of restaurant chains such as Red Lobster, Chili's, and Applebee's round out the mall experience.

Just outside mall proper is **Borders** (2130 Haines Avenue), a mighty peak in a small city's literary landscape. The chain bookstore is particularly unchain-like, mostly because it carries so many regional authors and showcases local performers in the coffeehouse section. The sunny color scheme of this store, too, made it hard for me to peel myself away one summer night. There, I discovered *The Prairie in Her Eyes,* by Ann Daum, and *Feels Like Far: A Rancher's Life on the Great Plains,* by Linda Hasselstrom. Both women, who were raised on western South Dakota ranches, write eloquently about working, knowing,

The Ballad of Brooks & Dunn

Growing up in South Dakota, my musical palate was whetted early with the sounds of Merle Haggard, Loretta Lynn, and Johnny Cash. Country-western songs were in tune with the daily struggles of plains people who dreamed of a better life.

Later, working as a journalist at the Rapid City Journal, it was my duty to interview the stars. One time the country duo Kix Brooks and Ronnie Dunn was to perform in Rapid City. I had scheduled a telephone interview with their publicist. The time came to call, and I dialed up the number, confident of my interview skills as I reviewed my questions. Brooks and Dunn, however, took control and had me in the interrogation chair from the time we said hello.

"What kind of girl are you, a makeup girl or a natural girl?" they asked good-naturedly, which is the cowboy way.

"What color is your hair?"

"How tall are you?"

"How much do you weigh?"

My coworkers crooked their necks as they tried to catch snippets of the conversation.

The interview was flattering, startling, and irreverent all at the same time, and one that I won't forget.

and loving the prairie. Borders is open from 9:00 A.M. to 10:00 P.M. Monday through Thursday, from 9:00 A.M. to 11:00 P.M. Friday and Saturday and from 9:00 A.M. to 9:00 P.M. Sunday. Call (605) 394–5334 for more information.

Just north of the downtown district along Omaha Street is **Memorial Garden,** a rose grower's fantasy: The All-American Rose Gardens show off the long-stemmed beauties in many varieties, such as Summer Fashion and Red Pinocchio. At the center of the gardens, the simple yet stately Memorial Fountain is dedicated to the 239 people who lost their lives in the devastating flood of 1972. Dedicated city planning prevailed, and now part of the floodplain has been developed for recreational use. Music can be heard from the park bandshell during the summer.

Not far from the garden is **The Journey** (222 New York Street), one of Rapid City's newest museums that incorporates local history and the nature of the universe. This incredible museum—which is described as an excursion through time—unifies collections from five sources: the Museum of Geology, the South Dakota State Archaeological Research Center, the Sioux Indian Museum, the Minnilusa Museum Collection, and the Duhamel Collection, which was a gift to the city from Helen and F. A. "Bud" Duhamel in 1985. The museum tour begins with a twenty-minute video, which details pioneer and Native

American history. The self-guided tour begins with 1,000 points of light that represent the immense nature of a universe deep in space and time. The time line takes you from the formation of the Black Hills billions of years ago to the present day. Visitors are given sound sticks so they can listen to historical stories and descriptions at each exhibit. Open daily from 9:00 A.M. to 5:00 P.M. Admission is $6.00 for adults, $5.00 for seniors, $4.00 for children eleven to seventeen; free for children ten and under. For more information and hours call (605) 394–6923 or visit the Web site at www.journeymuseum.org.

The romantic notion of the Old West comes alive each fall as the Journey Museum hosts the **Wild West Days.** Historians, actors, and re-enactors take the stage to bring to life the colorful and sometimes infamous characters of the Dakota past. Local artisans and craftspeople show their wares, and ropemakers, weavers, woodcarvers, spinners, quilters, and storytellers add undeniably Old West flair to the celebration. For more information call (605) 394–6923.

The **Black Hills PowWow** also is held each fall at the nearby Rushmore Plaza Civic Center. The Lakota, Nakota, and Dakota nations come together for this celebration, highlighting the Native Americans' vast cultural heritage and pageantry. It is an unforgettable and mesmerizing experience to see the dancers perform. For more information, call the Black Hills PowWow Association at (605) 341–0925 or visit the Web site at www.blackhillspowwow.com.

Follow Omaha Street east and see why folks from Rapid City are so crazy about dinosaurs. It seems they're everywhere. The **Museum of Geology** (located in the O'Harra Memorial Building on the South Dakota School of Mines and Technology campus) is filled with high-quality fossils of dinosaurs, giant

Four Seasons

We have a saying about the climate in South Dakota, which is part deadpan humor and part reality: "Summer is three months in South Dakota, and winter lasts nine months." That is an exaggeration, of course, but snow in June is not unheard of. In general, here's what you can expect from South Dakota's four seasons:

Summer—Warm (sometimes hot) days and cool nights are the norm from mid-June to mid-September.

Fall—Comfortable warm weather through September and crisp cool weather into November is typical.

Winter—Although temperatures can be dastardly cold from December to early March, cold spells usually alternate with milder weather. Snowfall is prevalent, providing excellent conditions for winter sports.

Spring—You'll find mostly sunny days late March to mid-June, but this can be the rainy season. Spring snow showers are a possibility through early May.

A Landmark Taste

The Landmark Restaurant has been a favorite of mine, whether for lunch or for a romantic evening.

The restaurant has graciously shared this recipe for Old-Fashioned Buffalo Stew, which reflects South Dakota cuisine in a savory way.

1 pound buffalo chuck, trimmed, and cut into 1-inch cubes

2 tablespoons all-purpose flour

2 tablespoons vegetable oil

2 large onions

2 cups sliced mushrooms

2 cloves garlic, minced

2 teaspoons tomato paste

4 cups sliced carrots

2 medium russet potatoes, thinly sliced (about 2 cups)

1 cup 1-inch green bean pieces

1 tablespoon cornstarch

1 tablespoon water

½ cup chopped fresh parsley

Coat meat with flour, shaking off excess. In a large nonstick pot, heat oil over medium-high heat. Add meat; sauté until browned, about 6 minutes. Remove.

Add onions and mushrooms to pot; sauté for 6 minutes. Add garlic; sauté, stirring, for 1 minute. Pour off fat. Return meat to pot; stir in tomato paste. Add enough water to just cover, and bring to a boil. Reduce heat to low; simmer until meat is tender, about 1¼ hours. Skim off any foam.

Add carrots, potatoes, and green beans. Cover partially; simmer for 15 minutes.

In a small bowl, mix cornstarch and cold water; stir into stew. Increase heat and boil uncovered for 1 minute. Sprinkle with parsley and serve. Makes six servings.

fish, and prehistoric mammals. Dioramas tell the story of the Badlands and the strange and wild creatures that once lived there. Rock hounds can find a collection of local agates, minerals, and ores. (Remember that the state gemstone is the Fairburn agate, which is considered among the most beautiful of all agates.) The museum is open 8:00 A.M. to 5:00 P.M. Monday through Friday, 9:00 A.M. to 4:00 P.M. on Saturday, and 1:00 to 4:00 P.M. on Sunday. For information call (605) 394–2467. Admission is free.

Take St. Joseph Street west and you can see more museums in Rapid City's historic downtown district. Helpful tip: The downtown district basically spreads from two one-way streets: Main and St. Joseph Streets. (Be mindful of this, for during summer many near-collisions and several fender benders have been seen as newcomers try to go against the flow of traffic on a one-way street.) Like so many other communities across the nation, the city's downtown has been on an economic seesaw as malls redefined where America shopped. Rapid City's downtown wholeheartedly met the challenge and lined its streets with restaurants, galleries, one-of-a-kind boutiques, and a movie house. Before you browse in the shops, take a good look at the architecture. Each building is distinctly unique, and as one adjoins another, you get a mini-lesson in architecture. Notice the ornate Italianate facades, as well as the European onion-shaped domes. A walking-tour guide of the historic downtown district is available at the Rapid City Area Chamber of Commerce office. Call the chamber at (605) 343–1744.

At the corner of Main and Sixth Streets is the Elks building, which was built in 1911 as an Elks lodge and opera house. At present it's home to the **Elks Theatre,** where you can enjoy second-run movies for just $1.50. The theater also features a balcony, which is perfect for movie dates. The cushy seats and big screen (which hides a vaudeville stage) make the Elks Theatre the grandest movie house in town. Call (605) 341–4149 for show times.

Across the street at 523 Sixth Street is the **Hotel Alex Johnson** (605–342–1210; www.alexjohnson.com), which was built in 1925. This hotel, one of the city's finest, is listed on the National Register of Historic Places. If a celebrity or government official is visiting the area, he or she likely will be staying here. The 143 rooms have been refurnished, and they continue the Old World charm of the hotel—with a decidedly American twist. Rates start at $107.50 in summer.

With its own gift shop, restaurant, and bar, the Alex, as locals affectionately call it, offers full-service luxury under one roof. Moderately to expensively priced, The **Landmark Restaurant & Lounge** menu includes native game, whereas **Paddy O'Neill's Pub & Casino** is the place to be for a yard of imported beer, a bowl of popcorn, and a chance at one of the slot machines.

And while you're soaking in the elegant, romantically Western atmosphere of the Alex, pick up a walking tour brochure of the hotel. The self-guided tour will take you to points of interest inside and outside of the hotel. For instance, if you look upward in the lobby, you will see the hotel's unique chandelier of wood, copper, and glazed tile. Suspended with chains, the chandelier is formed of war lances. The fixture is shaped like a teepee and it is made of concentric, copper-clad wooden rings, each decreasing in size. The rings are decorated in authentic Sioux Indian patterns.

For the most part, downtown shop owners have pledged allegiance to the original architecture of their properties. ***Prairie Edge Trading Co. and Galleries*** (605–342–3086 or 800–541–2388), located at 606 Main Street, is a stunning example of what restoration can do. You'll find an extensive collection of Plains Indian arts, crafts, and jewelry. Several Native American artists have their studios here, providing visitors an opportunity to see works in progress. Prairie Edge's Sioux Trading Post features an enormous selection of glass beads, trade beads, hides, furs, shells, teeth and claws, and many other craft supplies. It's like getting lost in a candy shop, but calorie-free. For a sneak preview of this ingeniously conceived store, check out the Web site at www.prairieedge.com.

Grab a hearty bite to eat next door at ***The Firehouse Brewing Co.*** (610 Main Street; 605–348–1915), which bears the distinction of being the first brewpub in the state. It features great beer and great food. The Firehouse has always been one of my favorite haunts, and I highly recommend it. And yes, it's located in an honest-to-goodness 1915 firehouse, complete with historic photos and memorabilia.

Across the street at 611 Main Street, ***Dakota Interiors*** (605–343–8331) carries decorative home furnishings and accessories that capitalize on the ever-popular rustic lodge look. The shop itself has hardwood floors and natural colors that flatter the wide selection of goods. Candles, potpourri, lamps, bath accessories, imported and custom-made furniture, birdhouses, bedding, and more will definitely put you in the redecorating mood. The shop is open 10:00 A.M. to 5:30 P.M. Monday through Friday, and 10:00 A.M. to 5:00 P.M. Saturday, with extended holiday hours.

Chocoholics have nowhere to run—and nowhere to hide—once they enter the doors of ***Mostly Chocolates.*** The charming downtown store features more than twenty-three kinds of truffles, including chocolate raspberry, Black Forest, apricot brandy, Irish crème, lemon chiffon, and rum. If you happen to be at the store during Christmastime, you can sample such red-and-white treats as the candy-cane truffles. To keep the sugar buzz going, the store also has recently added a gelato (that's Italian ice cream) bar. The fudge is equally tempting, especially in such seasonal themes as pumpkin pie and fresh strawberry. If it can be covered in chocolate—and potato chips, coconut, cookies, pretzels, and fresh and dried fruit qualify—Peggy Kelly and her staff will do it. (The chocolate factory is in Rapid City, adjacent to Black Hawk.) For more information call (605) 341–2264.

A jazz club–like decor—turquoise walls accented with black-and-white photographs of famous jazz musicians—marks ***Art's Southern Style Smokehouse BBQ*** (609 Main Street). Art explains all the meat, including pulled pork, chicken wings, and beef brisket, is seasoned, marinated, and slowly smoked to perfection for up to fourteen hours. Coleslaw, fried okra, hush puppies, and cornbread muffins are the supporting cast at this welcome, change-of-pace eatery. Call (605) 348–5499 or fax at (605) 348–5503. Good news: There is a carryout menu as well.

For a totally different experience, walk down the street to **Global Market Imports** (605–343–4051). Choose from hemp jewelry, dishes, clothing, local arts and crafts, silver jewelry, unique gifts, and twig baskets. This is a favorite of mine. The store is open from 9:00 A.M. to 9:00 P.M. Monday through Saturday and 11:00 A.M. to 7:00 P.M. Sunday.

A few blocks away, at the corner of Seventh and Quincy Streets, is another arts facility that boasts three galleries and a live theater. The **Dahl Fine Arts Center** (605–394–4101) houses the Dakota Art Gallery, which features local and regional artists; the Cyclorama Gallery, a unique 180-foot oil-on-canvas panorama spanning 200 years of United States history; and the Central Gallery, which brings world-class exhibits to Rapid City. Black Hills Community Theatre (BHCT) also stages its productions in the 170-seat Dahl theater. A group of professional and amateur thespians skillfully performs classics such as Arthur Miller's gripping *Death of a Salesman* and shows equal finesse with newer productions like *Dancing at Lughnasa*. BHCT presents five productions each year during the fall and winter months. Dahl hours June through August are 9:00 A.M. to 7:00 P.M. Monday through Thursday, 9:00 A.M. to 5:00 P.M. Friday and Saturday, and 1:00 to 5:00 P.M. Sunday. Hours from September through May are 9:00 A.M. to 5:00 P.M. Monday through Saturday and 1:00 to 5:00 P.M. Sunday. Free admission.

Can haute couture be found in the Heartland? Yes, indeed. The fine staff of **Kay's Next Door 2** in downtown Rapid City (625 St. Joseph Street) dresses the best in Rapid City. The lines are elegantly borrowed from Kenar, Regina Porter, Harvé Benard, Karen Kane, Howard Wolf, and D'oraz, just to name a few. The best thing about this boutique is the classy staff who will help you dress up for any event—whether a rodeo or a glamorous night on the town. The jewelry selection is fantastic as well. Store hours are 9:30 A.M. to 5:00 P.M. Monday through Saturday, with the store closing at 1:00 P.M. on Saturday during the summer season. Nearby at 613 Sixth Street, the ultrahip **Eclipse on Sixth** beauty salon can style your hair in an equally fashionable manner. For appointments call (605) 343–2107.

If you like browsing for antiques, you won't want to miss the **Antique & Furniture Mart** (605–341–3345) at 1112 West Main Street. The store is packed with antiques and used furniture. The items move quickly, so if you see something you absolutely can't live without, it's best to make a purchase decision right away. Keep in mind that South Dakota has been a state for only 115 years, and settlement didn't occur much before that; as a result, most of the antiques you find in the region are only three to four generations old. Simple oak furniture in particular is found here, pedestal tables, china cabinets, and picture frames. Other well-represented lines include crockery, spongeware, Depression glass, barbed wire, Indian artifacts, and anything that could be found on an old ranch. Interior designers, however, have caught on to the ranch-theme decor in recent years, and the functional nature of plains furniture and accessories mixes in nicely with just about any style.

With the many talented artists practicing in the Black Hills, it's no surprise that another gallery has opened in Rapid City. *Smatterings: Art for All People,* is located in the Old Metz Bakery building at 601 Twelfth Street. The gallery features such regional artists as Richard DuBois, a former teacher of mine who specializes in watercolors; Judy Lehner, another watercolor artist; Jennifer Braig, who works in oils; and James Van Nuys, whose print of *House in Buffalo Gap* graces my kitchen-nook wall. These artisans fit well into the gallery's mission statement: to assemble an eclectic collection of artwork, filled in with Dakota integrity.

Many of the building's original fixtures have been left intact, giving a slightly industrial, loft-like effect to the gallery and enhancing the artwork. Smatterings also does framing and offers art-related classes and workshops.

Hours are 9:00 A.M. to 5:00 P.M. Monday through Friday and 10:00 A.M. to 4:00 P.M. Saturday. Closed Sunday. For more information call (605) 342–6197 or visit the Web site at www.smatterings.com.

Halley Park is just across the street, and although small, its rose arbor and garden bring visual joy to passersby. The park forms a triangle where West Main Street forks into two one-way streets. It's one of the more beautiful, yet less-occupied, parks in town.

Located at the park is the *Children's Science Center* (515 West Boulevard). This is one of the newest ways the city has piqued the imaginations of young people with interactive programs on math, physical science, technology, space science, and more. A giant sand pendulum and a simulated fossil dig are two ways the center helps teach kids about scientific principles and the laws of nature in a fun way.

The center is open from 9:00 A.M. to 4:00 P.M. Tuesday through Saturday. For more information call (605) 394–6996.

If you travel south on *West Boulevard,* you'll see the grand homes that have made it possible for this street to bear the designation of a historic district. The best way to see it is to take a leisurely stroll down its tree-lined median. The boulevard is so stately that it's common to see walkers, joggers, day-dreamers, and artists getting wrapped up in its turn-of-the-twentieth-century grandeur. English Tudor, Neoclassical, Queen Anne, Federal, and many more styles are represented on this street. Residents take great pride in their homes, and it shows through their vigilant upkeep of the properties and some fantastic flower gardens. If you're here in wintertime, take a slow drive up and down the boulevard to see some ornate Christmas-light displays that make the area shine like an enchanted village.

If the quiet elegance of West Boulevard leaves young people in the group a little restless, follow Quincy Street west to the top of the hill. Kids' imaginations will roam free at **Dinosaur Park** (605–343–8687), where seven life-size replicas of dinosaurs, including a triceratops and a tyrannosaurus rex, await to be climbed upon, photographed, and gleefully admired. The park is a free attraction that is appropriately listed on the National Register of Historic Places. Adults will be impressed by the scenic view as well. When you're at the park, you also are on Skyline Drive, which affords one of the finest views of Rapid City. It also geographically divides the town in half. A gift shop and sandwich bar are located at the park, which is open 8:00 A.M. to dusk during summer and 8:00 A.M. to 5:00 P.M. after Labor Day. (South Dakota has its own state fossil: the veggie-eating triceratops. A skeleton of the horned dinosaur, which lived in the late Cretaceous period, approximately sixty-eight million years ago, was found in Harding County in 1927. It's now on display in the Museum of Geology, located at 501 East St. Joseph Street on the South Dakota School of Mines and Technology campus.)

A comfortably elegant stay can be found in one of the four Victorian-themed guest rooms available at **Morning's Glory B&B,** located at 820 South Street. Room rates range from $95 to $135. For more information call (605) 355–4550 or visit the Web site at www.morningsglorybnb.com.

Wilson Park, located on Mount Rushmore Road, a main drag that runs parallel to West Boulevard, is small, but its charm is enormous. An outdoor skating rink sets a Currier-and-Ives scene during winter, and arts festivals in summer continue the neighborly feeling as visitors flock around the flower gardens and gazebo.

Located 5 miles west of the downtown district on Chapel Lane (Route 11) is **Chapel in the Hills** (605–342–8281). Stavkirke, as it also is known, is an exact replica of the famous 860-year-old Borgund Church in Norway. Wood carvings, Christian symbols, and Norse dragon heads adorn the building, which features pegged construction. It's a favorite and most romantic place for couples to exchange their wedding vows. Evening vespers are held daily 8:00 P.M. to 8:30 P.M. during the summer months. The chapel itself is open 7:00 A.M. to sunset May 1 to October 1. While you're there, check out the nearby **Norwegian Log Cabin Museum.** Admission is free.

Home is where the bear, elk, wolves, bighorns, and other North American wildlife roam at **Bear Country USA** (605–343–2290), 8 miles south of Rapid City on Highway 16. Bear cubs, wolf pups, and other park offspring are featured in the walk-through Wildlife and Welcome Center at the end of the driving tour. Bear Country is open daily, from May through October. Visit the Web site at bearcountryusa.com. Call for admission prices.

Not too far away from the Old World-charm of the Stavkirke is the contemporary lodge attitude of the **Canyon Lake Chophouse** (2720 Chapel Lane). A relative newcomer to the fine dining roster in Rapid City, the Chophouse serves an incredibly peaceful view of the west shore of Canyon Lake. The menu features beef, seafood, native game, imported beers, and wine. The ultimate comfort food for lunch? The cowboy meatloaf sandwich with mashed potatoes. Heavenly. Call (605) 388–8000 for more information.

One of the newest additions to the Black Hills bed-and-breakfast scene is **Where Rosemary Grows,** which is located 1-miles off Highway 79 on Highway 40 West in Hermosa. "Where Rosemary Grows is a place that my imagination dreamed of where all is balanced," says owner Cheri Santana. "A place of joy where romance is the language spoken and children's laughter is the music played." Rosemary does indeed grow here, along with perennials, annuals, and antique roses. The house overlooks seventeen rolling acres of land, with a seasonal creek running through it, in the foothills of the Black Hills. To the east you can see all the way to the plains, while just to the north the foothills begin. Evenings on the decks give glimpses of eagles, deer, and distant coyote. Rates are $115 a room. For reservations call (605) 394–5431.

For the most part, western South Dakota has taken advantage of its handsome surroundings, and tourism is vital. The tourist trappings are evident in Rapid City—sometimes elegant, sometimes cheesy—but to get a true snapshot of what South Dakota's second-largest city is like, just get in the car, drive, and go wherever the wind takes you.

The Southern Hills

If you take U.S. Highway 16 west, you'll find a plethora of tourist attractions as you get closer to the heart of the **Black Hills National Forest.** Actually a domed mountain region, the Black Hills extend over an area of about 6,000 square miles. They often are described as intimate because the natural surroundings invite you to hike, bike, explore, and experience the Black Hills. Fishing, camping, skiing, mountain climbing, rock hunting, and daydreaming round out an outdoors-lover's menu for magic.

Because of their unfettered plains and gorgeous summits, the Black Hills and Badlands have been a natural movie site for producers eager to capitalize on America's ongoing romance with the West. Probably the most well-known film shot in the Hills is *Dances with Wolves,* Kevin Costner's Academy Award–winning tale of a young Union soldier who deserts his post to live with the Lakota Indians in the 1800s. TNT productions also filmed *Crazy Horse* near the Hot Springs area.

Aside from the occasional limelight from these productions, the Black Hills and Badlands are more likely to bathe in the spirit of their people and under the glorious blue skies midday or the stunning sunsets as the evening draws near. As a summer day winds down, you can see the soft black fringe of the pine trees on the horizon. Barely there, clouds hover low over the hills, adding a wisp of rich orange and cotton-candy pink.

South Dakota's Badlands and Black Hills region ranks among the top five localities in the United States for a variety of minerals and rocks.

The Black Hills are famous for gold, copper, silver, iron, lead, tin, zinc, feldspar, spodumene, and more than 140 other minerals.

Expansive surface outcroppings of all three major rock types—igneous, metamorphic, and sedimentary—yield not only rock specimens, but embedded crystals, ores, and fossils. Beds of alluvial outwash on the perimeter of the Black Hills offer a colorful mix of all kinds of stones.

Tunnel Mania

There are a lot of tunnels in the Black Hills, and children will especially love them if you honk the horn while passing through. There are several narrow tunnels you should be aware of, however, particularly if you're driving a recreational vehicle, camper, truck, or bus. Here are the locations of these tunnels:

ROUTE	LOCATION	WIDTH	HEIGHT
US 16A	6 miles SE of Keystone	13'6"	12'6"
US 16A	4 miles SE of Keystone	13'6"	12'6"
US 16A	3 miles SE of Keystone	13'6"	12'6"
US 16A	1 mile N of Keystone	42'	14'6"
SD 87	6 miles SE of Sylvan Lake	9'	12'
SD 87	2 miles SE of Sylvan Lake	8'7"	11'5"
SD 87	1 mile N of Sylvan Lake	10'	10'8"

While it's a no-no for rock hounds to go collecting at Badlands National Park, the surrounding public lands—*Buffalo Gap National Grasslands*—hold some fine rock beds that produce Fairburn agates, funny eye, gay prairie, and bubble-gum agates, red jasper, blue chalcedony, and petrified wood.

The region is probably best known for its tourism appeal, but agriculture, mining, Ellsworth Air Force Base, higher education, and the timber industry add to the economic profile. The entrepreneurial spirit is alive and well in the Black Hills, a testament to the dogged independence of its people. Black Hills residents shudder at the thought of becoming a trendy, upscale haven for the rich and famous, as have surrounding states with their nouveau ranches. Oftentimes, East or West Coasters leave the fast track behind for the wholesome lifestyle found in the Hills. Because of the area's unabashed beauty, artists, musicians, and writers frequently set up studios here.

Did we mention that this is the way to *Mount Rushmore National Memorial?* Who could write about South Dakota without mentioning the Four Faces? Even though it's a busy place in summer, you still might want to check it out. It's located 25 miles southwest of Rapid City on U.S. Highway 16A; follow the signs. If you follow Mount Rushmore Road (a can't-miss main drag in town) south, you'll soon, and effortlessly, be on US 16A.

You'll drive through Keystone on your way to the Four Faces. Keystone's carnival atmosphere will stand out as one of the most raucous and colorful in the communities of the Hills. Think of Keystone as a dear but gaudy friend whose baubles are fascinating to observe, but only for short periods. This pint-size town epitomizes the best and worst of tourism; some attractions border

A Girl and Her Dog

The Black Hills are a natural place to have a dog or cat, horse, or any other pet to call your own. When I was a child, our little mutt, a part Scottish terrier named Whimpie, was anything but wimpy. Whimpie had an aversion to noise of any kind, and she would ferociously try to attack the thunder and lightning if she thought it was threatening us. She even took on a noisy street snowblower. (She suffered three broken ribs from that encounter. The veterinarian said he would have hated to have seen the snowblower.)

Whimpie once tangled with a skunk under our camper at Sheridan Lake, located southwest of Rapid City in the Black Hills National Forest. The skunk won. The foul odor woke our entire family—Mom, Dad, and four kids—and we had to pack up in the middle of the night and go back to our sweeter-smelling home in Rapid City. Needless to say, Whimpie was immersed in several tomato baths the next day to counter the lingering scent. Whimpie was a brave, courageous, and loyal dog, and, as my Mom always says, "a real sweetie with a heart bigger than all outdoors."

on tacky, yet others show elegant restraint. You be the judge. Whatever the verdict, the taffy shops are well renowned for pleasing the sweet tooth.

The Four Faces are one of the most recognized and beloved national symbols. The 60-foot granite images of George Washington, Thomas Jefferson, Abraham Lincoln, and Theodore Roosevelt were carved by Gutzon Borglum. Mount Rushmore was commissioned as a national memorial by Congress in 1929, although work actually began in 1927. The project was not always the media darling of its time. Back East, a newspaper blasted: "Borglum is about to destroy another monu-

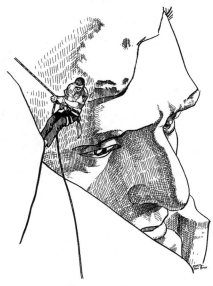

Mount Rushmore

ment. Thank God it is in South Dakota, where no one will ever see it." Fortunately, Borglum and others had more foresight. When President Calvin Coolidge dedicated the project in 1927, he proclaimed that Mount Rushmore was "decidedly American in its conception, magnitude, and meaning. It is altogether worthy of our country."

Over the next twelve years, Borglum and his crews, using pneumatic drills and dynamite, carved four massive heads out of the mountaintop. Although the sculptor died before the project was finished, his son, Lincoln, made sure his father's vision would be complete. At present, more than two million visitors each year see the Borglums' legacy to America and the four men who contributed to its greatness.

The Orientation Center, the first facility you will enter after parking your car, explains the physical layout of the visitors facilities at Mount Rushmore, outlines the different interpretive buildings and programs, and shows the day's schedule of special activities. At the Sculptor's Studio, built in 1939, you'll find winches, jackhammers, and pneumatic drills that date from the time of construction. Borglum's original model of Mount Rushmore also can be viewed here. Rushmore personnel offer five impromptu presentations from 9:00 A.M. to 6:00 P.M. daily. They outline topics such as the original location of the Jefferson face (different from where it appears today).

Sculptor

The sculptor-in-residence program at Mount Rushmore allows visitors to see an artist working—and a sculpture in the making. Sculptor Lisbeth Sabol works in marble, limestone, and alabaster. As part of the Mount Rushmore summer program, she makes herself available to the general public to answer questions. She showed me her set of hammers and chisels, explaining what each does. Her piece one particular summer was a portrait of a woman's face.

"Rodin said you know that you have truly captured a person in portrait if he or she doesn't like it," she told me.

I wonder what Abe, Teddy, George, and Tom would think of Borglum's interpretation of their famous mugs. . .

A $56 million redevelopment was completed in 1998, with the addition of a new parking structure, amphitheater, museum/theater complex, Visitor Orientation Center, Presidential Trail, gift shop, bookstore, and dining facilities.

A patriotically fitting end to a day at Mount Rushmore is watching the evening lighting ceremony from the outdoor amphitheater. Evenings can be downright chilly, so bring a light jacket. The ceremony is held nightly at 9:00 Memorial Day through Labor Day. Mount Rushmore National Memorial is open year-round, and admission is free—no doubt Abe, George, Teddy, and Tom would have approved.

The Gaslight in tiny Rockerville (truly a one-pony town 10 miles south of Rapid City on US 16) offers family dining in an Old West saloon; don't forget to sample the ice cream sodas from an old-fashioned soda fountain. Antiques also are carried in this charming establishment, located at 13490 Main Street. Call (605) 343–9276 for more information. Hours are 4:00 to 9:00 P.M. weekdays and from 11:00 A.M. to 9:00 P.M. weekends. After mid-October, the Gaslight is open Wednesday through Sunday from 4:00 to 9:00 P.M.

For the shopper who plans ahead, or just enjoys unique gift items, the ***Mistletoe Ranch*** (605–574–4197), a half mile south of the U.S. Highway 385 and US 16 junction, is a must-see. The bi-level historic home (1890) is peacefully nestled in the pine trees. A "Christmas welcome" with wreaths adorns the stairs and porch. Lawn ornaments include Santa's reindeer, and candy canes fill the yard with holiday cheer. Naturally Christmas colors explode once you step inside, and more than fifty trees are decorated in a variety of themes—from Walt Disney to Native American. The staff likes to celebrate Christmas every day and does so with holiday ornaments, decorations, porcelain dolls, specialty foods, and collectibles to fit almost any holiday theme. Open daily year-round.

And if you love European sensibilities, then the ***Coyote Blues Village Bed & Breakfast*** is just your cup of tea. Swiss-born Hans Peter and Christine Streich built their cedar-lodge haven seven years ago, and they have implemented European design and cuisine into their business. Located 12 miles north of Hill City off US 385, the bed-and-breakfast offers four rooms with international style. Pick your theme: European Antique, Middle Eastern, Turkish, or African. Each is equipped with a deck, a hot tub, and a private bath. The thirty-acre facility also taps into local heritage, offering summer classes in Lakota arts and crafts. Guests have included rock star Dave Matthews, a Lakota medicine man, and many travelers from Europe. Rates start at $90. For more information call (888) 253–4477. The Web site is www.coyote bluesvillage.com.

If you're thoroughly enjoying your Southern Hills trek, stay overnight at the ***Abend Haus Cottage & Audrie's Cranbury Corner Bed and Breakfast*** (605–342–7788). Located west of Rapid City on State Highway 44, this country home and five-acre estate is surrounded by the Black Hills National Forest. Each suite and cottage has a private entrance, bath, hot tub, and patio. Rates are expensive but well worth it to sample Old World charm and hospitality. Open year-round.

The prices at local antiques shops would make vendors at big-city flea markets blush. There is almost always a deal to be found in the Black Hills, making the area a quaint destination for treasure seekers. Some stores are cluttered and require a thorough dig to find something collectible, and others thoughtfully display their goods. ***Talking Leaves Gifts & Antiques*** (605–574–9090), on the way to Hill City, is an example of the latter. Along with antiques, I found Western-theme pillows, Parisienne and Victorian linens, candles, and baby items. The shop, at 23849 Highway 385, is open from 10:00 A.M. to 5:00 P.M. Monday through Saturday and from noon to 5:00 P.M. Sunday. Call (605) 574–9090 for details.

Hill City, with a population of 650, is affectionately considered to be one of the most unpretentious towns in the Black Hills. The attitude is whatever goes. If you're looking a bit disheveled after three days of camping, don't fret. You can visit any of the Main Street establishments, and no one will make you feel out of place.

The oldest town in Pennington County, Hill City was a bustling region when gold first was discovered in the Palmer Gulch area. Bigger strikes in the Deadwood area left the town almost deserted, but when the Burlington Railroad ran its Hot Springs–Deadwood line through Hill City in 1892, the town reclaimed its place as gateway to the central Black Hills. It's hard to imagine that the town had a population of 3,000 in the 1890s.

Sylvan Rocks Climbing School & Guide Service & Granite Sports (605–574–2425 or 605–574–2121), on Main Street, promises high adventure in the Needles and Devils Tower. Starting at $115 a day, the skilled and friendly staff will take beginners or advanced climbers on full-day expeditions. Packages also are available. The school was named one of the top ten by the American Mountain Guides Association. Reservations are recommended. Granite Sports carries a full line of climbing, hiking, and camping equipment. Check out the Web site at www.sylvanrocks.com, or e-mail the store at info@sylvanrocks.com.

Mount Rushmore Brewing Co., also located on Main Street, features an extensive menu, including Italian entrees, prime rib, seafood, specialty pizzas, and pub cuisine such as white chili and vegetarian lasagna. For libations, choose from microbeers, wine, and espresso. The three-story historic building is tastefully decorated with hardwood floors, high ceilings, historic photos, and antiques. Casual dining is available in the old-fashioned pub on the first floor. The third floor is dedicated to the display of local artists' work. Call (605) 574–2400.

Hill City is being touted as the new Jackson Hole, Wyoming. The comparison is justified. The Hill City artscape is growing. Case in point: The classy ***Warrior's Work Studio & Gallery*** (310 Main Street), where Randy Berger specializes in creating leather frame designs for Native American and other fine art. The frames are covered in deerskin, buffalo hide, or elk leather. Embossing and beadwork, all done in the studio, quietly enhance the frames. Some of the contemporary artists featured include Joe Geshick, Frank Howell, Del Iron Cloud, Roger Broer, Jim Yellowhawk, and Alison Dearborn Rieder. Randy can describe the latest art trend or technique—like the fancy-sounding gicleé (French for "spraying in ink")—in plain terms for the layperson. Call (605) 574–4954 for more information.

Next door, ***Jewels of the West*** (308 Main Street) presents jewelry, Western art, pottery, and more. Stoneware and porcelain by local artist Gail J. Heilmann is featured. Open 9:00 A.M. to 8:00 P.M. daily. For details call (605) 574–2464.

The Old World Plaza features a collection of shops, including Vintage Cowboy, the Coffee Garden, and Snow Creek Gallery.

Across the street, the Hershey Ranch Gallery promotes the artwork, among others, of owner Brooke Hershey's former high school classmates: Joan Buckles, Charlene Hare, and Cherril Cobb. This is a fine place to see Western art in many media. The gallery is open from 9:00 A.M. to 9:00 P.M. weekdays and 11:00 A.M. to 5:00 P.M. weekends.

Jon Crane Watercolors (605–574–4441 or 800–288–1948; www.joncrane watercolors.com) next door is filled with watercolors by one of South Dakota's favorite artists. Crane's trademark is capturing the landscape of the region, and his work readily evokes the gentle yet determined spirit of the pioneer. Summer hours are 9:00 A.M. to 8:00 P.M. Monday through Saturday and 10:00 A.M. to 4:00 P.M. Sunday. The shop sells and displays Crane's artwork, and custom framing is done here as well. Call the gallery for off-season hours.

Another good place to eat is the ***Alpine Inn Restaurant*** (605–574–2749), located in the classic 1886 Harney Peak Hotel. The lunch menu (offered 11:00 A.M. to 2:30 P.M.) has a European flair, whereas the filet mignon dinners with salad, baked potato, and Texas toast are the main fare from 5:00 to 9:30 P.M. The homemade dessert menu is scrumptious; it's hard to choose from so many tempting goodies, but a sure bet is always the apple kuchen. Open Monday through Saturday. Meals are very affordable. The six-ounce filet mignon dinner is $6.95, and the nine-ounce dinner runs $8.95. Moderately priced bed-and-breakfast arrangements also are available.

The ***1880 Train*** in Hill City is one of the town's most familiar and endearing tourist attractions. Years ago, the iron horse pulled cars carrying equipment and ore from Hill City to Keystone. The movie industry has tapped the historical significance of both the railroad and the area for productions such as *Orphan Train* and *Gunsmoke*. Modern-day travelers can board the train for a two-hour round-trip excursion that will take them from the Hill City Depot or the Keystone Junction several times a day from mid-May through early October. For more information call (605) 574–2222 or visit the Web site at www.1880 train.com.

Just 2 miles east of Hill City off Highway 16, the ***Country Manor Bed & Breakfast*** offers four themed guest rooms and a family suite for up to eight people. The inn is located in a sun-filled meadow bordered by Spring Creek. The Rhineland Room turns the spotlight on the owners', Blair and Mindy McCaskell, European ancestry. The Heartland Room remembers the farmers who settled the Midwest region, and it is appropriately dressed in down-home charm. The Dreamland Room re-creates memories of the American family, and antiques and stuffed toys will appeal to the young at heart. The Native American culture, too, is honored in the Badlands Room, which reflects a calm and peaceful atmosphere through Indian designs. Last, Frontierland, a three-room suite, captures the spirit of the Wild West. Rates range from $85 to $135. Call (888) 560–5508 for reservations. Visit the Web site at www.countrymanor bb.com.

Not too far away from Hill City on US 16A, you can see a mountain carving in progress at ***Crazy Horse Memorial*** (605–673–4681; www.crazyhorse. org). The late Korczak Ziolkowski began work on a sculpture of the famous Oglala Lakota leader at the request of several chiefs. Chief Henry Standing Bear's invitation said, "My fellow chiefs and I would like the white man to know the red man has great heroes, too." The sculpture shows Crazy Horse astride his warhorse. Although Ziolkowski died in 1982, his wife, Ruth, and their children continue the sculptor's dream. Their work is guided by his scale models and detailed plans.

Locals will confirm that the process has been slow but steady and precise; Ziolkowski insisted that no federal or state monies be used to fund the project. The nine-story-high face of Crazy Horse was completed in 1998. Most recently, the project reached the halfway mark in blocking out the horse's 209-foot-high head. The public is permitted to hike up the mountain on the annual 10K Volksmarch in June. Travelers can view drilling and blasting on the mountain. Crazy Horse is open year-round; admission is $9.00 per adult (children under age six free), $20.00 a carload.

Bison and Mammoths

The 73,000-acre *Custer State Park* is famous for its bison herds, other wildlife, scenic sites, fishing lakes, and interpretive sites. There are seven campgrounds with 323 sites, but book early (call 800–710–2267) because they fill quickly. Here you'll have the chance to walk on the wild side: *Buffalo Safari Jeep Rides* (605–255–4541) offer a chance to scout bison in the Dakota backcountry or hope for a chance encounter with the many other animals that roam the park: elk, mule deer, white-tailed deer, coyotes, bighorn sheep, turkeys, and eagles, just to name a few.

The *Badger Hole* was home of the state's first poet laureate, Charles Badger Clark (1883–1957), whose most popular poem is "A Cowboy's Prayer," which, incidentally, is frequently misprinted and rarely attributed to its author. After a tour of the four-room cabin where Clark spent most of his literary career, hike the Badger Clark Historic Trail and read his poetry at quiet stops amid the pines. The Badger Hole is open from Memorial Day to Labor Day. Hours are 10:00 A.M. to 5:00 P.M. weekdays and 1:00 to 4:00 P.M. on Saturday and Sunday.

The *Black Hills Playhouse* (605–255–4141 or 605–255–4551), nestled in Custer State Park, offers top-drawer entertainment. You can dress up or dress down for performances because your presence is valued much more than your attire at this nonprofit professional theater and training program. The summer troupe works, lives, eats, and breathes theater at this rustic site. A visit here can be a fun expedition for the theatergoer. As you're walking to the cozy theater for an evening of Shakespeare, you might see a chipmunk scurry by or hear soothing sounds from a nearby stream. As bucolic as this might seem, the performances are anything but homespun. The professionally trained cast and crew present five productions each summer, and the schedule can include anything from *Fiddler on the Roof* to *Godspell*. (Trivia note: Jarrod Emick, winner of the

1994 Tony Award for best supporting actor in the Broadway play *Damn Yankees,* is not only a South Dakota native, he's also an alumnus of the Playhouse.) The price is more than right here, too. All shows start at 8:00 P.M., with matinees on Saturday and Sunday at 2:00 P.M.

Your drive home can be a theatrical experience as well, if you take State Highway 87. The 14-mile-long **Needles Highway** takes you on an electrifying spin around and through majestic granite spires. Along the way you can pull over and take in the spectacular views. Drive slowly because this is a long and winding road—not to mention narrow. (In winter the Needles Highway is closed to allow snowmobiling and cross-country skiing.)

After you catch your breath, you'll be at **Sylvan Lake Lodge** (605–574–2561), one of the four historic lodges in the park. Choose from cozy lodge rooms or rustic cabins that range in price from moderate to expensive. This magnificent mountain resort overlooks Sylvan Lake and the granite outcroppings of Harney Peak. So romantic is this establishment that many couples choose to marry here. It's open May through September. Rates start at $95.

Rich in history and natural beauty, Sylvan Lake is designated as Custer State Park's "crown jewel." The lake was created in 1881, when Theodore Reder built a dam across Sunday Gulch. In 1921 this unique lake became a part of the newly created Custer State Park.

In 1895 a Victorian-style hotel opened its doors on the shores of Sylvan Lake. The hotel was a popular site for many Black Hills vacationers until it burned to the ground in 1935.

The current hotel opened in 1937, and the new wing was added in 1991. The hotel features cozy lodge rooms, a lobby, a lounge, and a restaurant, The Lakota Dining Room, which specializes in native game entrees and seafood.

Hike to **Harney Peak,** which is the state's highest point at 7,242 feet, but only if you're in decent shape. This 6-mile trek is a challenge but well worth it. When you get to the summit, the castlelike fire post gives you a spectacular 60-mile view and the chance to breathe clean, rarefied

Bison herd at Custer State Park

air. Without question Harney Peak has inspired people of all faiths. When he was only nine years old, the Oglala holy man Black Elk had his first vision here. "Then I was standing on the highest mountain of them all, and round about beneath me was the whole hoop of the world," he said. At present Harney Peak is part of the Black Elk Wilderness. Dr. Valentine T. McGillicuddy, or *Wasichu Wakan* ("Holy White Man") to the Lakota, was the first white man to climb Harney Peak, and his ashes were scattered there in 1939.

There is Custer the park, which is splendid in its own right, but be sure to visit Custer the town, too. Custer is expanding its creative side throughout the business district, which you can find by taking US 16A west from Custer State Park.

One of my favorite pastimes is to check out new restaurants, and I was pleased to discover Nancy Gellerman (formerly of the Sixth Street Deli in Rapid City) has brought her culinary talents to Custer. At my first visit to her *Sage Creek Grille,* I had the English Grill Sandwich, which paired sautéed onions, mushrooms, and tomatoes with melted Swiss and cheddar cheese on grilled sourdough bread. My friend Peter, a devout vegan (and picky eater), ordered the Grilled Vegetable Salad. We were both thrilled with our selections. Meat

A Cabin of Memories

Our family's log cabin is nestled in the forest west of Custer, and I cherish each day I have hiked through the meadows and collected wildflowers. Likewise, I have wistfully recalled the starry nights I have lain in the antique four-poster bed and listened to the lonesome cry of the coyotes, wondering how close they really were.

The cabin's remoteness summons images of the pioneer days when people actually worked for food. There is no electricity, and an outhouse, however stylishly marked, is a necessity, not just a cute building.

Certainly one of my loveliest memories of the cabin is the year we celebrated Christmas there. It was the last time I spent that holiday with my father before he died. My younger sister and her family were unable to travel home, but my brothers, Matt and James, our parents, and I feasted on homemade chili for Christmas Eve, and, as was our family's tradition, opened our gifts around the wood-burning stove. My brother Matt chose a sports theme for his gifts. He gave me running tights, and he gave my father, an avid golfer, an umbrella to affix to his golf cart.

It is those days that I often recall—the days when we children, even as adults, felt our parents were immortal. But the following year, my Dad passed away. Dad, a timber-man, wanted to be buried in Custer, as he so loved the Black Hills. The cemetery is sweet and consoling in a rustic way, but during the moments when I miss my father, I think of the cabin and all the happy times we spent there.

lovers, too, will find some wonderful entrees, such as top sirloin, served with mushroom wine sauce and grilled potatoes, or the Buffalo Burger, which is best grilled to medium rare to medium.

Of course, like most eateries in the Black Hills, the friendliness of the wait staff and the cozy, creative atmosphere add extra seasoning to the dining experience. The walls are painted a sunny yellow or a soft sage green. The pine floor and furnishings are further enhanced by the casual bouquets of fresh daisies on every table. Located at 607 Mount Rushmore Road, this no-smoking restaurant is open from 11:00 A.M. to 2:00 P.M. and 5:00 to 9:00 P.M. Monday through Saturday, Memorial Day through Labor Day. Off-season hours are 11:00 A.M. to 2:00 P.M. and 5:00 to 8:00 P.M. Tuesday through Saturday. For more information call (605) 673–2424.

Just next door, at 611 Mount Rushmore Road, Gellerman has expanded her culinary world to include the *Wild Sage Wine Bar.* A wine and beer bar, a full menu, and live music will appeal to the connoisseur. Wild Sage is open from 4:00 to 10:00 P.M. daily. For information, call (605) 673–6400.

Walk across the street and find the lovely *A Walk in the Woods Gallery & Gifts,* which is operated by Koko Hunsaker, whose bubbly enthusiasm makes you feel right at home. This is the best the Lodge Look has to offer: wonderfully crafted bison leather chairs, plump pillows, candles, pottery, specialty foods, books, and, upstairs, an expansive art gallery with many regional artists featured. For information call (605) 673–6400.

Next door, the handmade chocolates of the *Custer County Candy Factory* (506 Mount Rushmore Road) are worth every single luscious calorie. My sister Jean observed—and approved—the wantonly buttery taste of the truffles. I find the prices equally irresistible: an assortment of twelve truffles, for instance, is $10.95. A bargain anyday in my book. Call (605) 673–3912 for more information.

And to indulge the senses yet again, schedule a spa treatment at *Bella Day Spa* (605–673–5700). Here, you can receive head-to-toe treatments, from hair styling to body massages and herbal body wraps to aromatherapy and pedicures. The shop, at 236 North Fifth Street, is set up to combine the best of shabby chic, Victorian, and Dakota decor. Indulge in the full-day treatments (allow about five or six hours), which include an hour massage, a European facial, a spa manicure and pedicure, a hair cut and style, and lunch from the aforementioned Sage Creek Grille. The package price is unbeatable: $185. Hours are 8:30 A.M. to 5:00 P.M. Monday through Wednesday, 8:30 A.M. to 8:00 P.M. Thursday, and 8:30 A.M. to 5:00 P.M. Friday. Open by appointment only Saturday.

Residents and businesses have lovingly contributed pieces of the past to fill the *1881 Custer County Courthouse Museum and Book Store* (411 Mount Rushmore Road). In this commanding brick Italianate building, which served

Trailside Bikes

One of the best ways to see the spectacular scenery of the Black Hills is by bicycle. Pedaling along the 114-mile George S. Mickelson Trail, for instance, puts the rider in the heart of the hills. (The Mickelson Trail follows the historic Burlington Railroad line from Deadwood to Edgemont.) Trailside Bikes in Custer offers Cannondale bikes for rent, starting at $10 per hour (and that includes a helmet). The business also organizes guided tours, and lodging, camping, and meals can be arranged. For more information call (888) 673–BIKE (2453). Or e-mail Trailside Bikes at tsbikes@trailside bikes.com.

the county for ninety-two years, visitors see slices of early Custer life, from artifacts of the timber and farming industries, which made the town prosper, to Victorian apparel and furnishings. On the museum grounds, printing equipment from Custer's 1879 first continuously operated newspaper and blacksmith forge and tools are also on display. A self-guided tour brochure takes visitors through the expansive collections. The first stop is a room dedicated to rocks and minerals and native birds and animals, which were mounted by a local taxidermist in the 1920s. The Custer room depicts photographs of the 1874 Custer expedition when General George A. Custer entered the Black Hills. Custer hunted antelope at Fort Hays, Kansas, with the gun on display. Custer's epaulets and a first edition of his book *My Life on the Plains,* are also displayed. Upstairs is the courtroom with the original cherry furniture and judge's chamber.

I am absolutely crazy about this museum, as its placards—which were obviously typed years ago and have the well-worn patina of the past—and friendly staff echo back to gentler times. Admission is $3.00 for adults, $2.50 for senior citizens, $1.00 for kids ages twelve to eighteen and free for children under eleven. Summer hours are 9:00 A.M. to 9:00 P.M. Monday through Saturday and 1:00 to 9:00 P.M. Sunday. For more information call (605) 673–2443.

The Flintstones Bedrock City (605–673–4079; www.flintstonesbedrock city.com) was pure Stone Age id, pure indulgence to me as a child and, if the truth be told, it still has that effect on me as an adult. My siblings and I loved to play in the cartoon-themed park when we were younger, begging our parents to take us there to experience the Slideasaurus, the Iron Horse Train, and the Rockmore Theatre. The world of Fred, Wilma, Barney, Betty, and the gang is just as fun today with my nephews, Duke and Patrick. I still get a kick out of ordering the Brontoburgers and the Dino Dogs. Admission is $6.00 and free for children under five. A campground, too, is on site, with full-service hookups, a heated pool, a store, and a Laundromat.

The *Custer Mansion Bed & Breakfast* (35 Centennial Drive) serves home-cooked, full breakfasts, which have earned the establishment good words from *Bon Appetit* magazine. The 1891 Gothic Victorian home is on the National Register of Historic Places. Flower gardens and aspens cover the one-acre grounds. For more information call (605) 673–3333 or (877) 519–4948.

Just west of Custer on Highway 16, the *National Museum of Wood-carving* celebrates the art in grand fashion. Here, visitors can see the work of nationally recognized woodcarvers and twenty-five of the nation's top caricature carvers. Sure to entertain all ages, this unique museum also features The Talking Woodcarvings, more than thirty scenes created by an original Disneyland animator. The museum is open daily May 1 through October. For details call (605) 673–4404.

The *Strutton Inn Bed & Breakfast*, 2 miles west of Custer on Highway 16, features nine spacious rooms in a Victorian house. Innkeepers Cary and Denice Strutton are dyed-in-the-wool romantics themselves. The couple met in California, where they were both working as correctional officers. During a vacation in South Dakota, Cary proposed to Denice on bended knee in front of a crowd at Mount Rushmore. She said yes, and the couple received a standing ovation. Shortly after their wedding, they decided to open a bed-and-breakfast.

In May 1997 they began construction, and a year later the inn opened. The inn is open April through October. For reservations and room rates call (800) 226–2611 or (605) 673–4808.

In the late 1800s Hot Springs and its mineral springs attracted trainloads of wealthy visitors who sought the therapeutic benefits of "healing water." Although springs continue to flow up through the pebble bottom of *Evan's Plunge* (1145 North River Street; 605–745–5165), the accent today is more on fun. It's open from 5:30 A.M. to 9:45 P.M. weekdays and 8:00 A.M. to 9:45 P.M. on weekends.

Pedal Power

Bicycle touring and pleasure riding are popular in the Black Hills. Rapid City, for instance, boasts a 13½-mile bikeway along Rapid Creek, but most riding is done on the area's wide-shouldered highways. Some of the favorite routes are Rapid City to Mount Rushmore, the Needles Highway, Iron Mountain Road, Spearfish Canyon, and the Badlands Loop Road. All feature some steep grades and long climbs, but the spectacular scenery along the way makes the effort worth it.

Mountain biking is also becoming popular in the Black Hills, thanks to almost 6,000 miles of fire trails, logging roads, and abandoned railroad grades that crisscross the backcountry ridges, wind down canyons, and climb to mountaintops.

Stroll through the downtown district and see thirty-nine Romanesque sandstone buildings in soft shades of pink, buff, and red. History buffs in particular will enjoy the *Fall River County Historical Museum* at 300 North Chicago Street in a 1893 building that was once a school. Admission is free. The museum is open daily, except for Sunday, from June through September. Hours are 9:00 A.M. to 5:00 P.M. Monday through Saturday. Call (605) 745–5147 for information.

The Toal House Bed & Breakfast, owned and operated by George and Rebecca Toal, is a four-story octagonal bed-and-breakfast that sits high on a bluff at 801 Almond Street overlooking Hot Springs. The beautiful home, established in 1891, is listed on the National Register of Historic Places.

The couple has recently renovated the grand structure, restoring its original theme as a men's gaming club. As such, there is a common room called the Poker Room that sports a poker table. You need not be a gambler of any method, however, to enjoy the themed guest rooms, including the vintage-style Bicycling Room, or the gourmet meals. George and Rebecca serve guests a different breakfast every morning, and during the winter months, they offer five-course dinners. For information call (605) 745–4633 or visit the Web site at www.toalhousebnb.com.

See the Dakota prairie, as it must have looked 300 years ago, at the *Black Hills Wild Horse Sanctuary.* More than 300 wild horses roam free at this 11,000-acre private wilderness area. Two-hour guided bus tours are offered three times daily from May 1 through September 30. Hours are 10:00 A.M., 1:00 P.M., and 3:00 P.M. Closed Sunday. Prices are $20.00 for adults, $18.50 for senior citizens, and $12.50 for children twelve and under.

For another hearty bite into the Old West, sign up for the chuckwagon dinners. Guests are taken by a horse-drawn wagon up the spectacular grand canyon of the Cheyenne River to a cookout at 5:00 P.M. Tuesday, Thursday, and Saturday between June 1 and August 30. Reservations are required by 1:00 P.M. the day before the dinner. Prices are $35.00 for adults, $32.50 for senior citizens, and $25.00 for children. From Hot Springs, take Highway 71 South and turn right, just past the Cheyenne River Bridge. For more information call (800) 252–6652.

If you want to see where the big boys have been permanent houseguests, then visit the *Mammoth Site* (605–745–6017), located on the US 18 truck bypass. More than 26,000 years ago, large Columbian and woolly mammoths were trapped and consequently died in a spring-fed pond near what is now the southeast edge of Hot Springs. Experts estimate that as many as one hundred mammoths died here. Their remains might have gone undiscovered were it not for the beginnings of a housing project in 1974, when earth-leveling equipment revealed the white bones and tusks of these enormous creatures.

The Other Black Hills

Ninety percent of the Black Hills are in South Dakota, but the mountains also grace Wyoming for 10 to 40 miles. Even though they cross the South Dakota state line, the towns of Devils Tower, Hulett, Upton, Newcastle, and Sundance are very much part of the Black Hills community.

The Wyoming segment of the Black Hills includes a distinct branch known as The Bear Lodge. This is the site of the nation's first national monument, Devils Tower. The tower is actually a solitary, stump-shaped granite formation that looms 1,267 feet above the Belle Fourche River in northeastern Wyoming like a skyscraper against the rural landscape. The tower is popular with rock climbers and movie makers. Devils Tower was a location for *Close Encounters of the Third Kind*.

Scientists work with the fossilized bones of the extinct mammoths and other animals that were buried here: the camel, short-faced bear, antelope, gray wolf, mink, white-tailed prairie dog, and frog. The Mammoth Site is the only in situ (bones left as found) display of fossil mammoths in the United States. The 20,000-square-foot visitor center now covers the sinkhole and enables visitors to view firsthand this working paleontological site. Local residents are proud of this colossal graveyard and tout it as one of the Black Hills' more incredible sites. The site is open daily 8:00 A.M. to 8:00 P.M. in summer, 8:00 A.M. to 5:00 P.M. September and October, 9:00 A.M. to 3:30 P.M. November through February, and 8:00 A.M. to 5:00 P.M. March through May 14. Cyber-travelers take note: The Web site is located at www.mammoth site.com.

Located 13 miles west of Custer on US 16, *Jewel Cave National Monument* (605–673–2288; www.nps.gov/jeca) is the third-longest cave in the world and undoubtedly one of the prettiest. If stalagmites and stalactites intrigue you, trek down into the giant nooks and crannies of Jewel Cave. Guided tours will ensure that you won't get lost. Jewel Cave gets its name from the glittering calcite crystals that line its walls. The cave also features formations such as moonmilk, scintillites, and hydromagnesite balloons. The monument is open year-round. There is a fee for guided cave tours.

The exploration of Jewel Cave began about 1900, when Frank and Albert Michaud, two South Dakota prospectors, and their friend, Charles Bush, heard wind rushing through a hole in the rocks in Hell Canyon. Enlarging the hole, they found a cave full of sparkling crystals. They filed a mining claim on the "Jewel Lode," but they found no valuable minerals. Instead, they tried turning the cave into a tourist attraction.

The business was never a success, but the cave did attract attention. In 1908 Jewel Cave National Monument was established as part of the National Park System.

Fifty years later, exploration of the cave intensified as the husband-and-wife team of Herb and Jan Conn discovered new wonders and explored additional miles of passage.

For more cave exploration check out nearby **Wind Cave National Park** (605–745–4600; www.nps.gov/wica), which is the world's eighth-longest cave. It also features a 28,000-acre wildlife preserve aboveground. Bison, antelope, elk, and deer roam over this expanse of forest and grassland. Down under, delicate formations such as boxwork, popcorn, and frostwork abound. Open year-round, there is no entrance fee for Wind Cave, but there is a guide fee for cave tours. The park and visitor center are both open year-round.

You wouldn't think that there would be much difference between north and south in the Black Hills; after all, we're not talking about the state of the Union, but a small area in the grand scheme of things. The Northern Hills, however, are distinct from the Southern Hills. The Northern Hills area is more entrenched in tourism and not surprisingly turns a lot colder and snow-covered in the winter. If you take I–90 west from Rapid City, you'll be on your way to an all-seasons wonderland. Sometimes half the fun is getting there, so don't be in a hurry—this stretch of interstate has lots to offer.

Bikers and a Butte

If you're in Sturgis (26 miles northwest of Rapid City on I–90) for the first full week in August, put on a black T-shirt and head for the **Sturgis Rally & Races.** Even if you don't own a motorcycle, anything black or leather will have you dressing the part for this incredible gathering of bikers and curiosity seekers from around the world. Motorcyclists from near and far tour to the Black Hills to show their skills in the hill-climb and racing competitions. The rally attracts weekend warriors, biker gangs such as the Bandidos, and even celebrities. Peter Fonda, Emilio Estevez, and Neil Diamond are just a handful of the rich and famous who cruise into Sturgis for this spectacular show of chrome, leather, and heavy-metal thunder. J. C. "Pappy" Hoel, owner of a local cycle shop, started the Sturgis Rally in 1938 with only nine races and a less-than-capacity grandstand crowd. The rally has grown into a seven-day event, with attendance by more than 100,000 people. Just as Harley-Davidson implemented the "just-in-time" assembly line to produce better bikes, Sturgis seems to have many unique businesses that crop up just in time for the rally. Street vendors sell anything from T-shirts to gyros to jewelry and more. There are usually several booths where the brave-hearted can get a tattoo of their own design. Sources say that getting a tattoo feels like hot oil being poured onto your skin, so you be the judge of your comfort level.

If you're not a biker, the people-watching opportunities alone during the week will more than entertain. There's a Mardi Gras–like atmosphere here. The bikers' motto seems to be, to quote Neil Young, "It's better to burn out than fade away." Just be sure to bring your camera so that you can record some of this living, breathing, not to mention partying, history. For information, call (605) 347–4875.

Rally mania aside, Sturgis is a quiet farm and ranch community, which seems rather incongruous. You can drive down one of the main thoroughfares in this community of 7,000 people and see a SOD FOR SALE sign perched against a fence, and the neatly trimmed lawns and hedges of the city parks invite a cozy image of Small Town, USA.

The **Old Stone House Bed & Breakfast** (605–347–3007) was built in 1885, and present proprietor Diana Hayes entertains guests in this gracious setting. The home, located at 1513 Jackson, is furnished with family heirlooms, antiques, and collectibles. A swing on the veranda invites reverie on a lazy afternoon. Room rates are about $85 for two people and include a full breakfast on antique china.

On the more straight-and-narrow side, history abounds at the **Fort Meade Museum & Old Post Cemetery** (605–347–9822), located 2 miles east of Sturgis on State Highway 34. Fort Meade was built in the shadows of the majestic Bear Butte, a landmark that made it possible for early-day travelers to find the fort. Cavalry and infantry stationed here were assigned to keep the peace in those turbulent years, and so the fort gained the nickname "The Peacekeeper Fort." The site is open daily May through September. Hours of operation are 8:00 A.M. to 6:00 P.M. until September 1, then 9:00 A.M. to 5:00 P.M. until closing for the season on September 15. A National Byway winds between Fort Meade near State Highway 34 and the Black Hills National Cemetery near exit 34 on I–90.

Colonel Samuel D. Sturgis, a Union general during the Civil War, was commander of the Seventh Cavalry and the first permanent post commander at Fort Meade. He was a member of the company that founded the nearby town that bears his name.

It was at Fort Meade that "The Star Spangled Banner" was first ordered to be part of the evening military retreat ceremony, long before it became the national anthem.

The Bureau of Land Management manages approximately 6,700 acres of the former Fort Meade Military Reservation. Approximately one-third of this area is on the National Register of Historic Places, due to the numerous historical sites at Fort Meade, mostly remnants of early cavalry life. The area accommodates grazing, forestry, wildlife, and a variety of recreational uses that include camping, picnicking, horseback riding, and hiking. The 110-mile multiuse Centennial Trail also winds through this area.

Mato paha (bear mountain) is the name the Indians gave **Bear Butte State Park** (605–347–5240), an outstanding geographical formation located 6 miles northeast of Sturgis. This volcanic laccolith is still used today by Native Americans for religious ceremonies and vision quests, but visitors can hike to the summit on the scenic National Recreation Trail or browse through the visitor center. The park is open year-round, but the visitor center is open May 1 through mid-September. Because of its natural and historical significance, Bear Butte was designated a National Natural Landmark in 1965.

The abundant snowfall in the Northern Black Hills makes it a veritable mecca for winter sports. Snowmobiling, cross-country skiing, and downhill skiing are popular choices, but gambling, theater, and a good choice of restaurants provide entertainment year-round.

Ghost towns are a common theme in the Black Hills, but Mystic is one that still exists in an authentic, noncommercial manner, thanks to the pristine forest that surrounds and protects its remote location (9 miles off US 385, south of Lead-Deadwood; take the Rochford turnoff next to Trout Haven). Originally named Sitting Bull, the town was populated by miners, loggers, and railroaders hell-bent on profiting from the area's natural wealth. Today visitors can enjoy beautiful hiking and biking areas.

Eighteen miles northwest of Sturgis, Spearfish's downtown district is bustling with the passion of local businesspeople who still believe that Main Street is vital to a small-town economy. Where else could you find dress shops, thoughtfully planned gift shops, and an opera house, all within the expanse of 3 city blocks? Be sure to stop by **Langers Factory Outlet,** where locally made Black Hills silver jewelry makes wonderful gifts for the folks back home. The shop, located at 603 Main Street, also sells the famous Black Hills gold jewelry— easily recognized by its three-color, grape-leaf designs—and other western-themed gift items. For more information call (605) 642–2383 or visit the Web site at www.blackhillsgoldjewelry.com.

The **High Plains Heritage Center Museum** (605–642–9378) features Western art and artifacts from five states, along with outdoor displays such as antique implements, a log cabin, a sod dugout, a one-room schoolhouse, live buffalo, longhorns, and miniature horses. You can hear cowboy poetry and music in the theater every Wednesday at 7:30 P.M. during the summer season. The museum is open year-round 9:00 A.M. to 5:00 P.M. and 9:00 A.M. to 8:00 P.M.

during the summer season. The center is located off I–90 at exit 14.

Back in downtown Spearfish, you can visit the **Matthews Opera House** at 614 Main Street. The opera house was built in 1906, and although it sometimes veered from its original intent (it was once a dance hall), Spearfish residents returned it to its original charm. Summer community theater performances at the opera house draw audiences from throughout the Hills. Productions always have strong support from the college theater department. For a complete schedule of performances and other events, call (605) 642–7973 or visit the Web site at www.moh-scah.com.

There are women's fashions for every taste in Spearfish, and if you like a little flash, upscale labels, or just denim and lace, stop by **Kathleen's** (605–642–3843) and see what fine fashions the shop carries. The store is open from 9:00 A.M. to 5:30 P.M. Monday through Friday, 9:00 A.M. to 5:00 P.M. Saturday.

Once you open the antique door to the **Bay Leaf Cafe** (126 West Hudson; 605–642–5462), you've also entered one of the most refreshing eateries around. Serene and sensitive describe the ambience of the cafe and the attitude of its owners, French Bryan and Taffy Tucker. First, they've put together a healthful menu that tastes good, too. Second, they've made reading the menu fun. Each entree is described in detail and with good humor. A list explains what the more exotic foods are, like *seitan,* hummus, and tabbouleh. The cafe is open from 11:00 A.M. to 9:00 P.M. daily in summer, 11:00 A.M. to 8:00 P.M. in winter.

You don't have to be a bed-and-breakfast guest at the **Lown House** to enjoy breakfast, lunch, or dinner there, but you may want to be. The 1893 building features indoor and outdoor dining in an enchanting setting, and locals

OTHER ATTRACTIONS WORTH SEEING
IN WESTERN SOUTH DAKOTA

Boyd's Antiques, Custer

Broken Boot Gold Mine,
Deadwood

Dinosaur Park, Rapid City

Fife & Drum Corps Concerts,
Main Street in Hill City
(free performances every Monday
evening Memorial Day through
Labor Day)

Li'l Nashville Dinner Theatre, Custer

Old Style Saloon No. 10,
Deadwood

Parade of Presidents Wax Museum,
Keystone

Reptile Gardens, Rapid City

Springs Bath House, Hill City

rave about the food. The inn includes the Kemp Loft, the entire third floor, which can accommodate up to six people. Located at the corner of Fifth and Jackson Streets; call (605) 642– 5663 for more information.

For a place to toss a Frisbee, enjoy a steak hot off the grill, or just relax, *Spearfish City Park,* one of the most beloved parks in the Northern Hills, is the place to be. Walk across the footbridge over Spearfish Creek and discover the *D. C. Booth National Fish Hatchery* (605–642–7730), considered the premier facility of its kind (the hatchery is the site for the National Historic Fishery Records and Archive Repository).

Studies have shown that watching fish can lower blood pressure, and there is something mesmerizing about seeing a rainbow trout nonchalantly flick its fins as it moves through the water. The underwater viewing area lets you see just that—and notice the brown trout, too. It doesn't take an expert eye to discern between the two fish: The rainbow trout's fin is more translucent, with silvery undersides, whereas the brown trout's fin is more squarish.

The Booth family lived in the Superintendent's House. Guided tours of this gracious home prove why Ruby Booth was considered the extraordinary hostess of her time. Whether she was planning an Easter egg hunt for her children and their classmates or entertaining future President Herbert Hoover on her front porch, Ruby demonstrated a talent for hospitality. This is a must-see place for families, and, best of all, it's free.

"The Black Hills Passion Play," which re-creates the dramatic events during the last seven days of Christ's life, is a wonderfully presented and moving show the entire family will enjoy. The show recently marked its sixty-fourth anniversary, a testament to the commitment and vision of its creator, Josef Meier. Show times are at 8:00 P.M. Sunday, Tuesday, and Thursday during the summer months. The Passion Play is located at 600 St. Joseph Street. For more information call (605) 642–2646 or (800) 457–0160. Ticket prices start at $16. Backstage tours of the 6,000-seat amphitheater also are offered daily. The Web site is www.blackhills.com/bhpp.

Sanford's Grub & Pub (545 West Jackson Boulevard; 605–642–3204) is modeled after the junkyard theme of the popular 1970's TV sitcom *Sanford and Son.* No matter how many times you eat here, you'll notice something else hanging on the wall—or from the ceiling. Sheet music and a military uniform (from what war or branch we don't know yet) are tacked to the ceiling, an interesting collage but totally unrelated to the car theme on the back wall. When Sanford's first opened, word spread quickly of its amazing sandwiches and pasta dishes. Folks rave about the Freddies: thickly sliced potatoes dipped in buttermilk and seasonings, then fried. Served with a side of sour cream, these potatoes are a match for the venerable french fry. The beer list is one of the most extensive in the state.

Black Hills State University helps keep Spearfish in a robust, youthful state of mind. A football game in the stadium on a blustery fall day is a rare treat. The *First Lady Doll Museum* on the campus features an exquisite collection of porcelain miniatures of the nation's First Ladies in their inaugural gowns. All but two were made by a Spearfish resident, the late Rowena Rachetts. The museum is housed in the E. Y. Berry Library and Learning Center. Admission is free. Summer hours are 7:00 A.M. to 5:00 P.M. Monday through Friday.

Spearfish artist Dick Termes doesn't just paint on any canvas—he creates exciting worlds on spheres. In the *Termesphere Gallery* (605–642–4805; www.termespheres.com), the artist happily displays his works and explains how he reached this amazing mathematical process. Termes's latest creation greets visitors to Spearfish's city hall. The gallery is located on Christensen Drive, 1.7 miles southwest of Spearfish.

If you take U.S. Highway 14A, you'll cruise through *Spearfish Canyon,* which is a designated National Forest Scenic Byway. During fall the vibrant colors of crisp, changing leaves rival those of any New England landscape. The birch and aspen glow boldly against the backdrop of pine and spruce forests and the canyon's steep limestone walls. Colors usually peak around mid-October, which is a wonderful time for picture taking.

Located in the heart of Spearfish Canyon, the *Spearfish Canyon Lodge* (800–439–8544) provides top-of-the-line accommodations and dining amid pine trees. The lodge is located 13 miles south of Spearfish on US 14A. Rates range from $59 to $99 in winter and from $89 to $99 in summer. Suites range from $129 to $195. The lodge's Latchstring Inn Restaurant & Lounge serves meals on the veranda, where the fresh scent of pine trees can be intoxicating.

Crow Peak Trails are designed to allow access to the top of Crow Peak and the north end of Beaver Ridge. The Spearfish Ranger District has a brochure

Take a Trolley

One of the best ways to get around in Deadwood is to take the trolley. The trolleys run at regular intervals between the hotels, motels, and other key points throughout Deadwood. The cost is 50 cents per person. The schedule is posted on the back of the Main Street Trolley Signs. During the summer, from Memorial Day to mid-September, the hours of operation are 7:00 A.M. to 1:30 A.M. Sunday through Thursday and from 7:00 A.M. to 3:00 A.M. Friday and Saturday. Winter hours are from 8:00 A.M. to midnight Sunday through Thursday and 7:00 A.M. to 3:00 A.M. Friday and Saturday.

and a map that outlines the different trails. Call (605) 642–4622 for information, or pick up a brochure at the information center. Crow Peak is a key landmark in the Northern Hills. The name Crow Peak is the English translation of the Sioux name for the peak, *Paha Karitukateyapi,* which means "the hill where the Crow were killed." It is located 7 miles southwest of Spearfish on Forest Developed Road (FDR) 214, also known as Higgins Gulch Road.

About 14 miles southeast of Spearfish on Highway 85, Deadwood buzzes with the colors and energy of a mini–Las Vegas, and the sound of slot machines ringing over and over eventually becomes a gambler's mantra. Limited gambling in Deadwood keeps things hopping. In 1989 the state voted to allow $5.00 bets. The bet limit has since been increased to $100. It was an appropriate decision for Deadwood, because one hundred years ago, gambling helped the town flourish during the Gold Rush. This town of 1,860 residents has seen its share of ups and downs: Deadwood was wiped out three times in the 1880s, twice by fire and once by flood. It appeared that Deadwood's destiny was forever tied to sad times and a sad economy until gambling came back. The visage and the attitude of Deadwood were magically rejuvenated with the first shrill sound of a slot machine. Since then, many of Deadwood's Victorian buildings have been restored to their historic authenticity and grandeur. Several of the main thoroughfares have been repaved with brick, as they were more than eighty years ago. New buildings and businesses cropped up and continue to do so as businesspeople capitalize on the stream of people—and money— that gambling and its support industries bring to Deadwood. One industry, however, that didn't make a comeback was prostitution. Until houses of ill repute were shut down in the 1970s, prostitution was commonly practiced and acknowledged in Deadwood.

onetoughhorse

Tipperary was a bucking bronc who achieved fame along the rodeo circuit, and his name still remains a common and revered word for most Dakota rodeo folk. Born more than seventy years ago, no one knows what set Tipperary off on his one-horse campaign to rid the world of rodeo riders. Tales of Tipperary's vicious bucking and lightning speed spread through the West like wildfire. The legend even grew to the point that cowboys refused to ride him; however, a handsome purse did await the brave cowboy who could master this wild beast. But few did. Passing his prime, Tipperary spent his golden years in the pastures near Buffalo. Today, what could be the only monument erected in honor of a bucking bronc reads: TIPPERARY . . . WORLD'S GREATEST BUCKING HORSE.

Love Kevin Costner movies? You'll love the ***Midnight Star*** (a casino owned by Costner and his brother Dan), where Costner has displayed costumes and props from his many films—from his never-seen role as the dead friend in

The Big Chill to epics like *Dances with Wolves*. You can find the Midnight Star at 677 Main Street in Deadwood. An elevator sweeps you to the top of the Midnight Star and opens upon **Jakes** (800–999–6482), one of the most impressive restaurants in the Black Hills. The atmosphere is refined, and if you didn't know otherwise, you'd swear you were in New York City. Both the food and service merit the same high accolades. Jake's has consistently received the prestigious AAA Four Diamond Award. More moderate prices are on the menu at **Diamond Lil's Bar and Grill** (605–578–3550). Here the Costners have given their favorite sandwiches and appetizers unique names—those of their family, friends, and characters. The main level houses the casino. The Web site is www. themidnightstar.com.

Other casinos have matched the Costners' atmosphere with style and many perks for the gambler. You might get free drinks here or hors d'oeuvres there. It's all fun in the name of the game.

The historic **Franklin Hotel & Gaming Hall,** located at 700 Main Street, is one of Deadwood's largest restoration and preservation projects. The 1903, eighty-one-room hotel has been the choice of stars, including luminaries such as President William Taft, Robert Kennedy, Jr., President Theodore Roosevelt, John Wayne, Buffalo Bill, Pearl Buck, and Mary Hart (a South Dakota girl, too). Proprietor Bill Walsh, always charming and full of stories in an Irish way, serves a frosty mug in the downstairs pub, Durty Nelly's. Call (800) 688–1876 or visit the Web site at www.deadwood.net/franklin.

The **Deadwood History and Visitor Center** is a preservation success story. Built in 1897 as the Fremont, Elkhorn, and Missouri Railway passenger depot, the building looks as spanking fresh now as it did the day it was built. Visitor information and exhibits designed by the National Park Service are found inside. Here you can pick up a copy of the city's walking-tour guide, which will lead you through the commercial district to a series of interpretive signs.

Money may come and go in Deadwood, but the **Adams Memorial Museum** has been a cherished and steadfast fixture. There's something here to interest the entire family, from Wild Bill Hickok memorabilia to a rare plesiosaur dinosaur to folk art and photographs. One of the museum's most famous items is Potato Creek Johnny's gold nugget. At 7¾ troy ounces, the nugget ranks as one of the largest ever found in the Black Hills. It was recovered from a sluice on Potato Creek in western Lawrence County in May 1929. The massive chunk of gold was tucked away from public view until 1995, when it was on public display for two days to celebrate the museum's sixty-fifth anniversary. It now is safely back in the bank. The museum is open year-round. Admission is free. Call (605) 578–1714 for hours.

The city of Deadwood has restored the **Adams House Museum** (605–578–3724; www.adamsmuseumandhouse.org). A $1.5-million, two-part project refurbished the Victorian home, once owned by museum founder W. E. Adams, into a museum.

"It's one of the most significant pieces of architecture in the city. It represents the early history of Deadwood, including one of the most prominent families. It adds to the attractions we have that draw people to Deadwood," said historic preservation officer Chris Hertzel.

The house, which is located at 22 Van Buren Street in the so-called presidential neighborhood of Deadwood, was built in 1892, when it was originally owned by Harris Franklin. Adams purchased the majestic home in 1920. When he died in 1936, his second wife, Mary, took ownership. Bruce and Becky Crosswaite purchased the home in 1988 and opened it as a bed-and-breakfast.

The restoration project has returned the home to its mid-1930s glamour. Open year-round.

When you're in this residential area, you can see how Deadwood feels like a sliver of San Francisco, with its steep streets and historic homes. If you follow Lincoln Street uphill, you'll arrive at **Mount Moriah Cemetery,** the final resting spot for some of the Old West's more colorful characters. Here you can find the grave sites of Wild Bill Hickok, Calamity Jane, and Potato Creek Johnny. Also buried at Mount Moriah, with her parrot and her husband, is madame Dora DuFran, Calamity Jane's gal pal. Dora ran brothels in the Black Hills in the 1920s and 1930s but was known for her humanitarian work as well. Melanie Griffith portrayed Dora in the made-for-TV movie *Buffalo Girls.*

Just a few miles away is Lead, Deadwood's sister city. The bare-bones business district stands in stark contrast to glitzy Deadwood. Mining is the mighty force in this town, and **Homestake Gold Mine** has flourished economically, making it the largest underground gold mine in the Western Hemisphere. Founded in 1876 by three California investors, including George Hearst, the Homestake mine extends 8,000 feet below the surface of the Black Hills. In addition to the underground mine, Homestake operates the Open Cut surface mine, which was the original site of the Homestake claim. **Homestake Gold Mine Visitor Center** (605–584–3110) shows off both new and old mining technology, and you can watch the hoisting, crushing, and milling of gold-bearing ore.

For more on the history of mining, the **Black Hills Mining Museum** (605–584–1605) takes a detailed look at mining activity in the Hills during the past 118 years. Open seven days a week, the museum is at 323 West Main Street. For more information, visit the Web site at www.mining-museum.blackhills.com.

Deer Mountain Ski Resort and **Terry Peak Ski Resort,** located west of Lead, present lots of the fluffy white stuff for expert, intermediate, and beginner downhill skiers. Complete ski packages are available for sale and for rent. For more information call Deer Mountain at (605) 584– 3230, and Terry Peak at (605) 584–2165.

If snowmobiling is your choice of winter sports, the Black Hills is the place to be. The area offers more than 320 miles of interlinking, groomed snowmobile trails, with 64 miles of roadway outside the Lead-Deadwood city limits alone. Snowmobiles can be rented at several places in the Hills, including the **Deadwood Gulch Resort** (605–578–1294) in Deadwood, **Golden Hills Resort** (605–584–1800) in Lead, and the popular **Trailshead Lodge** (605–584–3464) on U.S. Highway 85 near the South Dakota/Wyoming border.

Points Northwest

The northwestern corner of South Dakota is not as familiar as the Black Hills (even to South Dakotans), but this is a perfect place to get away from it all. Tiny towns occasionally crop up on the plains landscape here, with names like Faith and Promise, Bison, Prairie City, Meadow, and Buffalo. The names reflect the ranch country and the determination of early settlers. Around here people automatically wave or tip their hats to fellow drivers as they tool down the highway—a warm gesture you'll never see in a big city. Folks assume they know you, or they know your kids, parents, employer, or whatever. It's a fine welcome, no matter what. If you stop at a Main Street store or gas station, you might get looked over once, but the unaffected congeniality of the residents extends to the out-of-town visitor.

If you take US 85 north 9 miles from Spearfish, you'll find the Western panorama of Belle Fourche (Dakotans say Bell Foosh). The town of 4,565 people earned the designation as the geographical center of the United States by the U.S. Coast and Geodetic Survey. An official marker and a sheepherder's monument called a "Stone Johnnie" note this distinction. Belle Fourche is proud of its Western image; after all, the community had its beginnings during the days of the dusty cattle drive when the wealth of the region attracted such notables as Butch Cassidy and the Sundance Kid. At the turn of the century, Belle Fourche became known as the largest cattle-shipping point in the world. Join in today's rough-and-tumble spirit July 3–5 each summer for the annual **Black Hills Roundup Rodeo,** with fireworks, a carnival, and historic parade. First held in 1918, this rodeo still attracts top PRCA cowboys. Indeed, many Pro Rodeo athletes call Bell Fourche their home, including four-time World Bareback Riding Champion Marvin Garrett.

Today the town is also the center of the largest concentration of sheep in the United States and ships more wool from its two warehouses than any other city.

Just 9 miles east of Belle Fourche, **Orman Dam** makes a fabulous playground for the waterskiing, boating, camping, fishing, or swimming enthusiast. The yearly Fourth of July fireworks display, too, is legendary, and the surrounding prairies make for the perfect patriotic backdrop.

The world's largest earthen dam, Orman Dam was constructed with the use of horses around the turn of the twentieth century to provide irrigation for a huge tract of sugar-beet farms downstream. Although corn, small grains, and alfalfa now dominate the agricultural scene, Orman Dam remains the area's primary dry-season water source. And there is plenty of water to go around: Orman has 185,000 acre-feet of water and 52 miles of shoreline with 13 square miles of water surface.

Continue on US 85 north, and you'll drive through cattle country, where one-pony towns like Redig and Ludlow can be missed with a blink of the eye. The sanctity of space keeps travelers mindful.

Historical landmarks like **Crow Buttes** crop up occasionally and offer interesting tidbits on the fascinating saga of the frontier. A case in point is the bizarre battle at Crow Buttes. Located in Harding County, Crow Buttes was the scene of a battle between Crow and Sioux Indians during the summer of 1822. Sioux men ravaged the Crow camp, destroying it and raping the women. Warfare ensued. The Crow warriors left the women, children, and older people at Sand Creek, north of the buttes, fleeing for a better vantage point on top of the Crow Buttes. The Sioux chased them. The Crow had no water with them, and no rain fell to soothe the sultry weather. The Sioux circled Crow Buttes and waited patiently for the trapped Crow to die from thirst. Subsequently, the nearby Canyon of Skulls to the northwest was filled with skeletons of the Sioux, who died en masse after contracting a fever from the Crow Indians.

Just before the town of Buffalo, take State Highway 20 east to find one of the best-kept secrets in South Dakota. Long before he became president, Theodore Roosevelt hunted bear in the region now known as Custer National Forest. (He later established forest reserves in the Cave Hills and Slim Buttes areas.) **Custer National Forest** is probably the most forgotten forest in the state. Even natives have a puzzled look on their faces when it's mentioned, which is understandable; there's Custer State Park to the southeast, so another Custer moniker seems at first repetitious, but that does not deter from the beauty of this rustic area.

The 73,000 timbered acres in the northwestern part of the state are anomalous to the barren, outlying landscape. Ride and hike, but don't expect a guide or user-friendly visitor center to take you by the hand. You're in the deep forest now, and there are no designated hiking trails.

The Cave Hills section of the forest was once a popular hiding place for outlaws. Ludlow Cave, the largest of the caves, sheltered many bandits during the stormy days of the Dakota Territory. Accordingly, ranchers have called this rugged, rough land the "jumping-off spot."

East of the Cave Hills lies the Slim Buttes section of forest, where lofty cliffs of limestone are split by dramatic canyons. The Slim Buttes battlefield is nearby, where Sioux veterans of the Custer battle were overtaken by the U.S. Cavalry. The Sioux were taken by surprise in the fall of 1876, but they took shelter high in the hills behind the limestone outcroppings and escaped during the night.

Stay east on State Highway 20 and you'll eventually run into State Highway 73. Take State Highway 73 north, and you'll inch your way toward literature and legend.

The first suggested stop on this stretch of highway is **Shadehill Recreation Area.** In addition to the customary sporting opportunities one expects, the reservoir also boasts an intriguing historical marker on the southern shore. The marker describes a saga that was the fodder for the book of a great regional writer and teacher, the late Frederick Manfred. *Lord Grizzly* is based on the legend of Hugh Glass, who survived incredible odds. In 1823, at the fork of the Grand River, Glass was hunting with the Ashley fur party when he was attacked by a grizzly bear. Horribly maimed, he could not be moved. Two members of the Ashley party were instructed to stay with him, but instead they took Glass's weapons and left him for dead. Amazingly, Glass survived on berries and buffalo meat acquired after driving away two wolves from a downed calf. Glass eventually crawled about 190 miles to Fort Kiowa on the Missouri River.

Lemmon, just 12 miles north on the South Dakota/North Dakota border, is the home of Kathleen Norris, another fine contemporary writer from the state. She captured the essence of small-town life in *Dakota: A Spiritual Geography.* Her collection of poetry, *Little Girls in Church,* also speaks from the heart. Other excellent writers of western South Dakota include Linda Hasselstrom, Virginia Driving Hawk Sneve, and Dan O'Brien.

The Lemmon **Petrified Wood Park and Museum,** located at 500 Main Avenue, is the poetry of simpler times in the form of petrified woods and fossils.

Petrified Wood Park was built in the early 1930s by the men of Lemmon under the command of Ole S. Quammen. Apparently this was a labor of love and necessity for some. A sign says: thirty to forty otherwise unemployed men received sustenance during this period. The park covers a city block in the heart of downtown and includes a castle, a wishing well, a waterfall, and the Lemmon Pioneer Museum—all made of petrified wood. One can envision trolls or at least gnomes pirouetting behind the cones, some of which stand at 20 feet.

The new *Grand River Museum,* located at 114 Tenth Street W, features local history, culture, and dinosaur fossils. In fact, it's a paleontologist's dream come true. It displays many of the dinosaur bones that have been dug up on ranches in the area. The outreach programs of the museum include dinosaur digs, scientific research, and community involvement. And there's a gift shop as well. The museum is open 10:00 A.M. to 5:00 P.M. daily. For more information call (605) 374–3911, or log on to its informative Web site, www.grandriver museum.org.

Where to Stay in Western South Dakota

BELLE FOURCHE

Candlelight Bed & Breakfast,
819 Fifth Avenue (US 85),
(800) 469–7572

CUSTER

Best Western Buffalo Ridge Inn,
224 Mount Rushmore Road,
(605) 673–2275

DEADWOOD

Best Western Golden Hills Resort,
located at US 14A and 85,
3 miles southwest of Deadwood,
(888) 465–3080

Bullock Hotel,
633 Main Street,
(800) 336–1876

Deadwood Gulch Resort,
US 85 South,
(605) 578–1294

First Gold Hotel,
270 Main Street,
(800) 274–1876

Mineral Palace Hotel & Gaming,
601 Main Street,
(605) 578–2036,
(800) 847–2522

HILL CITY

Best Western Golden Spike Inn,
106 Main Street,
(605) 574–2577

LEAD

Golden Hills Inn,
900 Miners Avenue,
(888) 465–3080

Whitehouse Inn,
395 Glendale Drive,
(800) 654–5323

RAPID CITY

Flying B Ranch Bed & Breakfast,
take exit 58 off I–90 then travel 3 miles north,
(605) 342–5324

Hayloft Bed & Breakfast,
9356 Neck Yoke Road,
(800) 317–6784

Holiday Inn Rushmore Plaza,
take exit 58 off I–90 then travel 1 mile south,
(605) 348–4000

Ramada Gold Key,
located at I–90 (exit 59) and LaCrosse Street,
(605) 342–1300

SPEARFISH

Fairfield Inn,
2720 First Avenue E,
(605) 642–3500

Kelly Inn,
549 East Jackson,
(605) 642–7795

Spearfish Canyon Lodge,
located in the heart of Spearfish Canyon,
(800) 439–8544

STURGIS

Super 8 Motel,
located off I–90 at exit 30,
(605) 347–4447

Where to Eat in Western South Dakota

CUSTER

Sage Creek Grille,
607 Mount Rushmore Road,
(605) 673–2424

Sylvan Lake Lodge,
junction of Highways 87 and
89 in Custer State Park,
(605) 574–2561

DEADWOOD

**Jakes Atop the Midnight
Star,**
677 Main Street,
(800) 999–6482,
www.themidnightstar.com

Silverado,
790 Main Street, (800)
584–7005

Tin Lizzie (American),
555 Main Street, (605)
578–1715

HILL CITY

Alpine Inn
(American/German),
225 Main Street,
(605) 574–2749

Continental Cafe
(American), 198 Main Street,
(605) 574–9422

Golden Spike Restaurant
(American), 106 Main Street,
(605) 574–2577

KEYSTONE

Powder House Restaurant
(American), (605) 666–4646

RAPID CITY

Carini's (Italian),
324 St. Joseph Street,
(605) 348–3704

Canyon Lake Chophouse
(American/steak),
2720 Chapel Lane,
(605) 388–8000

The Cattleman's Club
(American/steak), located
west of Rapid City off I–90
on exit 48,
(605) 787–4042

**Colonial House Restaurant
& Pub,**
2501 Mount Rushmore
Road, (605) 342–4640

The Firehouse Brewing Co.,
610 Main Street,
(605) 348–1915

The Fireside
(American/steak), 10 miles
west of Rapid City on
Highway 44,
(605) 342–3900

Outback Steakhouse,
665 East Disk Drive,
(605) 341–1192

Pirates Table
(seafood/steak), 3550
Sturgis Road,
(605) 341–4842

Tiffany Grille (American),
located in the Holiday Inn
Rushmore Plaza, 505 North
Fifth Street, (605) 348–4000

ROCKERVILLE

The Gaslight,
13490 Main Street,
(605) 343–9276

SPEARFISH

Bay Leaf Cafe,
126 West Hudson,
(605) 642–5462

Roma's Italian Ristorante,
701 Fifth Street,
(605) 722–0715

Sanford's Grub and Pub,
545 West Jackson
Boulevard,
(605) 642–3204

Valley Cafe/TCBY Treats
(American), 608 Main Street,
(605) 642–2423

STURGIS

Phil Town Country Kitchen
(American),
2431 South Junction,
(605) 347–3604

WALL

Elkton House (American),
exit 110 off I–90 and
Highway 240, (605)
279–2152

SELECTED CHAMBERS OF COMMERCE

Belle Fourche Chamber of Commerce,
415 Fifth Avenue, Belle Fourche 57717,
(605) 892–2676, www.bellefourche.org

Custer County Chamber of Commerce,
615 Washington Street, Custer 57730,
(605) 673–2244

Deadwood/Lead Area Chamber of Commerce,
735 Main Street, Deadwood 57732,
(800) 999–1876, www.deadwood.org

Hill City Chamber of Commerce,
P.O. Box 253, Hill City 57745,
(800) 888–1798, www.hillcitysd.com

Hot Springs Area Chamber of Commerce,
801 South Sixth Street,
Hot Springs 57747, (605) 745–4140,
www.hotsprings-sd.com

Rapid City Convention & Visitors Bureau,
P.O. Box 747, Rapid City 57709,
(800) 487–3223, www.rapidcitycvb.com

Spearfish Area Chamber of Commerce,
106 West Kansas Street,
Spearfish 57783, (800) 626–8013,
www.spearfish.sd.us

Along the Missouri River

For sheer wanderlust, travel the Missouri River section of South Dakota. There are few towns along this central strip and few people—except those of Old World and Native American heritage who proudly share their culture. The Missouri River winds through central South Dakota for 453 miles, offering not only a spectacular ribbon of blue water but also shore land rich in history, mystery, and adventure. Sliding past forts, monuments, ruins, reservations, and pioneer towns in South Dakota, the Missouri River ultimately flows into the Mississippi River and then to the Gulf of Mexico.

The powerful Missouri neatly divides the state into two dissimilar geographic and cultural regions. Along the west side of the river, wide stretches of prairie are broken by low hills and cut by ravines. Trees are sparse, and great cattle ranches fill the expanse of land. In the extreme west rise the forested Black Hills, one of the primary sources of the nation's gold. This is the hardy Old West of movies, memories, and dime-store novels—rowdy and independent. Fertile farmlands stretch out east of the Missouri River. Both the land and rainfall are generally good for crops. Culturally speaking, East River is the well-heeled cousin who needs to be sent away to the spirited West

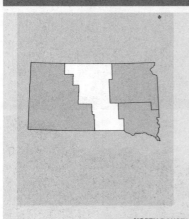

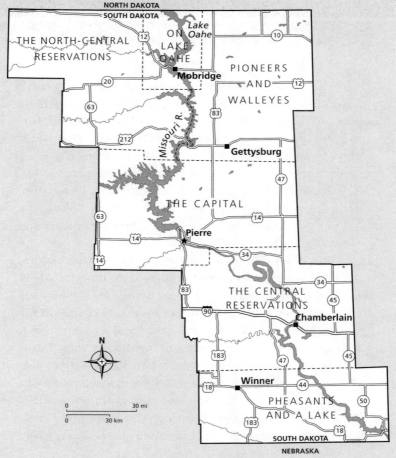

NORTH DAKOTA
SOUTH DAKOTA

THE NORTH-CENTRAL
RESERVATIONS

ON
LAKE
OAHE

Lake
Oahe

PIONEERS
AND
WALLEYES

Mobridge

Missouri R.

Gettysburg

THE CAPITAL

Pierre

THE CENTRAL
RESERVATIONS

Chamberlain

Winner

PHEASANTS
AND A LAKE

N

0   30 mi
0   30 km

SOUTH DAKOTA
NEBRASKA

TOP HITS ALONG THE MISSOURI RIVER

Al's Oasis	Scherr Howe Arena
Grand River Casino & Resort	Sitting Bull Monument
Indian Creek Recreation Area	South Dakota Cultural Heritage Center
Karl E. Mundt National Wildlife Refuge	South Dakota Discovery Center and Aquarium
Oahe Dam	Vérendrye Monument
Pierre Historic Homes Driving Tour	West Whitlock Recreation Area

River once in a while to get a good grasp of terra firma in his hand and in his soul. Likewise, this East River gentleman could rein in the wild Westerner.

The Mighty Mo, as residents like to call the river, served as the first highway into the region at a time when fur trappers pulled keelboats up the river by hand. Later, fur traders arrived in steamboats, beginning with the arrival of the *Yellowstone* in 1831. They sang the now-familiar folksong "O Shenandoah," and you can almost hear the strain of ". . . across the wide Missouri."

River traffic became a thing of the past as the railroad reached the area at the turn of the century and the number of settlements increased rapidly thereafter. The river in those days was known as the Muddy Mo, and the standard joke was that a person didn't know whether to plow it or drink it. Stand-up comedy had its last laugh under the Pick-Sloan plan and the construction of four dams across the Missouri, which created Lewis and Clark Lake, Lake Francis Case, Lake Sharpe, and Lake Oahe. These reservoirs have transformed Old Muddy into a series of crystalline blue lakes that have become popular recreation areas for South Dakotans and nonresidents.

Today life along the Missouri River isn't as bustling as life in East River or as animated as that in West River. But isn't new geography or culture what we crave? Feel doubly blessed along the Mighty Mo.

On Lake Oahe

South Dakota's claim to a portion of the Missouri River begins at the north-central edge of the state. The river was formed when glaciers to the east blocked the flow of western rivers, and the town of Mobridge enjoys the prosperity that the river has afforded. Mobridge calls itself the Walleye Capital of the

World, and no one is likely to dispute that moniker, since both the Missouri and the Oahe Reservoir envelop this town of 3,400. In 1906 the Milwaukee Railroad built the first bridge to cross the Missouri River in South Dakota, at what was formerly the site of an Arikara and Sioux village. A telegraph operator used the contraction *Mobridge* to indicate his location, and the name has stuck.

Lake Oahe, with a shoreline of more than 2,250 miles, is the longest lake on the main stream of the Missouri River, stretching 231 miles from Pierre to Bismarck, North Dakota. Begun in 1948, it is the largest of the four impoundments. The shoreline is virtually devoid of trees, making it a curious earthbound moonscape. The lake's azure waters and native stands of grass on the bluff, however, make it appealingly endless and warm.

The genuinely down-to-earth people of Mobridge are eager to accommodate the visitors who flock to the town during hunting, fishing, and boating seasons. The choices in lodging are appropriate for both the serious-minded and casual sportsperson. The sparsely furnished but clean rooms of the **Mo-Rest Motel** on U.S. Highway 12 are perfect for no-frills fishermen. Owners Denny and Glenda Palmer have ensured that there are special amenities for anglers. For instance, they provide aerial river maps. The motel is across the street from two bait shops with boat repair. Outside the rooms, electrical outlets are available for battery charges. Denny himself is a veteran Missouri River guide, tour-

A Stone's Throw Away

The City Park on North Main Street in Mobridge was dedicated to the public in 1910, after it was platted by the Grand Crossing Company. Beautification and planting of the large variety of trees, however, did not begin until 1925.

The Conqueror's Stones are on the north side of the park. How they arrived in Mobridge and who placed them there remains a mystery. Originally, there was a marker with this inscription:

NOTE THE GROOVES ACCORDING TO TRADITION DEFEATED INDIAN WARRIORS WERE REQUIRED TO PLACE THEIR HANDS IN THESE GROOVES AS A SIGN OF SUBMISSION SHETAK CAPTIVES RESCUED HERE

NOVEMBER, 1862
BY FOOL SOLDIER BAND

Further investigation found that these stones were commonly referred to as prayer rocks and that natives would place their hands in the grooves in the rocks when taking an oath as part of initiation ceremonies. Some believe the grooves are the handprints of the Thunderheads, the gods displayed on totem poles. According to this belief, by putting their hands in the prints before they died, the Indians would be taken to the Sky World or heaven.

ROBIN'S FAVORITES

Akta Lakota Museum,
Chamberlain, (800) 798–3452

Grand River Casino & Resort,
located 2 miles west of
Mobridge on US 12,
(800) 475–3321

Oahe Dam,
4 miles north of Pierre

**Samuel H. Ordway Jr.
Memorial Prairie,**
50 miles northwest of Aberdeen
on U.S. Highway 281

**South Dakota Cultural
Heritage Center,**
900 Governors Drive, Pierre,
(605) 773–3458

nament fisherman, speaker, and outdoor writer. The Palmers' MoPro Guide Service offers on-the-water instruction using the latest fishing techniques and boat control. Call the motel at (605) 845–3668.

For more luxurious surroundings, the *Wrangler Motor Inn,* 820 West Grand Crossing (0.5 mile west on US 12), offers civilized respite for the evening. An indoor swimming pool and the Windjammer restaurant (with a stunning view of the river) and bar round out the accommodations. Call (605) 845–3641 or (888) 315–BEST (2378), or visit the Web site at www.wranglerinn.com for more information.

Adjacent to the Wrangler Inn is the *Wheel Restaurant* (820 West Grand Crossing), where we always went during a visit to Grandpa and Grandma DeSart's home in Mobridge. It still seems a special place with a noon buffet and evening salad bar, homemade pies and soups, and even fruit smoothies. For more information, call (605) 845–7474 or (877) 363–5884.

The *Mobridge Country Club* (located 1.5 miles north of Mobridge on State Highway 1804) serves mouth-watering cuts of steak and has a nine-hole golf course. Call (605) 845–2307 for hours of operation.

History buffs will find a profusion of items to marvel at in the *Scherr Howe Arena* on Main Street. Colorful murals by the late Oscar Howe, a highly esteemed Dakota Indian and art professor at the University of South Dakota, depict both the history and ceremonies of Native Americans. Each mural measures about 16 feet high by 20 feet wide. For instance, one mural depicts the Social Dance, a prenuptial ceremony common among the Sioux. Custom prescribed a well-established routine for courtship and marriage, but the marital relationship was mostly the result of an agreement between the parties. Since marriage involved being taken into the families of the contracting parties, there were usually group meetings of the relatives with feasting, dancing, and ceremonies that sometimes lasted four or five days. Members of the family wishing to honor the bride and groom brought appropriate gifts. The bride was suitably honored, her hair combed and braided, and she was given face paints and beautiful garments. Earthenware vessels and other household goods also were common wedding presents.

The groom's father also brought gifts that he bestowed upon his son. Spirited horses and weapons used in the chase and war were among the gifts to honor the new union. Songs of praise about the newlyweds were sung, and small gifts were distributed to the elderly and needy people of the camp. Admission to the center is free. Open 8:00 A.M. to 5:00 P.M. Monday through Friday. Call (605) 341–8649 for more information.

For more history on the Arikara and Sioux Indians, head 2 miles west on US 12 to the *Klein Museum* (605–845–7243), where Arikara and Sioux artifacts

Range Club

In small Dakota towns, a supper club is often the heart of social activity.

In Mobridge, my grandparents once operated The Range Club. I remember as a child performing on its wonderfully spacious stage during the day with my sister, Jean Beth, and my two cousins, Marva Jo and Lorrie. We always chose songs we thought Grandpa DeSart would enjoy, like those of Glen Campbell, and we tossed in some quickly choreographed moves as well. Britney Spears we were not, but we always had a captive audience in our parents and grandparents.

Grandpa DeSart had moved this huge building from Stanton, North Dakota, to Mobridge. He remodeled and it became The Range Club, just east of town near the airport. It had a wooden floor that was ideal for dancing, and many dances were held there on Saturday nights. The Range Club had a restaurant, which my Grandma DeSart managed. My parents' wedding party and dance was held there, too, in 1959. In my mind now, it was straight out of a Walker Evans photograph.

The Range Club is no longer; in its place is the Eagles Club (605–845–9126) on Airport Road, which carries on the tradition of small-town dining and nightlife. The Fireside Supper Club (605–845–2936), at Sixth Avenue West and Grand Crossing, is a popular spot, too.

Granny

My maternal grandparents lived in Mobridge, so the area holds many dear memories. Of holidays. Of fishing expeditions in my Grandpa DeSart's hippie van. Of Granny DeSart's dill pickles and her lovingly made baked goods. She is well-renowned in our family for her cinnamon rolls, apple pie, and date cookies. When I copied this recipe, it had two smiling stick men in the corner—a sign drawn years ago by Grandpa DeSart that these were fine cookies indeed.

Jumbo Date Cookies

For the filling:

1 package dates, chopped

1 cup water

¼ cup sugar

Boil together until thick. Stir frequently to prevent burning.

For the cookies:

2 cups brown sugar

1 cup Crisco (Cream the Crisco; and Granny insists on using Crisco)

3 eggs

3¼ cups flour

1 tsp soda

½ tsp salt

1 tsp vanilla

Chill dough. Then form dough into small balls and make dents in the center. Place 1 teaspoon cooled date filling in each dent. Then make another small ball, flatten it, and put it on top of the date filling in the cookie. Pinch the edges together to seal.

Bake at 350 degrees for 8 to 10 minutes.

share space with relics of the pioneer past, such as old farm machinery and a restored schoolhouse. It was the dream of an early homesteader, Jake Klein, long before the building was ever designed. His dream was to have a top-notch museum that would represent the counties of Campbell, Corson, Dewey, and Walworth, where he traded, homesteaded, and finally retired.

The museum building, with its native stone front, was a gift from Klein to the city of Mobridge and the surrounding area with the help of a $15,000 grant from the South Dakota Bicentennial Commission.

The museum displays focus on prairie and Native American artifacts. More than twenty pictures of Sitting Bull are featured, along with stone and bone artifacts. The culture of the Sioux and Arikara Indians is reflected in the many articles of clothing, beadwork, pottery, tools, and implements that are on display.

The daily tasks of the early pioneers also come alive through the room scenes. For instance, the 1900s pre-electric kitchen features a wood/coal stove, large doughmaker, berry press, kraut cutter, and wooden icebox. A one-room schoolhouse and the original Glencross post office are also located on the museum grounds.

The museum is open April 1 through October 31, from 9:00 A.M. to noon and from 1:00 to 5:00 P.M. on weekdays, except Tuesday. It is open from 1:00 to 5:00 P.M. Saturday and Sunday. Admission is $2.00 for adults, $1.00 for children. Preschoolers and school groups are admitted free.

The Fool Soldier Band Monument also is located at the Klein Museum. On August 20–22, 1862, a group of young Teton Sioux negotiated for white captives of the Santee Indians and returned the captives to their families. They expected no rewards or reimbursement, and their actions seemed to be motivated by purely humanitarian concerns. This act of heroism took place in what is now Walworth County.

In Mobridge the Missouri River and Lake Oahe are the center of outdoor leisure. Fishing isn't the only sport in town; the Mobridge area is also a hunter's paradise, with open seasons on pheasant, grouse, turkey, deer, and antelope. Waterskiing, swimming, boating, or just soaking up the brilliant South Dakota sun can easily fill an afternoon.

Indian Creek Recreation Area (located 2 miles east on US 12, then 1 mile south) is an outdoor sports heaven right on the Oahe Reservoir. The area offers swimming, boating, fishing, picnicking, playgrounds, and tent and trailer sites. For more information call (605) 845–7112.

Sitting Bull Monument

Some 135 million years ago, the area around Mobridge was covered by a great shallow sea, teeming with marine mollusks and shellfish. Clues to their prehistoric existence have turned up along the shores of Lake Oahe in the form of fossil ammonites, baculites, and belemnites that range from 1 to 6 inches long. If you look hard enough, you might find one of the ancient treasures.

Sitting Bull Monument, in Dakota Memorial Park, west of Mobridge on US 12, marks the burial site of the famous Hunkpapa medicine man. Like many chapters in the collective Plains Indian story, Sitting Bull's is one of a fascinating, enigmatic man who met an untimely death. Sitting Bull was born in 1834 on the Grand River,

Norwegians in America

My maternal great-grandmother, Anne Olsen, came from Norway by boat when she was three years old. Her family settled in Iowa, where they eventually became wealthy farmers. Much to their dismay, she met and married a poor Norwegian man, Olous Njos, from a neighboring village. He would walk 20 miles just to court her. Olous was born in the United States, and he, too, was 100 percent Norwegian.

Anne and Olous eventually filed a homestead claim northwest of Isabel, South Dakota, which is about an hour's drive southwest of Mobridge. Eight children were born to this union, and somehow Anne and Olous eked out a living on the 160 acres and also managed to send most of their children to college to become teachers.

Anne would not allow her children to speak Norwegian, as she wanted them to become Americans in the fullest sense of the word. Consequently, my grandmother, Alice Njos DeSart, speaks no Norwegian, but she cooks a great meal of lutefisk and lefse (a flat, tortilla-like bread made from potatoes). I must say lutefisk, a strong-smelling fish that my mom swears can turn forks black, is enough to make Norwegian cuisine an oxymoron. The lefse and sweets, however, are adequate damage control.

a few miles west of Mobridge, and his tragic demise years later occurred in the same place. The last known leader of the Cante Tizna, an elite warrior society, Sitting Bull also helped to defeat General George Custer's troops in 1876 at the Battle of the Little Big Horn. Sitting Bull met his own death, however, after he was arrested and then shot at his camp on the Standing Rock agency near Fort Yates in North Dakota.

The bodies of Sitting Bull and his men were buried in the corner of a post cemetery at Fort Yates. On April 8, 1953, descendants, with the help of the Dakota Memorial Association, moved Sitting Bull's remains to the present location and dedicated the memorial.

The giant granite bust of Sitting Bull was carved by Korczak Ziolkowski, who also started the Crazy Horse Memorial in the Black Hills. The marker today seems desolate and rather forgotten. Sitting Bull's remains, encased in a steel vault, are embedded in a twenty-ton block of concrete on which the monument stands. The grave site is open to the public free of charge.

It is also fitting that a memorial to Sakakawea (an alternate spelling of Sakagawea), the indomitable guide of Lewis and Clark, is located near the Sitting Bull Monument. Sakakawea, or Bird Woman, was a Shoshone Indian princess of the Big Horn Mountains of Montana. She was captured and taken to North Dakota. There she married a French fur trader, and together they were hired by Lewis and Clark for their first trip west in 1804.

Sakakawea guided the expedition over seemingly insurmountable obstacles. Much of the credit for the venture's success is given to her. She died later of "putrid fever," in 1812, at the age of twenty-five, at Fort Manuel in Corson County, a short distance north of Mobridge.

In 1929 Mobridge schoolchildren donated pennies to erect a monument to honor this illustrious Indian woman. On September 27, 1929, a graceful cement shaft with a bronze plaque was erected at the Dakota Memorial Park in her memory.

The North-Central Reservations

Two of the state's more sparsely populated Indian reservations abut Mobridge to the west. The **Standing Rock Indian Reservation** covers 562,366 acres of land in South Dakota (it extends into south-central North Dakota). The **Cheyenne River Indian Reservation** covers 1.4 million acres, making it the second-largest reservation in the state.

Adjacent to the Sitting Bull Monument on the bank of the Missouri River, you can find the **Grand River Casino & Resort,** with more than 15,000 square feet of gambling fun, as well as a lounge, an outdoor amphitheater, and a restaurant, perched high on a bluff overlooking Lake Oahe. The Grand River casino, owned by the Standing Rock Sioux Tribe, features slots, blackjack, and poker. The casino walls are decorated with the artwork of Del Iron Cloud. The casino is located 2.5 miles west of Mobridge on US 12. For more information call (800) 475–3321 or visit www.grandrivercasino.com.

For a true Western adventure, tours can be made to see the Cheyenne River Sioux tribe's buffalo herd, which numbers more than 500. The Lakotas recognize the tatanka's significance and have incorporated traditional methods of raising buffalo to restore them in a culturally and environmentally sound manner. For more information about the tours, call Pte Hca Ka, Inc., at (605) 964–4010.

Cheyenne River Tribe Flag

Color is magically represented in the Cheyenne River Sioux Tribe's flag. The tribe's name appears in a banner framed by color. Blue represents the thunderclouds above the world where the thunderbirds that control the four winds live. The rainbow is for the Cheyenne River Sioux People, who are keepers of the Most Sacred Calf Pipe, a gift from the White Buffalo Calf Woman. The eagle feathers at the edges of the rim of the world represent the spotted eagle, which is the protector of all Lakota. Underneath the banner, two pipes fused together represent unity. One pipe is for the Lakota, the other for all the other Indian nations. Behind the pipes are yellow hoops symbolizing the Sacred Hoop, which shall not be broken. The Sacred Calf Pipe Bundle in red, in the center, represents Wakan Tanka—The Great Mystery.

In Eagle Butte southwest of Mobridge, the ***H. V. Johnston Cultural Center*** (605–964–2542) displays traditional beadwork and murals that depict the Lakota way of life. You also can buy beadwork and paintings by contemporary artists here. The center is located on US 212 near State Highway 63 on the Cheyenne River Indian Reservation. Free admission.

One of the area's more famous residents is Arvol Looking Horse, a nineteenth-generation keeper of the Sacred Pipe of the Great Sioux Nation. In this position he cares for the Sacred Pipe, presented by the White Buffalo Calf Woman many years ago. Looking Horse leads the annual Sacred Pipestone Run, which was formed to stop the sale of sacred pipestone. He holds an honorary degree from the University of South Dakota and has been profiled many times by local and national media. Looking Horse also is featured in the book of portraiture *Visions Quest*, the story of contemporary Lakotas, Dakotas, and Nakotas who have chosen to carry on the traditions and culture of their people. The book was a collaborative project between Jesuit Don Doll and prominent Native American men and women. This handsomely arranged book features fifty contemporary members of the Sioux nation from five states and fifteen reservations, as well as Sioux lands, sacred sites, and photographs of dancers in traditional costume.

site selection

Founded in 1901, Pollock, northeast of Mobridge in Campbell County, thrived until the early 1950s, when construction of the Oahe Dam threatened to leave the town under water. For several years the people of Pollock struggled with whether to move, abandon their town, or consolidate with nearby Herreid. After much consideration the town decided to move. But in what direction? A vote was held and ballots cast, some with a touch of humor. One vote called for Pollock to be put even deeper under the waters of Lake Oahe. Groundbreaking ceremonies for the "new" town were held on June 4, 1955. Today Pollock is surrounded on three sides by water and enjoys its reputation as one of South Dakota's most mobile cities.

Pioneers and Walleyes

Whereas Native American history swells from the central plains of the state, the tiny town of Eureka (www.eurekasd.com), northeast of Mobridge on State Highway 10, shows the Old World's contribution to America's melting pot.

For more than a hundred years, beginning in the late 1700s, German colonists had been permitted to live in Russia and retain their culture, customs, and language; then, in 1871, Czar Alexander II revoked the agreement, which spurred a mass exodus. Thousands of German-Russian immigrants made their way to Dakota Territory, and eventually to Eureka.

LewisandClark

Like many other points along the Missouri River, the stretch in central South Dakota swells with the historical exploits of Lewis and Clark. Near Greenwood in the south-central part of the state, for instance, Captain Lewis wrapped a newborn Sioux in a United States flag and predicted the babe would always be a friend of the whites. The child grew up to become Chief Struck by the Ree. Farther upstream, at Mobridge, the explorers camped with the Arikara Indians and met with French fur traders.

You can find colorful touches of Germany throughout Eureka, whether they be in a church, Kauk's Meat Market (praised for its German sausage), or just in the conversations of locals. Many of Eureka's 1,225 residents still speak German, often slipping between English and German without a thought. Ron Bender, a Eureka homeboy and now city editor at the *Rapid City Journal,* remembers that the Lutheran church had two pastors—one English-speaking and one German-speaking—well into the 1960s. "As a kid, I worked in my dad's hardware store, and customers would do their business in German. I knew just the basics of German, so we almost had to conduct business in sign language," said Bender.

Eureka still is a great place for a child to grow up in, and Eureka Lake, with its gently sloping beach and perfect swimming waters, enhances the deal. In fact a child's rite of passage in Eureka is to swim in the lake alone. Like many towns in rural America, Eureka's nature is conservative, even staunchly Republican. "I remember my mom telling me, in almost a whisper, that she voted for Jim Abourezk (a former U.S. senator who is a Democrat)," said Bender. "It's a real close-knit community with a lot of big extended families."

While you're in Eureka, dubbed "The Gem of Highway 10," hang up your hat at the **Lakeview Motel,** which overlooks beautiful Lake Eureka. With thirty-two rooms and a full-service restaurant, this establishment knows how to cater to guests—especially if they happen to be hunters. The motel also has a bird-cleaning room and a pheasant freezer. The motel is located at 49 West Highway 10. Call (605) 284–2400 for reservations and room rates.

Neuharth is a common name in this part of the country, and it's also the last name of one of its most famous natives: Al Neuharth. Neuharth, founder of Gannett Newspapers, recalls his impoverished youth in his book *Confessions of an S.O.B.* The Neuharth name is not forgotten in Eureka. The town's information booth, located on the west edge of town, is dedicated to Al Neuharth's father, Daniel J. Neuharth.

Appropriately, Eureka citizens celebrate their heritage with the annual **German-Russian Schmeckfest** during the third weekend in September. Visitors are welcome to the celebration of Russian-German food and heritage.

A Prairie Romance

My parents' marriage on September 23, 1959, seemed to be fated at birth. My mother, Norma Jean DeSart McMacken, was born in Mobridge April 24, 1933. My father, Robert Edmund McMacken, was born in a log cabin on the McMacken ranch near the Grand River north of Trail City, South Dakota, on August 11, 1934. Trail City was southwest of Mobridge. My grandmother, Bertha Dawes McMacken, had been in labor for quite some time, so someone went to Mobridge for a doctor. The physician was Dr. Sarget—the same doctor who had delivered my mother. My maternal grandfather, Pat DeSart, used to drive this doctor on emergency runs since he was usually the only one who could get him through the snowdrifts, my mother recalls. Dr. Sarget was French like the DeSarts, and he had followed the family to the Mobridge area from DeSart, North Dakota, to continue his practice.

My mother and father met years later at the radio station where my mom was working at the time. The McMacken-DeSart connection proved to be a strong and loyal one.

You can discover Eureka's frontier past at the ***Eureka Pioneer Museum of McPherson County,*** located on State Highway 10 at the west edge of Eureka. Look inside the country schoolhouse or see an early-day pioneer kitchen. The complex also includes a thoroughly furnished sod house. There is no admission charge, but donations are always appreciated. Call (605) 284–2711 for more information.

For the dauntless explorer, the ***Samuel H. Ordway Jr. Memorial Prairie*** (50 miles northwest of Aberdeen on U.S. Highway 281) offers a rare, unspoiled pocket of native America, albeit an out-of-the-way jaunt. On the 7,600 acres of pristine land here, wild grass and more than 300 species of plants flourish, thanks to the foresight of the Nature Conservancy. See big bluestem, needle-and-thread, and other native grasses weave through colorful patches of wildflowers. Waterfowl and shorebirds nest on the waters, while buffalo, deer, antelope, coyotes, and other animals populate the uplands. But hang onto your hat, it's awfully windy here.

If you drive on U.S. Highway 83 south from Eureka, you'll come to tiny towns like Selby and Akaska, which, like so many others in rural America, are small enough to become instant acquaintances of the traveler. If you take US 212 east for just a few miles, you will have a formal introduction to Gettysburg (population: 2,200), located in the Whitlock Bay area on the eastern shore of Lake Oahe. The Forest City Bridge spans Lake Oahe at Whitlock Bay, and the Potter County seat of Gettysburg is near the intersection of US 212 and 83. Gettysburg was settled in 1883 by 211 veterans of the famous Civil War battle after which the town was named. Many of the streets, townships, and communities in the area share names intrinsically associated with the Civil War.

The *G. L. Stocker Blacksmith Shop* served as the Grand Army of the Republic Hall during the post–Civil War years. Later it was home to the blacksmith shop, which has been renovated to its original condition. It includes an interpretive center, so visitors can see how blacksmith shops operated in the early part of the twentieth century. The *Potter County Courthouse,* built in 1910, is a splendid example of a Classical Revival courthouse building. It is located on Exene Street 1 block east of Main Street. For more information call the Gettysburg Historic Preservation Committee at (605) 765–9480. Other noteworthy historic sites include the *National Hotel* and the *Odd Fellows Re-Echo Lodge,* which was moved to its present site by eighty teams of mules. The 1908 *Holland House* reflects a combination of Colonial and Queen Anne styles of architecture.

Innkeepers Norma and Don Harer promote privacy at their five-room bed-and-breakfast, the *Harer Lodge,* which also features a separate honeymoon cottage. The lodge sells South Dakota–made products in its country store, and visitors can try horseback riding as well. A full breakfast is included. Open year-round. For more information call (605) 765–2167, or write to the Harers at Rural Route 1, Box 87A, Gettysburg 57442. You also can visit them at www.bbon line.com/sd/harerlodge. The inn has been featured in *Country* magazine.

Both state-run and privately operated camping facilities are available near Gettysburg. The town's city park offers free camping.

For a look at how even farming can contribute to the world's architectural style, visit *Sloat's Round Barn,* 13 miles north on Old U.S. Highway 83, then 2.5 miles west. C. B. Sloat designed this round barn as a college mechanical-drawing and carpentry project, and it was built after he graduated from college in 1915. The 100-foot-diameter barn was designed to house hogs and beef and dairy cattle. A track is located inside the barn around the top and bottom of the wall to facilitate feeding and cleaning.

Back in Gettysburg, the most popular exhibit in the *Dakota Sunset Museum* at 205 West Commercial Street is the mysterious Medicine Rock. Considered sacred by local Native Americans, the rock is embedded with footprints believed to have been made by the Great Spirit. The museum is open daily. For more information call (605) 765–9480.

Wheat Kings

From 1887 to 1902, Eureka was known as the greatest primary wheat market in the world. As many as thirty-two grain buyers worked day and night, storing and shipping wheat brought in by horses and oxen. In 1892, 3,330 freight-car loads of wheat were shipped from the town.

Gettysburg is just fifteen minutes east of **West Whitlock Recreation Area,** on giant Lake Oahe. West Whitlock was once a popular campsite for the Arikara and Mandan people. Today it is treasured by campers, boaters, and anglers— especially for its 103 camping sites. Although a thirty-six-pound northern pike was caught from shore in 1993, the main sport fish here is walleye. The annual **Whitlock Bay Walleye Tournament,** which is held each summer, offers competitors big prizes and lots of action. Call (605) 765–9410 for more information. The reservoir's newest sport fish is the chinook salmon. Each year thousands of eggs are taken from adult salmon at **Whitlock Spawning and Imprinting Station;** after hatching, fingerling salmon are returned to the lake. When adult salmon return in the fall, these fast and furious swimmers will test the skills of even the most avid fishermen.

The *South Dakota Sportsman's Atlas* contains maps of each South Dakota county, with all State Game Production Areas, State Parks and Recreation Areas, and Federal Waterfowl Production Areas marked in color. It is available for $5.00 through South Dakota Game, Fish, and Parks, 523 East Capitol Street, Pierre 57501.

History buffs and mountain bikers will find their own adventure schools in this rugged land, first explored by Lewis and Clark. West Whitlock is open year-round. Call (605) 765–9410 for more information.

Hunters will feel right at home on the **Paul Nelson Farm.** Consisting of nearly 10,000 acres of farmland, 5,000 acres are dedicated to pheasant hunting. For more information call Paul and Cheryl Nelson at (605) 765–2469 or visit the Web site at www.paulnelsonfarm.com.

North-central South Dakota seems sparse and lonely at times, yet the landscape is provocative. As you head south along the Missouri, the capital of South Dakota awaits and quietly renews one's faith that central South Dakota is anything but a cultural wasteland.

The Capital

Pierre is the state's capital, and the easiest way South Dakotans can spot a newcomer is by how he or she pronounces the name. French students, don't be mortified, but in South Dakota the town of Pierre is pronounced "pier." How this hazy pronunciation arrived is a mystery; one can only speculate that the ruggedly autonomous forefathers were trying to downplay the *très français* beginnings of the state—funny nonetheless, because it was indeed a Frenchman who started the first permanent white settlement in the state in 1832. American Fur Co. agent Pierre Chouteau Jr. piloted his steamboat, the Yellowstone, to the mouth of the Bad River and established Fort Pierre Chouteau. Representatives from nine Sioux tribes brought their furs to trade, principally buffalo, which were valued at the time from $3.00 to $4.00 per hide. An average of 17,000 buffalo robes were traded each year. The site of the settlement is now a designated landmark on the National Register of Historic Places. Presently Pierre is an out-of-the-way center for government and agriculture with 13,200 residents. Pierre is the nation's second-smallest capital. Its location on the Missouri conveniently makes the town of Pierre nonpartisan when it comes to East River–West River favoritism. The issues in the more thickly populated areas of the state are wisely left to state legislators to argue.

The **Oahe Dam,** 4 miles north of Pierre, is the nation's largest rolled-earth dam. The chamber of commerce boasts that the lake formed by the dam has more shoreline than the state of California. It was dedicated by President Kennedy in 1962. Today its power plant houses seven of the world's largest generators.

Tours of the power plant run Memorial Day through Labor Day from 8:30 A.M. to 3:30 P.M. Tours begin every half hour. During the winter months, reservations can be made by calling (605) 224–5862.

Overlooking the Oahe Reservoir, the Oahe Visitor Center offers information on anything from recreation to local hotels and restaurants. The center has numerous informational displays, which include Lewis and Clark, the Oahe Chapel, Oahe intake structures, and a Kid's Korner. The center is open from Memorial Day through Labor Day, from 9:00 A.M. to 5:00 P.M.

In 1874 the Reverend Thomas L. Riggs, a Congregational minister, and his wife, Cornelia Margaret Foster, established the Oahe Mission to serve the Dakota Indians. The mission was originally located on the site of an old Arikara Indian village, about 5 miles from the location of the modern-day chapel.

In the 1950s, when it became evident that the completion of the Oahe Dam would flood the mission location, the chapel was given to the South Dakota

Merry Christmas

The nation's capitol building received a special gift from South Dakota for Christmas 1997: a 60-foot white spruce tree from the Black Hills. After the November 14 tree-cutting ceremony, the spruce was carefully wrapped and secured on a semitrailer for its 2,500-mile journey to Washington, DC. The tree was appropriately adorned with thousands of ornaments crafted by South Dakota students and groups.

South Dakota artist Jon Crane captured this momentous occasion in his painting, *America's Holiday Tree,* which depicts the snow-flecked spruce in the forest before all the holiday fanfare.

Historical Society. In 1964 it was relocated at the eastern end of Oahe Dam, where it stands today.

Nondenominational Sunday services start at 8:00 A.M. Memorial Day through Labor Day. The chapel is also a popular wedding location.

Fishing on Lake Oahe or Lake Sharpe is legendary. The Walleye Capital of the World also is known for its trophy northern pike. Chinook salmon, white and smallmouth bass, brown and rainbow trout, and catfish also are caught here. Eminent filmmaker Ken Burns, creator of the popular PBS documentaries *Baseball* and *The Civil War,* made a documentary of the Lewis and Clark expedition along the Missouri River system. His crews visited Pierre in the summer of 1995 to capture sections of the river and to film buffalo near the Lower Brule Indian Reservation. "We're looking for stretches of river that represent how it really was," Burns told *The Lincoln* (Nebraska) *Star Journal.* "We want to see it as [Lewis and Clark] might have seen it."

The French connection is underscored at the **Vérendrye Monument** in Fort Pierre, just off US 83 across the Missouri River. The two French brothers Vérendrye were the first white people to set foot in South Dakota in 1743. They buried a lead plate on a bluff that overlooks Fort Pierre to claim the area for King Louis XV of France. Safely covered by dirt for generations, the plate was accidentally unearthed by schoolchildren in February 1913. Now the artifact is on display at the Cultural Heritage Center (900 Governors Drive; 605–773–3458). A monument in Fort Pierre marks the spot where the plate was discovered. The lead plate is only ⅛-inch thick. Scratched onto the back with the tip of a knife are these words: PLACED BY THE CHEVALIER DE LA VÉRENDRYE WITNESSES LOUIS, LA LONDETTE, AMIOTTE 30 OF MARCH 1743. Interestingly, a second plate was found by a man who was canoeing on the Cheyenne River in the summer of 1995. It also was dated 1743 and presumably was buried by the Vérendrye party. The plate was much sought after by museums, various government agencies, and individuals. The man eventually became so overwhelmed by all the attention that he took an airplane over the river and dropped the plate back where he found it.

For a walk on the historic side, the Pierre Historical Society has prepared a pamphlet, **Pierre Historic Homes Driving Tour,** that lists homes of historic interest. Several homes are listed on the National Register of Historic Places: For instance, a Georgian Revival home built by a physician later served as the governor's mansion during Peter Norbeck's term from 1917 to 1921. Now an apartment building, this stately home can be seen at 106 East Wynoka Street. Queen Anne, Tudor, Neoclassic, Victorian, Dutch Colonial, and Gothic Revival styles also are represented on this list of twenty-four homes. The number-one home, located at 119 North Washington Street, is the governor's mansion, which was built in 1936 as a WPA project. Although the eighteen-room private residence of South Dakota's first family is not open to the public, visitors are welcome to drive by or walk along the south lawn, which adjoins Capitol Lake. For a copy of the tour pamphlet or more information, call the Historical Society at (605) 773–3458.

During the Thanksgiving and Christmas seasons, the Capitol Rotunda is awash in the lights and color of beautifully hand-decorated trees. The annual *Capitol Christmas Trees* extravaganza was begun more than fifteen years ago by Dottie Howe, who is now retired from state government. Dottie and her friends couldn't find a perfect tree to display in the rotunda, so the group took a dozen or so and bunched them together—kind of like an exaggerated version of Charlie Brown's Christmas tree. Now the display has grown to include about one hundred trees—Black Hills spruce, pine, and other evergreens—that are decorated with a holiday theme. See a teddy bear tree, a Victorian Christmas tree, a music tree, even a pheasant tree. More than 50,000 people visit the striking display each year. Capitol Christmas Trees is open 8:00 A.M. to 10:00 P.M. daily November 26 to December 25. For more information call (800) 962–2034.

The capitol building, which more than casually resembles the nation's capitol in Washington, DC, is dazzling. You can see for yourself during guided tours, which are offered Monday through Friday. Call (605) 773–3765. Built upon a foundation made of South Dakota boulder granite, the building is resplendently graceful with terrazzo floors, coolly elegant marble staircases, stained glass skylights, and a solid copper dome. This striking limestone structure, which looks

much as it did when it was completed in 1910, is one of the most fully restored capitols in the United States. The state seal, which bears the motto "Under God the People Rule," symbolizes the way of life in South Dakota and the resources that keep it vital: farming, ranching, industries, lumbering, manufacturing, and mining. The seal was adopted in 1885, four years before the state was admitted to the union, and it is repeated on the state flag. A blazing sun encircles the seal, and the state's motto encircles the sun.

Fed by a warm artesian well, *Capitol Lake* never entirely freezes. It has become a winter haven for Canada

**The South Dakota
state capitol in Pierre**

The Oyate Trail

The concept of a scenic route to the Black Hills of South Dakota has been around since before the Missouri River was dammed and before Mount Rushmore was even finished. Since the day the state could boast of having a "fully improved road" along its southern border, South Dakotans have been promoting this 388-mile stretch of highway as an educational alternative to interstate travel. Travelers will discover diverse geography, as well as the cultural and historical contributions of both the Sioux Nation and European immigrants.

The Oyate Trail of today turns off Interstate 29 at Vermillion and heads west on Highways 50 and 18 to Edgemont near the Wyoming border. For local attractions along the way, write: Oyate Trail of Southern South Dakota, P.O. Box 234, Herrick 57358.

geese, mallards, wood ducks, and many other varieties of migratory waterfowl. The *Flaming Fountain* perpetually glows as a memorial to all veterans, while the *South Dakota Korean & Vietnam War Memorial* stands as a tribute to the valiant South Dakotans who lost their lives in those two wars. The names of these slain veterans are carved in granite next to the Flaming Fountain.

A reproduction of Korczak Ziolkowski's *Fighting Stallions* also stands on the capitol grounds. It was erected in remembrance of the late Governor George S. Mickelson and seven staff members and state leaders who died in a plane crash in 1993.

While the goings-on of state government present a busy and intriguing scene in Pierre, this town has more to offer than just politics.

Culturally, Pierre is the quintessence of East River and West River. The *South Dakota Cultural Heritage Center* (900 Governors Drive) preserves the state's multifaceted heritage. *Oyate Tawicob'an* ("The Ways of the People"), a permanent exhibit at the center, showcases Native American culture. More than 300 Native American artifacts are displayed, including an eagle feather headdress, a full-sized tepee, and a mounted buffalo. The research room, museum, gallery, and gift shop are open 9:00 A.M. to 4:30 P.M. Monday through Friday and 1:00 to 4:30 P.M. Saturday and Sunday. For more information call (605) 773–3458. Admission is $3.00 for adults; children under eighteen are admitted free.

Would you like to see a Sherman Tank? General Custer's sword? A Civil War horse-drawn gun? A jeep or an A-7D jet fighter? These and many other items of military memorabilia are on display at the *South Dakota National Guard Museum.* The museum, at 301 East Dakota Street, is open from 9:00 A.M. to 4:00 P.M. Monday, Wednesday, and Friday. Tours can be arranged by calling (605) 224–9991. There is no admission charge.

Another hot spot is the **South Dakota Discovery Center and Aquarium** (805 West Sioux Avenue), a former Pierre power plant that now houses hands-on science and technology exhibits and much more. Three aquariums feature native species of fish. Visitors can experience the universe through astronomy in the Sky Lab planetarium or test their reflex skills in the reactionary car. The center (605–224–8295) is open Sunday through Friday 1:00 to 5:00 P.M. and Saturday 10:00 A.M. to 5:00 P.M. Summer hours are from 10:00 A.M. to 5:00 P.M. Monday through Saturday, 1:00 to 5:00 P.M. Sunday. Admission is $4.00 for adults and $2.00 for children.

Nightlife thrives in the state's capital. A favorite watering hole is the **Longbranch Saloon** (106 East Dakota Street; 605–772–9783) in downtown Pierre. Live music provides entertainment six days a week. Open from 10:00 A.M. to 2:00 A.M.

It's not too often a restaurant is mentioned in the illustrious *Bon Appetit* magazine, but Pierre's **La Minestra** was touted recently for its Crostini with Sun-Dried-Tomato Tapenade. The feature focused on great neighborhood restaurants of the Midwest. Stacey and Mark Mancuso restored an 1886 tavern, revealing the building's wainscoting and original pressed metal walls and ceiling. The Italian restaurant is known for its freshly made pasta dishes and hand-cut steaks.

If the restaurant walls could talk, they would tell some interesting stories. The building originally was a funeral parlor. In 1947 the grand mahogany bar was added when the building got a new life as Hensey's Pool Hall and Card Room. In 1982 the historic site was home to a country-western bar.

La Minestra is located at 106 East Dakota in downtown Pierre. For more information call (605) 224–8090.

Add a touch of class to your visit and stay at the affordably elegant **Governor's Inn** (700 West Sioux Avenue). Room rates start at $59 for two people. Call (800) 341–8000 for reservations. For luxury and convenience, the **Best Western Ramkota River Centre** (920 West Sioux Avenue) is the place to stay. Room rates are $69 to $200, but the difference in price is well worth it. It is also home of the Freedom Shrine, where you can see and read twenty-eight authentic reproductions of historic documents, from the Mayflower Compact to the World War II Instrument of Surrender. The inn also is adjacent to the River Centre convention facility. Call the Best Western at (605) 224–6877.

Much of the Academy Award–winning movie *Dances with Wolves* was filmed 25 miles northwest of Pierre, on a private ranch along State Highway 1806. The 53,000-acre **Triple U Buffalo Ranch** is home to a herd of some 3,000 buffalo. A bed-and-breakfast and a gift shop also are on site. Call (605) 567–3624 or visit the Web site at www.tripleuranch.com for more information.

Birds of a feather flock together, and in Pierre, the residents unite through annual festivals that spotlight the area's charm and scenic landscape.

The *Goosefest,* held every September, celebrates the return of migrating geese to the Pierre area. Each year, their return signals the beginning of fall in South Dakota's capital city. The three-day event is held outdoors along the shores of the Missouri River. The South Dakota Arts Showcase, craft booths, children's activities, and live entertainment prove what's good for the goose is indeed good for the gander.

Vendors also sell a variety of unique products, including South Dakota honey, Arikara-style pottery, dried flower arrangements, and Indian tacos. Entertainment in the park's bandshell ranges from goose-calling demonstrations to folk music.

For more information on the Goosefest, call (800) 962–2034.

The annual *Riverfest* celebrates summer. This three-day event is also held along the Mighty Mo, affording participants a water ski show, car and air shows, a Kiddie Parade, kids carnival and fishing events, a buffalo chip flip, paddle boat, kayak rides, and races. Call (800) 962–2034 for more details.

Because of the central and mountain standard time differences, late-night revelers can party in the Pierre nightclubs until closing time, then head just 3 miles southwest to Fort Pierre bars for another hour of merriment. Every evening the *Silver Spur Bar* (605–223–9560) on Main Street in Fort Pierre turns on the light over a portrait of Casey Tibbs, indisputably the greatest bronco buster in the United States. Tibbs was born on a family homestead some 50 miles north of Fort Pierre in 1929. At nineteen he was the youngest man ever to win the world saddle-bronc riding championships, and more prestigious awards and titles followed. Although he died in 1990, Casey's name is still heard on the rodeo circuit. His life is also commemorated in a display at the National Buffalo Association headquarters in town and at the South Dakota Heritage Center in Pierre.

To the south of Pierre is the *Fort Pierre National Grassland.* Call (605) 224–5517 for more information on the area's native grasses.

The Central Reservations

The *Lode Star Casino* in Fort Thompson is accessible from the Native American Loop just north of Chamberlain. Owned by the Crow Creek Sioux tribe, the Lode Star boasts 160 slot machines, eight blackjack tables, and two poker tables. The Lode Star also offers a full-service RV park and campground; there are two camping areas free of charge. Call (605) 245–6000 or (605) 245–2240 for more information.

Just west of the Crow Creek Indian Reservation on the Native American Loop is the Lower Brule Indian Reservation. Driving through the area, you can appreciate the beauty of Lake Sharpe or Lake Francis Case or catch a glimpse of a buffalo herd. For a more modern-day indulgence, test your luck at the **Golden Buffalo Casino** (605–473–5577). To get there, take Interstate 90 to exit 248 at Reliance; then turn north for a fifteen-minute drive to Lower Brule. Slot machines and live blackjack and poker keep the adrenalin flowing. Overlooking Lake Sharpe, the casino also features a resort motel and convention center, restaurant, lounge, and gift shop. The house special is prime rib. RV parking, fishing and hunting permits, and shuttle service are some of the perks at the Golden Buffalo.

Considered the gateway to the Old West, Chamberlain lies just east of the Missouri River. Its vast shoreline was surveyed by Lewis and Clark. Their adventurous spirit continues in this modest-sized town of 2,626. Chamberlain was named for Selah Chamberlain, who was director of the Milwaukee railroad in 1880, when the town was started. Rumor has it that, before 1880, natives called Chamberlain *Makah Tepee,* or "mud house," because a hermit had a dugout there.

When South Dakotans travel from the Black Hills to Sioux Falls, one of the most popular stops is **Al's Oasis,** off exit 260 on I–90. A great almost-halfway-there (or over-halfway-there, depending on which way you're traveling) place, the restaurant is highly acclaimed for its food, especially the homemade pie and buffalo burgers and 5 cent coffee. This restaurant has been a respite for weary travelers for more than seventy-five years. Owners Albert and Veda Mueller moved the Oasis to its present location, right off I–90, in the 1950s. At that time the grocery store consisted of a ten-stool lunch counter. Since then Al's Oasis has expanded into a full-menu, 400-seat restaurant and lounge. Meal prices are moderate ($6.95 to $15.25 per person). The Oasis Trading Post and General Store has anything and everything you forgot or need on your trip—from food and toiletries to men's, women's, and children's clothing and cowboy boots. The Oasis has everything, including a campground and an eighty-five-room inn. For information call (605) 734–6054.

nativeamerican facts

A self-guided driving tour starts in Chamberlain and covers the nearby **Crow Creek** and **Lower Brule Indian Reservations.** Highlights include the Akta Lakota Museum, the Big Bend Dam, and the Lower Brule Game Lodge. In the summer the Lower Brule and Crow Creek tribes hold powwows, and visitors are welcome. The tribes also operate casinos. Maps and audiotapes of the Native American Loop are available from the Chamberlain Area Chamber of Commerce (605–734–4416).

The **Cedar Shore Resort** (888–697–6363; www. cedarshore.com) is the first resort erected on the shores of the Missouri River. The 80,000-square-foot facility, on 164 acres, features a marina breakwater, a ninety-nine-room hotel, a full-service convention center, and a 200-seat restaurant with lounge, art gallery, and more. The marina facility is one of a kind, with one hundred boat slips and a floating concession. The interior design centers on themes indigenous to the area such as buckskin, the pasque flower, yucca, coyotes, horses, and prairie wind.

The **Riverview Ridge Bed & Breakfast** (www.bbonline.com/sd/riverview ridge) is a contemporary home that overlooks a scenic bend on the Missouri River about 3.5 miles north of downtown Chamberlain on State Highway 50. Innkeepers Frank and Alta Cable promise country peace and languorous quiet. They start the day off right by serving a full breakfast for visitors. Call (605) 734–6084 for more information.

Founded by the Priests of the Sacred Heart in 1927, **St. Joseph's Indian School,** nestled on the banks of the Missouri River, is surrounded by prairie, rolling hills, and blue waters. St. Joseph's fosters the spiritual and educational growth of more than 200 Lakota and Dakota Indian children and young adults of all religious backgrounds. The school uses the concept of *tiospaye,* or "extended family," in its four communities. In recognition of the Native American heritage, St. Joseph's opened the **Akta Lakota Museum and Cultural Center** on its campus, which features exhibits and art that represent the past and present Lakota way of life. The museum rightly lives up to its name, which means "to honor the people." The Akta Lakota Museum hosts one of the finest collections of artifacts and contemporary Lakota art in South Dakota. Summer hours are 8:00 A.M. to 6:00 P.M. Monday through Saturday and 1:00 to 5:00 P.M. Sunday; winter hours are 8:30 A.M. to 5:00 P.M. Monday through Friday. For information on the school or museum, call (800) 798–3452 or visit the Web site at www.stjo.org.

Family heirlooms and antiques tell a lot about the Sweeney family and their life in Presho, largely a ranching community, located 39 miles west of Chamberlain on I–90. **Sweeney's Bed & Breakfast** (132 Main Avenue) is a perfect halfway stop between Rapid City and Sioux Falls. Its convenience is further enhanced by the fact that the inn is open year-round, and the rooms are refreshingly affordable. Call Paul and Wanda Sweeney at (605) 895–2586 for more information.

Pheasants and a Lake

The town of Winner is located on the Oyate Trail (Trail of Nations), the scenic east-west route across South Dakota. Winner, a community of 3,354, is internationally known as a hunter's paradise, and justifiably so. The wily ring-necked pheasant, grouse, prairie dog, and big game lure hunters from around the world. Fishing in the many stocked dams and lakes of Tripp County is also excellent. Also located in Winner is the ***Tripp County Museum,*** which houses antique autos, steam engines, tractors, a frontier law office, a millinery shop, and more. Call (605) 842–1533 for more information.

Each fall thousands of hunters aim for Gregory County on the western edge of the Missouri River in central South Dakota. Accessible via State Highways 44 or 47, the area is renowned for its pheasants. Officials say that hunting is the second-largest industry in the county, behind agriculture. Appropriately, a large, artificial pheasant greets visitors at the west entrance to the town of Gregory.

The tantalizing smell of cinnamon French toast, blueberry coffeecake, and caramel-pecan rolls will gently rouse guests from their deep slumber at the ***Gray House Inn Bed & Breakfast*** (605–835–8479). A complete breakfast is just one of the many charms found at this spacious eight-room inn (six of which have private baths). Conveniently located off U.S. Highway 18, the Gray House Inn is open year-round and offers an affordable bed-and-breakfast experience. Write to innkeepers Bruce and Alice Shaffer at Rural Route 2, Box 29, Gregory 57533.

If you take State Highway 50 southeast from Chamberlain, you'll discover Platte, conveniently located at the end of the railroad line. Coffee's on the house at the ***Dakota Country Inn*** (605–337–2607 or 800–336–2607). Located 0.5 mile east on State Highway 44, this comfy inn sells handmade toys and antiques in its lobby. From the inn it's just a short walk to ***Dyke's Garden,*** a colorful bloom of Dutch tradition with its many bulbs. The garden is noteworthy because Platte was originally settled by immigrants from the Netherlands.

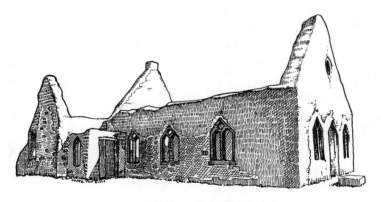

1875 Fort Randall Chapel

Just minutes from Platte (population: 1,366), the Missouri River is spanned by the longest bridge this side of the Mississippi. Just over 1 mile long, the bridge is located 15 miles west of Platte on State Highway 44.

To reach the tiny town of Pickstown, go east on State Highway 44, then southeast on State Highway 50 for about 30 miles. This community of just 170 people has mammoth-sized *Fort Randall Dam–Lake Francis Case.* A part of the Missouri River Basin project, Fort Randall Dam is 10,700 feet long and 165 feet high. At the base of the huge earthen dam is the Fort Randall Historic Site, which commemorates a military outpost established in 1856 to keep peace between white settlers and the Sioux. Its visitors list reads like a Who's Who in Plains history: George Custer, Philip Sheridan, and Hunkpapa Sioux leader Sitting Bull (who was held prisoner at the fort for two years). At present the only visible sign of the fort's existence is the *1875 Fort Randall Chapel,* which looks like crumbling Gothic. You can tour the dam's powerhouse daily from Memorial Day through Labor Day. Many recreation areas along the reservoir have swimming, fishing, boating, picnicking, and camping. Call (605) 487–7847 for more information.

Find everything you need at *Fort Randall Bait & Tackle* (605–487–7760)—from live and artificial bait to sporting goods, beer, ice, souvenirs, two campgrounds, and a full-service cafe.

Did we save the best for last? That depends on whether you love eagles, because the *Karl E. Mundt National Wildlife Refuge,* the nation's first federal eagle sanctuary, marks the end of the trail for this region. Bald eagle watchers will find an observation point directly below Fort Randall Dam on the west side. Call (605) 487–7603 for specific directions. The refuge was named for the late South Dakota senator and ardent conservationist. The refuge itself is not open to the public, but the endless sapphire skies of South Dakota are.

Where to Stay Along the Missouri River

CHAMBERLAIN

Cedar Shore Resort,
(888) 697–6363

EUREKA

Lakeview Motel,
49 West Highway 10,
(605) 284–2400,
(888) 666–9306

MOBRIDGE

Mo-Rest Motel,
US 12, (605) 845–3668

Wrangler Motor Inn,
820 West Grand Crossing,
(605) 845–3641,
(888) 884–3641

PIERRE

Best Western Ramkota River Centre,
920 West Sioux Avenue,
(605) 224–6877

Comfort Inn,
410 West Sioux Avenue,
(605) 224–0377

Governor's Inn,
700 West Sioux Avenue,
(605) 224–4200,
(800) 341–8000

PRESHO

Hutch's Motel,
exit 225 or 226 off I–90,
(605) 895–2591

Where to Eat Along the Missouri River

CHAMBERLAIN

Al's Oasis (American),
take exit 260 off I–90,
(605) 734–6054

MOBRIDGE

Wheel Restaurant,
820 West Grand Crossing,
(605) 845–7474,
(877) 363–5884

SELECTED CHAMBERS OF COMMERCE

Chamberlain-Oacoma Area Chamber of Commerce,
115 West Lawler Street,
P.O. Box 517, Chamberlain 57325,
(605) 734–4416,
www.chamberlainsd.org

Mobridge Chamber of Commerce,
212 Main Street, Mobridge 57601,
(605) 845–2387, www.mobridge.org

Pierre Convention and Visitors Bureau,
800 West Dakota Avenue, P.O. Box 548,
Pierre 57501, (800) 962–2034,
www.Pierrechamber.com

Platte Chamber of Commerce,
P.O. Box 236, Platte 57369,
(605) 337–2275

Western North Dakota

Wallace Stegner once said that the West is America, only more so. In North Dakota you're privileged to experience an inconceivably huge chunk of the real West. There is no drugstore-cowboy posturing here. The ranchmen and ranchwomen work tirelessly, and their careworn faces reflect the daily rigors of ranch life—from falling cattle prices and the unpredictable turns the weather can make to the inner knowledge that their children will likely graduate from college and leave the state.

The traveler will find long, lonely stretches of land—just like those that the settlers and Plains Indians of the past encountered—west of the Missouri River and few things of beauty to break up the monotony. The ranches are large; the towns are unfailingly small and weather-beaten. Go farther west and the jagged edges of the North Dakota Badlands interrupt the landscape. It serves the soul well to roam over the plains of North Dakota. The self-reliance espoused by Ralph Waldo Emerson years ago is infectious in North Dakota. As Teddy Roosevelt once said, "My experience when I lived and worked in North Dakota with my fellow ranchmen, on what was then the frontier, was the most important educational asset of my life."

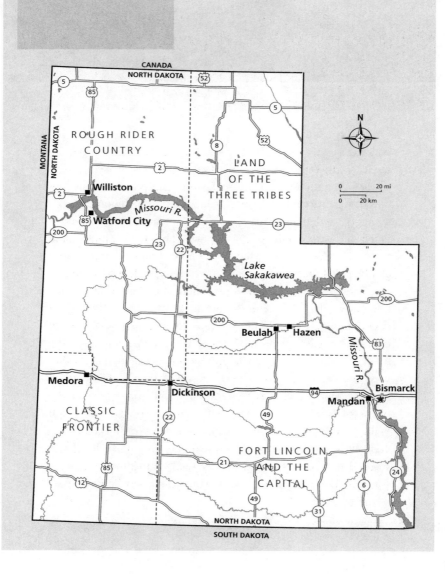

Classic Frontier

South Dakota may have Mount Rushmore, but when North Dakota pulls out its big guns for tourism promotion, you can be sure that Medora will hover at the top of the list. The frontier town of Medora was founded in 1883 by the Marquis de Mores, a French nobleman whose thirst for adventure was matched only by his intense desire to be the richest financier in the world. In the early spring of 1883, de Mores and his beautiful wife, Medora, arrived in the tiny, yet tough, railroad town of Little Missouri, where he envisioned a unique meat-processing scheme that he hoped would launch his financial empire. Local residents called de Mores "the crazy Frenchman," yet it was Little Missouri that became a deserted pile of splinters when de Mores built his town of Medora. By 1884 Medora had a population of 251 and boasted not only the meat-packing plant but a newspaper, a brickyard, several stores and saloons, a hotel, and St. Mary's Catholic Church. The marquis often entertained neighbor Theodore Roosevelt at his twenty-six-room chateau that overlooked Medora. De Mores and the man who would be president did not always see eye to eye on everything, but they did agree on socializing over iced champagne. De Mores's dreams proved to be farfetched, however, and the town eventually proved to be his undoing. He shut down the meat-packing operation in 1886, and he and his wife returned to France the following year. After a severe winter in 1887–88, during which many ranchers lost 75 percent of their herds, Medora regrettably became another pale ghost town in the West. Even today, all that remains of the slaughtering plant is the towering brick chimney, standing in a meadow, and less significant bits and pieces.

What's in a Name?

On March 2, 1861, President James Buchanan signed the bill creating the Dakota Territory. It originally included the area covered today by both Dakotas as well as Montana and Wyoming. The word Dakota means "friend" in the Dakota and Sioux Indian language.

Beginning about 1887, efforts were made to bring Dakota into the Union as both a single state and as two states. The latter was successful, and on November 2, 1889, both North Dakota and South Dakota were admitted.

Since President Benjamin Harrison went to great lengths to obscure the order in which the statehood proclamations were signed, the exact order in which the states entered is unknown. However, because of the alphabetical position, North Dakota is often considered the thirty-ninth state.

WESTERN NORTH DAKOTA'S TOP HITS

Dakota Dinosaur Museum	Medora Musical
Fort Union Trading Post National Historic Site	North Dakota Heritage Center
	Peacock Alley
Knife River Indian Villages	State Capitol
Lake Sakakawea	Theodore Roosevelt National Park
Lewis & Clark Trail Museum	Tobacco Gardens
Maltese Cross Cabin	

The past would haunt Medora until 1958, when the Burning Hills Amphitheatre was built and the drama *Old Four Eyes* was presented to mark Roosevelt's one hundredth birthday. Four years later, history buff Harold Schafer reignited de Mores's dream and brought the town back to life, this time as a premier vacation destination. In 1986 the Schafer family donated its holding in Medora to the Theodore Roosevelt Medora Foundation, a public, nonprofit organization that operates the public attractions.

In the summer of 1995, the ***Harold Schafer Heritage Center,*** located at 335 Fourth Street in Medora, was dedicated. Exhibits in the center tell the story of Schafer's engaging life, his Gold Seal Company, and the development of Medora as the state's leading tourist attraction. A major feature is the ***Sheila Schafer Gallery,*** which is home to rotating art exhibits each year. For information call (800) MEDORA–1 (633–6721) or (701) 623–4444.

Today Medora touts itself as a place "where the West kicks up its heels." Promoters have a good time whetting appetites with pitchfork fondues, trailside barbecues, and theme restaurants.

The ***Burning Hills Amphitheatre*** has been renovated, with 2,900 seats, and there are thirteen family attractions. The ***Medora Musical*** (800–MEDORA–1, 800–633–6721 or 701–623–4444) is dedicated to our twenty-sixth president, and most likely Teddy would have enjoyed the rollicking variety show, with such songs as "The Wild West Is Gettin' Wilder" and "Harmony Ranch," as well as a grand finale that showcases Roosevelt's Rough Riders at the Battle of San Juan. Showtime is

surftheweb

North Dakota Travel & Tourism has one of the best Web sites I have seen for any organization. It's eye-catching, very well formatted, and easy to navigate. Check it out at www.ndtourism.com.

8:30 P.M. nightly in the Burning Hills Amphitheatre, with performances running mid-June through Labor Day weekend. (Call for current ticket rates.)

The elegantly appointed de Mores chateau is now the *Chateau de Mores State Historic Site.* Lavish furnishings, Oriental carpets, and fine details in this frame house greeted the family when it arrived in 1884. For three years the family occupied the home seasonally, returning to New York during the winter months. The marquis and his wife loved hunting, music, and art. The chateau was given to the state in 1936. The interpretive center and chateau building are open daily from May 16 through September 15, and the historic site is open year-round. Interpretive center hours are 8:00 A.M. to 5:30 p.m.; Chateau de Mores guided tours operate from 10:00 a.m., with the last tour ending at 5:45 P.M. For more information contact the Site Operator, Chateau de Mores Historic Site, Medora 58645, or call (701) 623–4355.

To see the softer side of this land, stroll through the *Medora Doll House* (485 Broadway), which features exhibits of antique dolls and toys, all displayed in the historic Von Hoffman house. (The Von Hoffmans were the marquis' in-laws, and he built this home for them in 1884.) The Old Woman in the Shoe sits on a bench outside her shoe house, watching her children play outside. Small, all-bisque dolls—which cost anywhere from 5 to 25 cents in 1905—are displayed, along with many other types. Adults may enjoy this museum more than children. Medora Doll House is open only during the summer from 10:00 A.M. to 7:00 P.M. Call (701) 623–4444 for more information. St. Mary's Catholic Church is located on the same block.

There are many other quaint shops—all within easy walking distance—in Medora, including the Joe Ferris General Store. Ferris, a hunting guide and friend to Theodore Roosevelt, was the original owner of the general store. In 1884 Joe expanded his business by building a new glass-fronted building with a large porch. Business was good and the store flourished as a drug store, hardware store, and saloon. Theodore Roosevelt stayed in the upstairs living quarters of the Ferris Store upon his arrival in Medora before he departed for his ranch.

Rough Riders Gift Shop features jewelry, including Landstroms original Black Hills gold and sterling silver. And you must certainly visit the good folks at Corner Corral to dress up right in Medora. The store is filled with outerwear and sharp-looking western wear for men, women, and children.

Other shops worth a look-see include Teddy the Sharp Shirter (yes, the teddy bear is ubiquitous throughout this charming business district), Stage Barn Gift Shop, Touch of Dakota, and Theodore's Candy & Toys.

If you want to see things as Teddy Roosevelt did, ***Dakota Lodge and Trail Rides*** (701–623–4897; www.dahkotahlodge.com) promises "the best rest in the West" and offers trail rides, pack trips, and meals as well.

The Medora Chamber of Commerce sponsors an ***Old-Fashioned Cowboy Christmas*** the first weekend in December, with most of the events taking place in the community center. The highlight is sleigh or hay rides, but the event also includes an antiques and crafts show, as well as a Christmas quilt show, a family Christmas dance, a cowboy poker game, cowboy poetry, and a Best of the West doll show. The kids are entertained with a children's story hour and art with chalk-art drawings. To round off the activities, the chamber hosts a traditional Christmas supper, Western Parade of Lights, and a cowboy Christmas jamboree. In conjunction with all the holiday wonderment, the chamber honors a veteran each year.

Famous North Dakotans

Theodore Roosevelt isn't the only famous person to have kicked up his boots in North Dakota. Other famous North Dakotans include:

- Warren Christopher, who served as deputy secretary of state in the Carter administration and was awarded the Medal of Freedom on January 16, 1981. In 1993, Christopher was sworn in as the sixty-third U.S. secretary of state.

- Angie Dickinson, who has appeared in more than fifty major movies and television productions but is best known for her roles in the movie *Dressed to Kill* and the TV series *Police Woman.*

- Phil Jackson, who will go down in National Basketball Association history not only for his dynamic leadership, but as the only person to both play and coach teams (New York Knicks, Chicago Bulls, and Los Angeles Lakers) to titles for the NBA and the Continental Basketball Association.

- Louis L'Amour, the award-winning western author and screenwriter, who published more than 400 short stories and more than one hundred novels. He wrote sixty-five TV scripts and sold more than thirty stories to the motion-picture industry, including *Hondo,* starring John Wayne.

- Roger Maris, baseball's former single-season home-run king, who hit sixty-one home runs during the 1961 season while he was a member of the New York Yankees.

- Lawrence Welk, who became one of the greatest entertainers in the world through his weekly TV show featuring his distinctive "champagne music."

TOP ANNUAL EVENTS

Cowboy Poetry Gathering,
Medora, (701) 623–4910

The Fort Union Trading Post Rendezvous,
held annually in June, (701) 572–9083

Frontier Army Days,
every summer in Fort Abraham Lincoln
Park in Mandan, (701) 663–9571

Old-Fashioned Cowboy Christmas,
Medora,
(701) 623–4910

The Roughrider Days Rodeo,
held over the Fourth of July weekend,
Dickinson,
(800) HELLO–ND

In February the chamber sponsors the *Sweetheart Breakfast* on the Sunday closest to Valentine's Day, and in the afternoon a variety show, aptly titled Romance of the Badlands, is featured. (The marquis and his wife were married on Valentine's Day.) Call (701) 623–4910 for more information.

After riding tall in the saddle, weary cowpokes can check into the *Rough Riders Hotel,* an agreeably handsome and historic inn (circa 1884) where Teddy Roosevelt once stayed. The hotel, located at 301 Third Avenue, inspired the name of Roosevelt's regiment in the Spanish-American War. This delightfully cozy nine-room inn is air-conditioned with private telephones and cable television. The antique furniture and decor provide a glimpse into its colorful past. Located in the heart of downtown Medora, the hotel is one of four buildings that still appear as they did at the time that Theodore Roosevelt ranched near Medora. The original structure was built in 1883 with the anticipation of a boom in Medora as the Marquis de Mores built his meat-packing plant, opened a stagecoach line, and started several other businesses.

The Marquis de Mores operated the hotel from the 1890s until 1917 when the family sold its interest in the property. Theodore Roosevelt frequented the Rough Riders Hotel and gave a political speech from the balcony in an early 1900 presidential campaign.

Since then, the hotel has been a cafe, bar, and a restaurant operated by different families. In 1962 the Rough Riders Hotel was reconstructed and refurbished on the original site by the Harold Schafer family and the Gold Seal Company of Bismarck, North Dakota. The hotel is now owned and operated by the Theodore Roosevelt Medora Foundation.

The Rough Riders Hotel Bed & Breakfast is open daily during the summer season, when room rates start at $76 for a single and $89 for a double. Also open every weekend October 6 through May 31. For more information call (701) 623–4444.

The popular Bed and Breakfast Package Plan, available for Friday and Saturday night stays only, includes a dinner with wine, an appetizer and a dessert, and breakfast. The Bed and Breakfast Package rates start at $75 for one person and $118 for two. Room-only rates start at $45.

Old West celebrations, shopping, camping, parades, rodeos, hunting, and canoeing are just a handful of other activities that add further appeal to the community of Medora. Visiting Medora is strictly a warm-season adventure, as the tiny town (fewer than one hundred people) basically rolls up the red carpet during winter months. For those who wear their hearts on their sleeves, an annual springtime event in Medora is the *Cowboy Poetry Gathering.*

When you're in Medora, you're also close to the wide-screen vistas of the south unit of the western Badlands.

Rough Rider Country

"It was still the Wild West in those days . . . and ours was the glory of work and the joy of living," Theodore Roosevelt said of North Dakota. The former president knew the Badlands intimately, and his passion for these endless buttes and clay-streaked bluffs inexplicably pulses through your own body when you come here. Caught in a surrealistic moment, you have to remind yourself that you are in the twenty-first century. The *Theodore Roosevelt National Park* (www.nps.gov/thro/) in North Dakota is one of the state's major tourist attrac-

Prairie Dogs in the 'Hood

One of the interesting sociable animals of the Dakotas is the prairie dog, a rodent that belongs to the squirrel family. The name prairie dog comes from their barklike call, not from their appearance. They were called *petit chien,* or "little dog," by early French explorers and were described in the journals of Lewis and Clark.

Prairie dogs rely on keen hearing, excellent eyesight, and a communal warning system for protection against predators. They dig burrows in the earth and live in towns or colonies, which may vary in size from an acre to several hundred acres. A typical prairie dog town comprises groups of prairie dogs that occupy and protect small areas within the town. These groups, known as coteries, may be compared to neighborhoods of human towns. Individual prairie dogs stay within their own neighborhoods. Communication between the members of a town is highly specialized. As many as ten different calls have been described, including sounds for danger, territoriality, fear, and fighting.

As a child, I remember seeing many prairie dog towns as we traveled across the state. They were easily recognizable because of the cone-shaped mounds of soil around the entrances of the main burrows.

Maltese Cross Cabin

tions, with hiking, trail riding, camping, and other facilities. This park is smaller than Badlands National Park in South Dakota but seems more untouched by commercialism. As you drive along Interstate 94 to reach the park, you might think you've missed it. There are no garish billboards to herald its presence, only land remarkably anchored in the 1800s.

The park is divided into three distinctly different units: the South Unit (accessible from Medora via I–94), the Elkhorn Ranch site, and the North Unit, which can be reached via U.S. Highway 85 near Watford City. Although the park is open year-round, some portions of the road system may be closed during winter. The park includes 110 square miles of Badlands, making it one of the smallest parks in the system. Since the withdrawal of an ancient salt sea 130 million years ago, rain, wind, and the Little Missouri River have shaped a curious, mystical landscape in the Badlands. Exposed seams of lignite coal create a band of black below one ridge and ignite to bake clay into red scoria on another butte. Painted canyons, ash coulees, and broad cottonwood river bends are breathtaking.

North Dakotans like to call the park Rough Rider Country, and no doubt it was the rough-and-tumble lifestyle of the West and the starkness of the North Dakota Badlands that primed the young Roosevelt for a much larger role later in his life, that of a Rough Rider leading his men to battle in Cuba. The ***Medora South Unit Visitor Center*** (701–623–4466) will formally introduce you to Teddy, and if you haven't already fallen madly in love with the former president, you certainly will here.

Just a few steps away from the visitor center is the ***Maltese Cross Cabin,*** a small, efficiently organized three-room cabin. The cabin was originally located about 7 miles south of Medora in the wooded bottomlands of Roosevelt's

Maltese Cross ranch near the Little Missouri River. At Roosevelt's request, ranch managers built a 1½-story cabin complete with shingle roof and cellar. In its day the cabin was considered a mansion, for it had wooden floors and three separate rooms. The steeply pitched roof, an anomaly on the Dakota plains, provided an upstairs sleeping loft for ranch hands. You can see the desk at which Teddy wrote his book, *Hunting Trips of the Ranchman,* which he completed between 1884 and 1885. The rocking chair in the living room was his favorite piece of furniture. During the Roosevelt presidency the Maltese Cross Cabin was exhibited in Portland, Oregon, and St. Louis, Missouri. It was then moved to the state capitol grounds in Bismarck and finally relocated to its present site and renovated in 1959.

While the cabin helps you visualize what life was like for Roosevelt in the 1800s, a real time-travel adventure awaits with an awe-inspiring drive through the flat, wide expanse of the park's South Unit. The **South Unit Scenic Loop Drive** covers 36 miles and leads back to the park entrance. Along this paved road you will see panoramic views of the Badlands in the 46,158-acre southerly unit of the park. A word to the wise: Drive carefully. Always be on guard for wildlife on the road, and wear your seat belt.

You'll likely see elk and bison in the park, and you'll literally be tripping over what seems like millions of prairie dog towns. Deer are abundant, too, and predatory birds such as eagles, falcons, and hawks soar majestically overhead. If you're out on the trails, be alert. Bison can be dangerous and may attack if provoked, so admire them from a distance. Even the seemingly timid prairie

The Great Survivor

As many as sixty million bison once roamed over one-third of the entire land mass of North America. It was not unusual for a herd to contain four million animals and cover an area 50 miles long and 20 miles wide.

On the Dakota prairies, bison provided food, clothing, shelter, arrow points, ropes, and ornaments for the Plains Indians. As late as 1866 a huge herd of bison estimated at 100,000 was sighted 18 miles north of Fargo. Often mistakenly called buffalo, bison are not related to the true buffalo of Africa and Asia. Their ancestors, wild cattle that found their way across the now-vanished land bridge from Siberia to Alaska, came to North America during the Pleistocene era.

Prized for their meat and hides and as trophies, bison were hunted almost to extinction; by 1891 the United States bison population had been reduced to a mere 541 animals. The species was saved from annihilation by concerned conservationists, ranchers, and lovers of the outdoors who protected the remaining bison, gradually replenishing their number and building today's herds.

dog can inflict a painful wound if you attempt to feed or tease it. And be on the watch for the prairie rattlesnake, especially in summer; it will try to avoid humans but will strike, often without warning, if surprised or provoked.

The North Dakota Game and Fish Department urges people not to touch baby animals that appear to be abandoned. It is illegal to take wild animals home, and captive animals returned to the wild will struggle to survive because they do not possess learned survival skills. According to Game and Fish authorities, most young wildlife aren't abandoned, even if they appear to be. More than likely, their mothers have their eyes on you while you're watching them. Handling wildlife can be risky. Wild animals can transmit a variety of diseases to humans, and aggressive actions are typical of mothers protecting their offspring. As a result, people should leave young wildlife alone, and allow Mother Nature to step in. Motorists also should watch for deer along roadways. June and November are the peak months for deer-vehicle accidents because young animals are more active during these months.

When T. R. first came to the Badlands, he was an asthmatic young man who chased the wild ravines—in bad weather for two weeks—until he finally found and shot a bison. The adventure thrilled Roosevelt so much that before he left he bought a cattle ranch about 7 miles south of Medora and renamed it the Maltese Cross Ranch. Unfortunately, when Roosevelt returned to North Dakota the next year it was for far grimmer reasons. His wife and mother had died within hours of each other, and Roosevelt was inconsolably grief-stricken. In a move to further isolate himself from civilization and his own pain, he bought another cattle operation, the **Elkhorn Ranch,** located 35 miles north of Medora. You can visit the ranch, but be forewarned that it can be reached only on rough dirt roads. Call the visitor center at (701) 623–4466 for conditions before attempting the trip.

Teddy's cattle ranches during the late 1800s constituted a laboratory in which his philosophy of practical conservation was faithfully worked. He also was aware of the problems of the West and possessed the rugged spirit of its settlers, an enviable asset when he became president in 1901. The national conservation policy of his presidency was based on wise use of the nation's natural resources in the public interest.

Theodore Roosevelt National Park and Medora are undeniably romantic episodes in the history of western North Dakota, and it's easy to let nostalgia overwhelm you. But don't forget that there are other pearls to uncover in this vast sea of plains. If you take I-94 east, you're on a sure and straight path to the state capital of Bismarck, located about 133 miles from Medora.

The stops along the way are worth investigating. For instance, Belfield, some 18 miles east of Medora, is a veritable paradise for weary travelers.

Hunt and Fish

The North Dakota Game and Fish Department's slogan is "Variety in Hunting and Fishing," and variety is indeed the operative word. Mourning dove, sharp-tailed grouse, Hungarian partridge, and ring-necked pheasant are just some of the upland bird-hunting opportunities. Wing-shooters take to the fields and prairie water holes on the first of September, as mourning dove hunting traditionally kicks off North Dakota's shotgun season.

For fur-bearing hunting, nonresidents may hunt only fox and coyote—the highest coyote populations are located in the western prairies and Badlands regions. Nonresidents may trap fur-bearers if their home state allows North Dakotans to trap.

For big-game hunting, nonresidents are welcome to apply for gun, deer, and bighorn sheep licenses.

For more information call the North Dakota Game and Fish Department at (701) 328–6300 or check out the Web site at www. state.nd.us/gnf/.

Trapper's Kettle (701–575–8585), a restaurant on US 85 in Belfield, is the place to be for down-home hospitality and food. The restaurant incorporates the hunting-trapping theme throughout its decor and menu. Authentic traps serve as door pulls in the restaurant, and the cedar dining tables have inlaid traps. Examples of taxidermy of almost every animal imaginable seem to stare vacantly in the dining areas. The hearty and well-prepared food is stick-to-your-ribs good here; the thick and beefy chili is served in a crock with grated cheese—perfect winter fare. Pan-fry dishes and minikettle soups also hit the spot. Prices are moderate: $6.00 to $12.00 a plate.

I was there in early November, and the deer season had just opened in North Dakota. This neck of the woods is called a hunter's mecca, and orange-clad hunters annually pounce on the land in search of the "big one." Even eastern North Dakotans favor the western part of the state for hunting, as I overheard men from Fargo, for example, remind their buddies to reset their watches to mountain standard time.

anybody got the time?

Like South Dakota, North Dakota has two standard time zones. The southwest corner uses mountain time and the rest of the state uses central time.

North Dakota observes daylight saving time. Clocks "spring ahead" an hour on the first Sunday in April and "fall back" an hour on the last Sunday in October.

White-tailed deer are found almost everywhere, but the mule deer tend to cluster in the jagged country of the Badlands and other broken terrain. Lightning-swift antelope inhabit the western borders of the region, and the regal white elk and bighorn sheep confine themselves primarily to the Badlands and the Killdeer Mountains.

If you take US 85 north from Belfield, you're well on your way to the North Unit of Theodore Roosevelt National Park. The highway first will take you through Grassy Butte, where you can find the **Old Sod Post Office.** Construction materials were scarce in 1912, so the Grassy Butte Post Office was built of logs and sod. The building was used until 1964. Now listed on the National Register of Historic Places as a historic site, the building serves as a museum that is filled with sundry antiques and relics from the 1800s and early 1900s. The museum is open from Memorial Day to Labor Day. During May and June the facility is open weekends 8:00 A.M. to 4:00 p.m.; from July through September it is open every day 8:00 A.M. to 4:00 P.M. Admission is free. Call (701) 863–6769.

In the **North Unit of Theodore Roosevelt National Park,** the buttes are taller and certain areas are heavily forested. Squaw Creek (1.1 miles) and Caprock Coulee (1.5 miles) nature trails are self-guided and interpret the Badlands, coulees, and breaks. Upper Caprock Coulee, Achenbach, and Buckhorn trails will take you into the backcountry. A 14-mile scenic drive has turnouts with spectacular views and interpretive sites.

Watford City, which bills itself as a slice of The New Old West, celebrates the beginning of summer each year with the three-day **Homefest.** Street dances, golf and bowling tournaments, and free swimming in the community pool are just a few ways the town welcomes visitors and renews friendships. Originally created as the focal point for school and family reunions, the event has rapidly grown to become one of the biggest events in the town. Likewise, the annual **Art-in-the-Park** festival brings together the best of art, entertainment, and food from western North Dakota and eastern Montana for one sunny day each June. Held in Watford City's Tourist Park, the festival also highlights demonstrations from ethnic performers.

For family fun, head for the **Wild West Water Park,** which offers two tower water slides, a

Hit the Trail

The Maah Daah Hey Trail is a 120-mile hiking, horseback, and mountain bicycle trail that traverses through the scenic and rugged Badlands of North Dakota. The trail begins at Sully Creek State Park (3 miles south of Medora) and ends at the USDA Forest Service CCC Campground in McKenzie County (20 miles south of Watford City). For maps or more information, call Sully Creek State Park at (701) 328–5357; Theodore Roosevelt National Park at (701) 623–4466; or the USDA Forest Service at (701) 225–5151.

children's play area, a large hot tub, and concessions. Swimming lessons and a senior program are also available.

Scheduled to open in spring 2004, the **Long X Visitor Center and Museum** will feature North Dakota's largest fossil. The petrified bald cypress tree stump, weighing about 25,000 pounds and measuring about 6 feet in diameter and 8-feet tall, was discovered in the Badlands south of Watford City during an archaeological dig in 2001. A trading post also will be on site. To check on its status, call McKenzie County Tourism at (800) 701–2804.

Situated 29 miles northeast of Watford City on the Missouri River, **Tobacco Gardens** is worth the extra travel because it offers premier fishing and recreational opportunities with modern facilities. Tobacco Garden Bay, formerly a stopping place for refueling steamboats, was organized as part of the Lewis and Clark Trail. Its name is derived from the Sioux and Assiniboin Indian name for the reed that grew in the area.

Twenty-two miles west of Watford City, the tiny town of Alexander has a charming museum that represents the educational, agricultural, and historical spirit of the West. The **Lewis and Clark Trail Museum** (701–828–3595) on US 85 is housed in an old schoolhouse and includes a country store, a hall of fame with memorabilia of outstanding citizens from the past, and a reading room stocked with historical material. Outside, antique farm machinery is displayed. A playground and picnic facilities are available just a few blocks away in **Alexander Park.** The museum is open from Memorial Day through Labor Day 9:00 A.M. to 5:00 P.M. on weekdays and Saturdays and 1:00 to 5:00 P.M. on Sundays. Plan a couple of hours to fully appreciate the museum, which is one of the largest and most interesting museums in western North Dakota.

Riding Tall in the Saddle

When in Theodore Roosevelt National Park, do as Teddy did—go on horseback. The South Unit of the park features more than 80 miles of marked horse trails, and endless unmarked trails carved by the park's buffalo herd. Riders are permitted in all areas of the park except for the camping and picnicking areas and nature trails. A group horse campground is available in the South Unit by reservation, and back-country horse camping is allowed. The Peaceful Valley Ranch offers horse rentals and guided trail rides. Popular riding areas include Petrified Forest, Peaceful Valley Ranch, Halliday Wells, and Painted Canyon. Be on the lookout for bison, wild horses, long-horned cattle, elk, and deer.

Call the **Peaceful Valley Ranch** (701–623–4568) for trail rides May 1 to October 1. A variety of rides and trails are available: You can ride across the high plateaus to the largest outcropping of petrified stumps in the forest or see trails used by the pioneers to cross the Badlands.

Some astounding history unfolds at the ***Fort Union Trading Post National Historic Site*** (701–572–9083 or www.nps.gov/focus/), which stands near the confluence of the Yellowstone and Missouri Rivers in the town of Buford. Open daily year-round, the site is accessible from State Highway 1804, a 24-mile drive southwest from Williston. From 1829 to 1867, the Fort Union Trading Post was the "vastest and finest" of a string of trading posts along the northern rivers. Twenty-foot-high whitewashed palisades, anchored by two-story stone bastions, surrounded Fort Union. Capitalist John Jacob Astor reasoned that the imposing structure would impress the local Native Americans. Here, Scots, Germans, French, and Spanish bargained with the Assiniboin, Crow, Cree, Blackfoot, and Sitting Bull's Hunkpapa band of Sioux. Furs and hides were traded for iron tools, guns, blankets, and other manufactured goods.

Trade flourished until smallpox ravaged most of the trading tribes. The friendly trade ultimately ended when Fort Union was occupied by the Thirtieth Wisconsin Infantry in 1864. It dismantled the private-enterprise fort to help construct the military's Fort Buford, now a state historic site about a mile upstream. The fort is probably best known as the place where Hunkpapa leader Sitting Bull surrendered in 1881. Not surprisingly, much of what we have learned about the cultures of the Northern Plains Indians comes from Fort Union's adventurous staff and often rich-and-famous guests. John James Audubon, Germany's Prince Maximilian, and renowned artists George Catlin and Karl Bodmer left lasting legacies in their paintings, sketches, and words about this incredible mosaic.

Twenty-two miles northeast of Fort Buford on State Highway 1804 is Williston, which, like Dickinson, has weathered the energy industry's ups and downs. Regardless of the economic climate, the town always takes pride in its history. ***Buffalo Trails Day*** each summer features a parade, a chuck wagon breakfast, old-time music, and lots of games. The ***Fort Union Trading Post Rendezvous*** is held annually in June. There people re-create the lifestyle of frontier traders with sets, costumes, and activities. The well-shaded ***Lewis and Clark State Park*** is 16 miles east of Williston. Call (701) 859–3071 for more information.

The ***Frontier Museum,*** northwest of Spring Lake Park on Main Street in Williston, has the flavor of the turn-of-the-twentieth-century town it resembles. The museum complex comprises a 1910 rural church, complete with furnishings, two modern buildings filled with artifacts, a 1903 two-story house filled with antique furniture, an 1887 grocery store, a restored Great Northern Depot, and a complete country school. The Williston Tourist Information Center is housed in the Great Northern Depot.

Frontier Museum is open June through September. To arrange a tour during the off-season, call (701) 572–9751 or (701) 774–9041. There is a small admission fee.

While driving through North Dakota, you eventually settle into a certain rhythm; you forget the distance and notice the brilliant sunsets, the windmills that infrequently dot the landscape, and the way the frost makes a lace pattern on the naked branches of cottonwoods. Occasionally you'll see an oil-drilling rig marring the scenery, but for the most part, this is a land of unspoiled beauty, where billboards and other contrivances of a capitalist society never interrupt.

If you climb out of your car in Dickinson (19 miles west of Belfield off I–94), you'll see honest-to-goodness cowboys and cowgirls there. Even country-western music blares through the loudspeakers over the gas pumps at the service stations. This is the way Dickinson, the Queen City of the Prairies, likes it. Put on your Stetson and your cowboy boots because this is the most natural-feeling way to experience Dickinson.

This sprightly community of 16,097 people is the rodeo capital of North Dakota, with two world champions and every level of rodeo from the young-

A Rodeo Family

Put on your cowboy boots, we're heading for the rodeo.

I can't think of anything more quintessentially Dakota than a good, old-fashioned rodeo.

My three siblings and I were regulars on the rodeo circuit. Our heritage presaged that life would be close to a chute. My father, Bob McMacken, was a saddle bronc rider. In fact, his father, Francis, and his three brothers were known worldwide as The Four Horsemen. Their prowess was legendary.

My Great-uncle Bill is featured in an artsy photo in *Life* magazine during the 1940s. The black-and-white image renders a brilliant summation of what must have been the rough-and-tumble glamour of rodeo. He was a saddle bronc rider whose finesse made him runner-up in the World Championship Saddle Bronc competition.

Great-uncle Joe bull-dogged; he was gored to death in Chicago during the 1940s. My grandfather, Francis McMacken, was considered to be the best of the four as a saddle bronc rider. Great-uncle Bud rodeoed as well, and my mother remembers his hands were like hams and he loved to fistfight.

My dad was still rodeoing in 1959 after he returned from his stint with the U.S. Army in Germany, and my mom saw one of his last rides in a Spearfish rodeo.

Although my own father died years ago, we children feel his rodeo spirit today in his— and my uncles'—spurs, saddles, tack, and chaps we so lovingly keep displayed at the family cabin.

Rough Riders and Art

The Rough Rider International Art Show arrives on the scene Mother's Day weekend at Airport International Inn in Williston. Professional artists, collectors, buyers, and visitors come from all over the country. The nonprofit show, sponsored by the Williston Convention and Visitors Bureau under the direction of an all-volunteer committee, offers free admission. This show provides an unusual cultural event for the region and scholarships to students involved in high school art classes. Art collectors and dealers will appreciate work from more than sixty professional artists and galleries in fifty exhibit rooms.

For more information, contact the Rough Rider International Art Show at 10 Main Street, Williston 58801, or call (701) 774–9041.

sters' "showdeo" to the Professional Rodeo Association. The **Roughrider Days Rodeo** and festivities are held during the Fourth of July weekend every year. Dickinson is just part of a statewide passion for rodeo: About fifty rodeos throughout the state attract hundreds of cowboys each year.

In case you didn't know, the word *rodeo* is actually derived from a Spanish word meaning "roundup." The history of the rodeo traces back to the 1800s when most ranches had untamed horses (or broncos). Cattle outfits often challenged one another to bronc-riding contests, and cowboys could prove their mettle. Eventually someone reckoned there would be good money to be made if there was an admission charge to see the battle between the bronc and the cowboy.

Rodeos remain a popular, breathtaking event in both North Dakota and South Dakota. Basically there are four types of rodeo: high school, college, amateur, and professional. For a listing of rodeos in North Dakota, call (800) HELLO–ND.

Interestingly, this cow town also is home to the **Dakota Dinosaur Museum** (701–225–3466), a fantastic earth science museum that features dinosaur bones found in North Dakota, including a complete triceratops, which lived in the Badlands when they were a swampy and warm area, and a duck-billed edmontosaurus. Ten other full-scale dinosaurs, a complete fossil rhino, and rocks and minerals are impressive displays as well. Located right on I–94 in Dickinson and attached to the Joachim Regional Museum complex, the Dakota Dinosaur Museum is a main attraction for visitors. It is open 9:00 A.M. to 4:00 P.M. Monday through Saturday, and 11:00 A.M. to 4:00 P.M. Sunday. Admission is $6.00 for adults and $3.00 for children.

The dinosaur museum is adjacent to the Joachim Regional Museum and Prairie Outpost Park, where through a self-guided tour you get an idea of how

Lewis and Clark Trail

Lewis and Clark are synonymous with American history. The men courageously reported on America's newest expanse with incredible depth and insight into the people and the lay of the land.

One of the ways in which North Dakota pays tribute to these all-American heroes is through the Lewis and Clark Trail, which basically comprises two developed highways along the Missouri River. The highway numbers—1804 and 1806—appropriately match the years that the explorers entered and returned to North Dakota. ND 1804 follows the eastern side of the Missouri River, while ND 1806 follows the western side. Historical sites and recreation can be discovered along both highways.

rugged pioneers settled southwestern North Dakota. The museum offers tours of a Norwegian *stabbur* (storage house), a Germans-from-Russia homestead house, a one-room schoolhouse, a railroad depot, a church, and other buildings that reflect the area's ethnic and immigrant past. For more information call (701) 456–6225.

During the summer, evening performances of the **Sosondowah Summer Theater,** weekly outdoor bandshell concerts, and the **Mind's Eye Gallery** on the Dickinson State University campus add a stroke of sophistication to the feral spirit of the western plains. For more on parks, pools, events, and accommodations, call the visitor center at (701) 483–4988.

If you travel 3 miles west on U.S. Highway 10, then 1 mile south, you'll be at **Patterson Reservoir** (701–225–2074) for swimming, fishing, boating, camping, and picnicking during the summer. The reservoir is part of the Missouri River Valley reclamation project. The park is open daily June through August.

In nearby Richardton, the twin spires of the historic **St. Mary's Catholic Church** on 418 Third Avenue West are quiet testaments to the faith that has steadfastly guided Dakotans through lean and prosperous times. Benedictine monks built this stunning structure a century ago. The original building and its immovable central altar are the focal point amid the vaulted ceilings, original medallion paintings, ornate altars, and more than fifty stained glass windows. St. Mary's is a wonderful example of Bavarian-Romanesque–style architecture. Today the church is lovingly tended by resident monks living in the Assumption Abbey, which is connected to the church. They warmly welcome visitors. Be sure to see their gift shop, printing facility, wine cellar, church, and library. Nuns of the Benedictine order at nearby Sacred Heart Monastery also welcome visitors. Call (701) 974–3315 for an appointment.

Land of the Three Tribes

North Dakota is a state carved with endless out-of-the-way excursions for the explorer. An easy and informative day trip from Dickinson can be found north on State Highway 22 into the *Fort Berthold Reservation*, centered on Lake Sakakawea. The trip affords some wonderful stops as well. One of the loveliest sites in the state, the town of Killdeer, which takes its name from the Killdeer Mountains to the northwest, is 32 miles north of Dickinson.

Hidatsa, Arikara, and Mandan Indians, known as the Three Affiliated Tribes, live on the Fort Berthold Indian Reservation. The boundaries for the reservation have changed many times since its inception in 1880, and today the reservation encompasses 450,000 acres of tribally and individually owned lands. Historically the Mandan and Hidatsa Indians were a peaceful and agricultural group, stable and not as nomadic as the other Plains Indians. The Arikara, previously part of the Pawnee, separated from their relatives on the Loup River in Nebraska, worked their way north, and eventually joined the Hidatsa and Mandan Indians. At present about 3,696 of the tribes' members live on the reservation.

Lake Sakakawea is named for the young Shoshone woman who guided the intrepid explorers Lewis and Clark from North Dakota to the Yellowstone River in 1805. The nation's "Sixth Great Lake" is artificially made, formed by the mighty barrier of the Garrison Dam. This massive body of water draws thousands of visitors each year because of its superb sailing, camping, hunting, and fishing. As the largest body of water in the state, it is 200 miles long, covering 909 square miles.

The *Three Affiliated Tribes Museum* is located on the Fort Berthold Indian Reservation about 4 miles west of New Town on State Highway 23. One of the newest exhibits at the museum honors Fort Berthold World War I veterans. At that time Native Americans were not allowed to vote, yet they valiantly volunteered to serve their country. Memorabilia, photographs, and a forty-eight-star United States flag are highlights in the display. The museum is open April through November. Call (701) 627–4477 for more information.

About 20 miles east of Dickinson, you'll pass one of the more kitschy sights in North Dakota. *New Salem Sue,* overlooking I–94, is the world's largest Holstein-cow replica—it's hard to miss her. In the town of New Salem, right over I–94 at its junction with State Highway 31, the *Custer Trail Museum*'s historic buildings and collections are open for visitors during the summer and by appointment (701) 843–7384. In nearby Glen Ullin the *Muggli Rock Shop and Museum,* open daily May through September, shows fossils and geologic minerals. *Lake Tschida,* 15 miles south on State Highway 49, is situated amid rugged buttes.

Ready for another excellent adventure off the beaten path? Take State Highway 49 North to Beulah, which prides itself on being the Energy Capital of the Midwest. And for good reason. The **Great Plains Synfuel Plant** is the nation's only commercial-scale coal gasification plant, which turns coal into natural gas. Tours are available by appointment Monday through Friday. For more information call (701) 873–6667.

While you're in Beulah, stop at the **Mercer County Historical Society Museum** (corner of Central Avenue and Seventh Street) to view pioneer and Native American collections. The museum is open during the summer Sunday 1:00 to 4:00 p.m., or call (701) 873–4740 for an appointment. In Beulah you also can step into a museum that resembles a medieval castle, the **Pfenning Wildlife Museum.** Local hunter Helmuth Pfenning shares his lifetime collection of exotic animals, which celebrates the art of taxidermy. The museum is open during the summer Tuesday through Saturday from 1:00 to 5:00 P.M. Call (701) 873–4889 for appointments at other times.

Northeast of Beulah, the **Knife River Indian Villages** is a national park that is set aside to commemorate Native Americans. The remains of the villages arc along the banks of the Knife and Missouri Rivers, approximately 60 miles

Tourist Information Centers in North Dakota

These official state Tourist Information Centers are generally open from May to October, except Fishers Landing, which is open all year. Many cities and attractions in North Dakota staff their own tourist information centers during the summer months. These centers are clearly marked and are conveniently located at the intersections of major highways. They include Bismarck/Mandan, Dickinson, Grand Forks, Medora, Minot, Rugby, Devils Lake, Dunseith, Bottineau, and Jamestown.

Lake Agassiz Tourist Center, northbound lane of I–29, Hankinson

Fishers Landing Tourist Center, 10 miles east of Grand Forks, on Highway 2 (in Minnesota)

Pembina Tourist Center, southbound lane of I–29, Pembina

Beach Tourist Center, eastbound lane of I–94, Beach

West Fargo Tourist Center, Bonanzaville USA, Main Avenue, West Fargo

Bowman Tourist Center, Highway 12 West, Bowman

Williston Tourist Center, Highway 2 and Sixth Avenue West, Williston

Oriska Tourist Center, Oriska Rest Area, on I–94, 12 miles east of Valley City

Fargo-Moorhead Visitors Center, exit 348 off I–94, Fargo

north of Bismarck. This is one of the oldest inhabited sites in North America, dating back 9,000 years. The Hidatsa and Mandan Indians, two of the oldest tribes on the continent, lived here in earth lodges, planting and harvesting gardens of corn, squash, beans, and sunflowers, which they exchanged in an ever-growing trading network between tribes. (The locally produced Knife River flint has been traced to villages in the far southeastern part of the United States.) In the winter of 1804–1805, they were gracious hosts to Lewis and Clark and the Corps of Discovery.

President Thomas Jefferson had appointed Lewis and Clark to explore and document America's new Louisiana Purchase territory. The Corps, which departed from near St. Louis, comprised forty-five men operating a 55-foot keelboat and five other boats. After arriving in North Dakota for the winter, the explorers met the teenage girl Sakakawea (the Dakotas' alternate spelling of Sakagawea). She helped guide them through her native Shoshone lands as they searched for a water route to the Pacific Ocean. In April 1805 the group left Fort Mandan to continue the westward expedition. Lewis and Clark returned to North Dakota in August 1806 on their way back to St. Louis.

Knife River Indian Villages can be reached via U.S. Highway 83 and State Highway 200A near Stanton. The site is part of North Dakota's American Legacy Tour. This world-class archaeological park boasts a newly constructed earthen lodge at the modern visitor center. Trails lead to three village sites, where remnants of earthlodges and scattered bones and tools are easily seen. Ten miles of hiking and Nordic ski trails offer opportunities to view wildlife. The center is open 8:00 A.M. to 6:00 P.M. Memorial Day through Labor Day; excluding federal holidays, the center is open 8:00 A.M. to 4:30 P.M. the remainder of the year. For more information call (701) 745–3300.

Fort Lincoln and the Capital

Most people think of South Dakota and Montana when they hear the name General George Armstrong Custer, and for good reason. He led the army expedition into the Black Hills of South Dakota, where he had been sent to quell rumors of gold on parts of Sioux land. Instead he found that the prospectors' tales of extractable quantities of gold throughout the area were bona fide. Later he and his troops were killed at the famous Battle of the Little Big Horn in Montana. Prior to these illustrious times in history, however, Custer was a young general stationed at Fort Lincoln in what was then the Dakota Territory. Today his home and the fort can be revisited at the ***Fort Abraham Lincoln Park*** (701–667–6340; www.state.nd.us/ndparks) in Mandan, which is located on I-94 just west of the Missouri River. Although most of the buildings at the fort were torn down in 1891, many of them were rebuilt in the 1930s. At this state park you can see the central barracks, the commissary store, the blockhouses standing guard over the old fort, and the cemetery where the marked graves of soldiers tell stories never found in history books.

See the last home Custer lived in before he took his last stand. After a fire destroyed the first Custer home at Fort Lincoln in 1874, Custer ignored standard army design and rebuilt the home according to his wife's more genteel tastes. The Custer home had a huge living room with a bay window, a billiard room on the second floor, a library, and plenty of rooms for Custer's relatives, gun collection, and hunting trophies. A sweeping veranda on the east and north sides completed the most impressive dwelling on officers' row. The Custer House has guided living-history tours from May to October.

Each summer, *Frontier Army Days* brings reenactment cavalry and infantry groups—the Frontier Army of Dakota—to Fort Abraham Lincoln for cannon firing, cavalry charges, drills, and the living history of Custer's pivotal presence in the development of the West.

The story of ill-fated Custer isn't the only legend at Fort Abraham Lincoln Park. Lewis and Clark camped here, and the Mandan Indians settled the *On-a-Slant Village.* Long before the white settlers arrived, the Mandan nation numbered 15,000. The Mandans farmed miles of Missouri River bottomland from ten or twelve fortified cities here on the Slant River. On-a-Slant Village had 1,000 people in the mid-1600s, but it was empty by the time Lewis and Clark visited. At the pinnacle of their wealth and power, the Mandans built remarkably cozy, round, earth lodges, like those seen at Fort Lincoln. Slant Village shows traces of seventy-five lodges, including the large ceremonial lodge that is 84 feet in diameter. Visitors also can capture the spirit of the time through trail rides and old-fashioned melodrama. The village is open 9:00 A.M. to 5:00 P.M. daily, Memorial Day through Labor Day. For more information call (701) 667–6340.

In downtown Mandan at 401 Main Street, the *Five Nations Arts Museum* (701–663–4663) brings the talent of local tribes into the present tense. Inside, the soothing sounds of Native American music can be heard and an amazing selection of native arts and crafts admired. Located in an old train depot, the Colonial Revival

a worldly capitol

The North Dakota Capitol was built in the early 1930s for $2 million. A Judicial Wing was completed in 1981. Although it ranks as one of the nation's most practical and economically built state capitols, this Art Deco structure is enhanced by a unique blend of raw materials, including Indiana limestone, Montana yellowstone, Belgian marble, Tennessee marble, Honduras mahogany, East Indian rosewood, English brown oak, Burma teak, and laurel wood.

redbrick building affords a unique sense of the architecture in 1929, the year in which it was built. The original interior is still gracefully intact, with stone floors, oak woodwork and trim, and a beautifully meticulous wainscoting of tan tiles. "We've had such great success," said manager Pat Schanandore, herself a Mandan-Hidatsa Indian. "Everything is handmade and locally produced." She says that the gallery carries the work of more than 200 artists from the Mandan, Hidatsa, Arikara, Chippewa, and Sioux tribes who manage this portion of Fort Abraham Lincoln State Park. The gallery is open 9:00 A.M. to 7:00 P.M. Monday through Saturday and noon to 5:00 P.M. Sunday during summer months. The hours October through May are 9:00 A.M. to 5:30 P.M. Monday through Saturday and noon to 5:00 P.M. Sunday.

Another jumping-off point for the adventurous is the ***Cross Ranch Nature Preserve,*** managed by The Nature Conservancy. The ranch is located 30 miles north of Mandan via Route 1806 (a gravel road). This 6,000-acre nature preserve has mixed grass prairies, Missouri River floodplain forest, upland woody draws, and a bison herd. You can hike along self-guided nature trails. Call (701) 794–8741 for more information.

Just across the Missouri River from Mandan, you'll find Bismarck, the state capital and the second-largest city in North Dakota. Located on a natural ford of the Missouri River, Bismarck served as an early-day steamboat port. It was named for German chancellor Otto von Bismarck in hopes of encouraging German investment in the railroad.

The near-downtown and the downtown district in Bismarck includes two great shopping opportunities. The ***Kirkwood Mall*** (701–223–3500), at Seventh Street and Bismarck Expressway, boasts more than one hundred stores, including major anchors like Marshall Field, Herberger's, Target, T.J. Maxx, and JCPenney. Just a few blocks away is an off-the-beaten path shopping area right downtown. One of the best downtown stores is ***Treasures of the Sea and***

On-a-Slant Village

Earth (701–224–0103), at 116 North Fifth Street, which sells rocks, crystals, shells, and custom-designed jewelry. I like the attitude of this store: gifts from the sea at one of the most inland spots on the continent.

A similar but altogether unique experience awaits at the *Country Barn* (701–222–1433; 110 North Fifth Street). Collectibles, folk art, gifts, and custom-designed furniture are specialties here, and the store gets major style points for displays and selections. During November a fireplace mantel and Christmas tree were fashionably decked out for the holidays in shimmering golds and bright whites—a stunning display indeed. Open Monday through Friday 10:00 A.M. to 5:30 p.m., and Saturday 10:00 A.M. to 5:00 P.M.

Another downtown favorite is *Caffe Aroma* (701–258–0204), in the Logan Building at the corner of Third Street and Broadway Avenue. Voted Bismarck's Best Coffee Shop, it features latte, cappuccino, espresso, mocha, and flavored coffees that are roasted and brewed daily. Open seven days a week.

After a cup of java, stroll over to *One World Imports* (701–250–6605), which features clothing, gifts, and jewelry from around the world. The store is at the corner of Fifth and Main Streets.

If you're like me, power shopping can lead to an enormous appetite, but, thankfully, there's *Peacock Alley* (701–255–7917) at the corner of Fifth Street and Main Avenue. Proprietor Bill Hixson has retained the aura of the former Patterson Hotel, which in its heyday was the off-hours headquarters for state and national politicos. Theodore Roosevelt, Calvin Coolidge, John F. Kennedy, and Lyndon Johnson swept through the hotel on presidential campaign stops, and legislators still meet in the bar and grill. Like the proud peacock, the restaurant's blue-and-green decor handsomely fans a posh yet down-to-earth attitude. This is the perfect place for drinks after the theater, but then again it's also the perfect place to take the family for Sunday brunch. There's nothing snooty about the restaurant—or anything in North Dakota, for that matter. Like most places in North Dakota, you can dine formidably on a modest budget. The Sunday buffet is only $4.95, and it is well-stocked with fresh fruits, muffins, sticky homemade caramel rolls, French toast, pancakes, hash browns, two kinds of sausage, bacon, ham, and more. Equally mouth-watering is the dinner menu. Temptations abound in dishes like sliced tenderloin with brandy peppercorn sauce, roast duckling, and cannelloni bolognese. The restaurant is open 11:00 A.M. to 2:00 P.M. and 5:30 to 10:00 P.M. (9:00 P.M. on Monday). Sunday brunch is served from 9:00 A.M. to 1:00 P.M. The bar is open until 1:00 A.M. except Sunday.

Across from Peacock Alley on Main Avenue is a Mission-style depot that sets the festive atmosphere for Mexican cuisine. *Fiesta Villa* (701–222–8075) is famous for its fajitas and chimichangas, and the margaritas are highly recommended to quench your thirst after a fiery meal. In the summertime diners can enjoy their meals on the outdoor patio. The restaurant is open 11:00 A.M. to 10:30 P.M. Monday through Thursday and 11:00 A.M. to 11:00 P.M. Friday and Saturday.

Now that everyone's appetite is sated, let's do some serious sightseeing in Bismarck. No trip to Bismarck would be complete without at least a walk or drive past the **State Capitol** (North Sixth Street). If you take Sixth Street north 10 blocks, you'll run into The Boulevard and be at the foot of the grand nineteen-story capitol, which is topped with an observation tower. It's hard to miss The Skyscraper of the Prairies—it's the tallest building in North Dakota. Built in the 1930s, the capitol's Art Deco interior is as fashion-forward now as it was then, with exotic wood paneling, stone, and metal. It's open year-round, and tours are available hourly Monday through Friday. Large groups can tour by appointment with one week's notice. Call (701) 328–2000.

The **North Dakota Heritage Center** (701–328–2666; www.state. nd.us/hist) is on the capitol grounds, and its permanent and changing exhibits reflect the history and settlement of the northern Great Plains. The artifacts cover the gamut of time periods, from a sinew-sewn buffalo-hide tepee to a mastodon skeleton. Admission is free, and the center is open daily, with limited hours on Sunday. For outdoor sculpture, the statue of Sakakawea—her baby on her back—is a lovely memorial to the woman who guided Lewis and Clark through the territory.

Just a few blocks south is the **Former Governor's Mansion State Historic Site** (701–328–2666), the restored Victorian mansion that was occupied by the state's first families from 1893 to 1960. Interpretive exhibits and governors' portraits now occupy this elegant three-story structure. Tour the mansion (corner of Fourth Street and B Avenue) for free; it's open mid-May through mid-September Wednesday through Sunday afternoons.

To see the great state of North Dakota in a similar fashion to Lewis and Clark almost 200 years ago, hop aboard the **Lewis and Clark Riverboat,** a 150-passenger boat. Charters are available from April through October for weddings, family reunions, and office parties, and the riverboat offers daily excursion cruises, dinner cruises, sunset cruises, and special events for the entire family. The riverboat is located at the Port of Bismarck on North River Road, exit 157 off I–94. Call (701) 255–4233 for more information or visit the Web site at www.lewisandclarkriverboat.com.

North Dakota is again timelessly joined to South Dakota through the **Standing Rock Reservation,** which extends into both states. The people of the Standing Rock Sioux Tribe are part of the Yanktonai and Teton Sioux Nation, which formerly controlled a vast domain that extended from the James

River in North Dakota and South Dakota, west to the Big Horn Mountains of Wyoming. In 1868 the Treaty of Fort Laramie reduced this area to the Great Sioux Reservation, setting the boundaries of a twenty-five-million-acre tract that covered all of South Dakota west of the Missouri. When gold was discovered in the Black Hills, Congress ratified an invalid agreement and took the Black Hills shortly thereafter. The Great Sioux Reservation was broken into six small reservations in 1889, one of which is Standing Rock (formerly called the Grand River Agency), situated on the North Dakota/South Dakota border between the Badlands and the Missouri River. On the western edge of Fort Yates, located on the Missouri River on the North Dakota portion of the Standing Rock Indian Reservation, is the original grave site of renowned Hunkpapa Sioux spiritual leader Sitting Bull.

On the Standing Rock Reservation, the ***Cannon Ball Powwow*** is held the second week in June; in Shields, the ***Porcupine Powwow*** takes place the third weekend in June. Shields is on the Cannonball River off State Highway 6. The powwow is a vital element of Lakota life today. Originally powwows were held in springtime to celebrate the beginning of life. In the Sioux tradition the celebration also was a prayer to Wakan-Tanka, the Great Spirit or Grandfather. Call (701) 854–7202 for more information on both powwows, which are highly educational and entertaining for all ages. The costumes are breathtaking.

Where to Stay in Western North Dakota

ALEXANDER
Ragged Butte Inn,
US 85, (701) 828–3164

BELFIELD
Bel-Vu Motel,
2 blocks west of US 85 on
US Highway 10,
(701) 575–4245

BEULAH
Super 8 Motel,
720 US Highway 49 North,
(800) 800–8000

BISMARCK
Americinn of Bismarck,
3235 State Street, (800)
634–3444

Comfort Inn,
1030 Interstate Avenue,
(701) 223–1911,
(800) 228–5150

Expressway Inn,
200 East Bismarck
Expressway,
(800) 456–6388

Kelly Inn,
1800 North Twelfth Street,
(701) 223–8001

Radisson Hotel,
605 East Broadway,
(800) 333–3333

BOWMAN
North Winds Lodge,
US 85 South,
(888) 684–9463

MANDAN
**Best Western Seven
Seas Inn,**
2611 Old Red Trail,
(800) 597–7327

**Colonial Motel and RV
Park,**
4631 Memorial Highway,
(701) 663–9824

MEDORA
Badlands Motel,
located on the east side of
Medora,
(701) 623–4422

Rough Riders Hotel,
301 Third Avenue,
(800) 633–6721

Sully Inn,
located at Fourth and
Broadway Streets,
(877) 800–4992

WILLISTON
Airport International Inn,
3601 Second Avenue
West, (701) 774–0241

El Rancho Motor Hotel,
1623 Second Avenue
West, (800) 433–8529

Where to Eat in Western North Dakota

BELFIELD
Trapper's Kettle,
US 85, (701) 575–8585

BISMARCK
**Bistro: An American
Cafe,**
1103 East Front Avenue,
(701) 224–8800

**North American Steak
Buffet,**
2000 North Twelfth Street,
(701) 223–1107

83 Diner (American),
1307 Interchange Avenue,
(701) 258–3470

Fiesta Villa,
Main Avenue, across from
Peacock Alley,
(701) 222–8075

**Golden Dragon
Restaurant and Lounge**
(Asian), 410 East Main,
(701) 258–0282

Kroll's Kitchen (German),
1915 East Main,
(701) 255–3850

Little Cottage Cafe
(American/German),
2513 East Main,
(701) 223–4949

Paradiso (Mexican),
2620 State Street,
(701) 224–1111

Peacock Alley,
corner of Fifth Street and
Main Avenue,
(701) 255–7917

Red Lobster (seafood),
1130 East Century,
(701) 222–2363

Rock'n 50's Cafe
(American), Gateway Mall,
(701) 222–4612

Space Aliens Grill & Bar
(American), 1304 East
Century Avenue,
(701) 223–6220

The Walrus Restaurant,
Arrowhead Plaza,
North Third Street,
(701) 250–0020

DICKINSON

China Doll Restaurant,
583 Twelfth Street West,
(701) 227–1616

German Hungarian Club
(German), 20 East
Broadway,
(701) 225–3311

**Rattlesnake Creek
Brewery and Grill**
(American),
2 West Villard,
(701) 225–9518

MEDORA

Cowboy Cafe,
½ block north of the
historic St. Mary's
Catholic Church,
(701) 623–4343

**Little Missouri Dining
Room** (American),
corner of Pacific and
Third Streets,
(701) 623–4404

WILLISTON

Kalley's Kitchen
(American), located at
Highways 2 and 86 North,
(701) 774–1103

**Gramma Sharon's Cafe
Inc.,** Highway 2 and 885
North, (701) 572–1412

**Missouri Flats
Steakhouse,**
10 Twenty-fifth Street W,
(701) 577–3848

SELECTED CHAMBERS OF COMMERCE

Beulah Convention & Visitors Bureau,
(701) 873–4585

**Bismarck-Mandan Convention and
Visitors Bureau,**
107 West Main Avenue,
Bismarck 58501, (800) 767–3555,
www.bismarck-mandancvb.org

**Bottineau Convention and
Visitors Bureau,**
519 Main Street, Bottineau 58318,
(701) 228–3849

**Dickinson Convention and
Visitors Bureau,**
72 Museum Drive, Dickinson 58601,
(800) 279–7391, www.dickinsoncvb.com

McKenzie County Tourism Bureau,
Box 699, Watford City 58854,
(800) 701–2804, www.4eyes.net/tourism

**Williston Convention and
Visitors Bureau,**
10 Main Street, Williston 58801
(800) 615–9041

Eastern North Dakota

Eastern North Dakota lures visitors today just as it did early settlers. Lakes, an especially symbolic garden of incredible magnitude, a fertile valley, and prairies make this area a virtual Eden.

In the north-central part of the state, big lakes—Devils Lake to the east and Lake Sakakawea to the west—lushly punctuate the Lakes and Gardens region. The International Peace Garden stuns visitors with its beauty.

As you travel toward the North Dakota–Minnesota border, the alluvial Red River Valley defines the history and economy of the far eastern third of North Dakota. It is one of the greatest agricultural regions in the world and is often compared with the Valley of the Nile. The Red River Valley is the form bed of the glacial Lake Agassiz, and its waters flow into the Hudson Bay and eventually into the Arctic Ocean. It varies from 10 to 40 miles in width from north to south along the border of North Dakota and Minnesota. The valley is relatively flat, with an average elevation of 900 feet. Rich chernozem (black) soils are found in the Red River Valley; promoters in the 1800s hailed the valley as the Garden of Eden, conveniently omitting the fact, however, that lack of water and a short growing season created conditions that were sometimes less than idyllic.

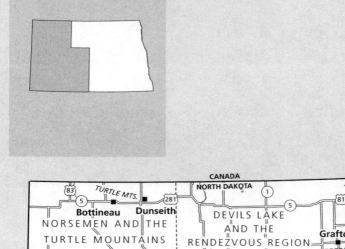

CANADA
NORTH DAKOTA

TURTLE MTS.

Bottineau   Dunseith

NORSEMEN AND THE
TURTLE MOUNTAINS

DEVILS LAKE
AND THE
RENDEZVOUS REGION

Grafton

Minot

Rugby

Devils Lake

NORTH
DAKOTA
HERITAGE

Grand
Forks

Carrington

LAND OF
LOUIS L'AMOUR

Valley
City

Jamestown

EDEN

Fargo

GERMANS-FROM-
RUSSIA POCKET

James R.

Wahpeton

Linton   Wishek

NORTH DAKOTA
SOUTH DAKOTA

MINNESOTA

NORTH DAKOTA

N

0   50 mi

0   50 km

North Dakota's livelihood, nonetheless, has always depended upon its soil, and that soil has made the state the land of plenty, whether in agriculture, crude oil, or lignite (a brown variety of very soft coal). North Dakotans simply call this long eastern corridor of woodlands in the north and agricultural bounty in the south The Valley.

Last, the Great Plains region, which stretches from Mexico to Canada, cuts through the heart of south-central North Dakota. The region of prairies and *coteaux* (hills) falls between the Sheyenne River to the east and the Missouri River to the west. The eastern part of the region is distinguished by rolling farmland and cattle and horse country. Glacial soils here are well suited for agricultural production, especially of wheat and other grains. Birds, too, take advantage of the region, and 10 percent of the bird species on the North American continent breed here. As you admire the scenery, look skyward for their winged beauty and listen for their songs.

Norsemen and the Turtle Mountains

Norwegians accounted for a large number of the immigrants who came to North Dakota. Given their native country's nonarable nature, that's highly understandable. Since 75 percent of the land in Norway was not suitable for agriculture, it was natural that Norwegians sought the fertile farmland of North Dakota. Only Ireland lost a greater percentage of its people to America.

The renowned **Norsk Hostfest** in Minot, which is located at the crossroads of U.S. Highways 2 and 83, brings in big-name entertainers and attracts 60,000 Scandinavians in a brightly ethnic celebration. Held each fall, the Hostfest also shows off delectables from Nordic kitchens at the All Seasons Arena, and arts

EASTERN NORTH DAKOTA'S TOP HITS

Bagg Bonanza Farm	Fort Abercrombie
Bonanzaville, USA	Fort Seward Historic Site and Interpretive Center
Campbell House	
Children's Museum at Yunker Farm	International Peace Garden
Devils Lake	National Buffalo Museum
Fargo Theatre	Norsk Hostfest
	Turtle Mountains

Livestock exhibit at the North Dakota State Fair

and crafts round out the list of attractions. Lefse, lutefisk, rosettes, and krumkaker are enjoyed by both Norwegians and non-Norwegians. Call (701) 852–2368 or log onto the Web site at www.hostfest.com for information.

The **Scandinavian Heritage Center,** located at South Broadway and Eleventh Avenue, is the world's only outdoor living museum that is dedicated to preserving the ethnic heritage of all five Scandinavian countries. Buildings on the premises include a visitor center, a *stabbur* (storage house) from Telemark, Norway, an eternal flame brought to North Dakota from Norway, and a 225-year-old house from Sigdal, Norway. Call (701) 852–9161 for the hours and other information.

The **Minot Holiday Inn** (located directly across from the State Fairgrounds and All Seasons Arena) combines modern architecture with contemporary, finely appointed interiors. The poolside restaurant, Ground Round Bar & Grill (a favorite in North Dakota), lounge, and casino complete a memorable stay. Rates start at $65. For reservations call (800) 468–9968. If you're in the bed-and-breakfast mood, try the **Dakotah Rose Bed & Breakfast** at 510 Fourth Avenue Northwest (701–838–3548). Call for rates.

In summer more than 300,000 people head to Minot for the **North Dakota State Fair.** Rodeos, parades, tractor pulls, car races, and carnival rides keep fairgoers entertained throughout the day and into the evening. For more state fair information, call (701) 852–FAIR or visit the Web site at ndstatefair.com. Also on the fairgrounds is the Ward County Historical Society Pioneer Village and Museum, open May through September.

The nineteen-acre **Roosevelt Park Zoo** (701–857–4166; www.rpzoo.com) is the home of a black-footed penguin collection. No doubt these flightless seabirds enjoy the chilly temperatures during North Dakota winters. Warmer-blooded residents include spider monkeys, kangaroos, a white Bengal tiger, giraffes, and llamas. Concessions, a children's zoo, a gift shop, and an educational center also are part of the zoo, which is located on the east side of town on the Burdick Expressway. The zoo is open daily 10:00 A.M. to 8:00 P.M. in the summer and 10:00 A.M. to 5:00 P.M. in September. Admission is $5.00 for adults, $2.50 for children ages six to twelve; free for children five and younger.

The Roosevelt Park and Zoo is the fifth point along the 2.5-mile *Riverwalk,* a walking and biking trail. Riverwalk starts at the *Railroad Museum* (701–852–7091) at 19 First Street Northeast. The museum presents the history and progression of the railroad through photographs and other memorabilia. A two-fifths scale train, located at the north end of Roosevelt Park, travels down a mile-long track.

The second point of interest is the *Lillian and Coleman Taube Museum of Art* (701–838–4445) at 2 North Main Street. The Minot Arts Association renovated the former Union National Bank building as a center for the visual arts, educational programs, and cultural and social events. Hours are 11:00 A.M. to 5:00 P.M. Monday through Saturday.

As you traverse the Riverwalk, you will also discover *Val's Cyclery* (701–839–4817) at 222 East Central, where Rocky and Rory Schell continue the cycling and fitness tradition started by their father, Valentine, more than forty years ago. *Eastwood Park* is the next stop. This is a splendid place to check out the architectural styles of homes from Minot's early days: Princess Anne, English Tudor, and Craftsman. In 1986 the neighborhood was designated a National Historic District.

Other sites along the Riverwalk are Lowe's Garden Center (701–839–2000), which is housed in a replica of an early North Dakota train depot; North Dakota State Fair and All Seasons Arena; Trax+, which features two go-cart tracks and an eighteen-hole golf course; MotorMania, which takes place every Labor Day weekend at the fairgrounds; and the Ward County Historical Society Pioneer Village and Museum (701–839–0785). Pioneer Village and Museum, located at the west entrance to the fairgrounds, is a collection of preserved and restored historic buildings, housing vintage automobiles and thousands of artifacts that illuminate Minot's past.

For more information about Riverwalk, call the Minot Convention and Visitors Bureau at (800) 264–2626.

And before leaving Minot, by air or by land, be sure to check out the *Dakota Territory Air Museum* (701–852–8500), which is adjacent to the northwest corner of the Minot International Airport.

If you love things that fly as much as I do, this is the place to be. You'll find civilian aircraft, from a 1928 Waco to a 1946 Piper J-3 Cub, as well as a Lockheed T-33 Jet Trainer, a Douglas C-47 World War II Transport, and a Curtis

P-40 Hawk. Also prominently displayed—and still operational—is the Minot Airport Beacon, which guided pilots in the area from 1949 to 1993. And the price can't be beat: $2.00 for adults and $1.00 for children ages six to seventeen. The museum is open from 10:00 A.M. to 5:00 P.M. Monday, Wednesday, Friday, and Saturday and from 1:00 to 5:00 P.M. Sunday. The museum is open late May through late September.

A drive north on U.S. Highway 52 through the Des Lacs River Valley in autumn shows off the colors of fall. In Kenmare, famous for its wheat and cheery sunflowers, the 1902 *Old Danish Mill* is a restored flour mill, with millstones that weigh 1,800 pounds. The *Des Lacs National Wildlife Refuge* is the perfect place to picnic and watch the birds.

The bustling community of Bottineau is the gateway to the Turtle Mountain area. To find it, travel 37 miles north of Minot on US 83, then 43 miles east on State Highway 5. Up north there's something to do every season at *Lake Metigoshe State Park,* a wooded natural area with numerous lakes. Lake Metigoshe is the most developed.

Bird Paradise

North Dakota is a paradise for birds, with more than 350 species of songbirds, shorebirds, birds of prey, wading birds, upland birds, and nesting waterfowl present. Birds unique to the pristine prairies include the western grebe, ferruginous hawk, Hungarian partridge, sharp-tailed grouse, piping plover, upland sandpiper, marbled godwit, clay-colored sparrow, and the chestnut-collared longspur.

Several endangered or threatened birds have been documented in North Dakota by the U.S. Fish and Wildlife Service, including the interior least tern, bald eagle, whooping crane, peregrine falcon, and piping plover.

Crossing the Border

For answers to questions about customs procedures, call toll-free (800) 435–5663, U.S. Customs at (701) 825–6551, or Canadian Customs at (204) 373–2524.

Both U.S. and Canadian citizens enjoy relatively unrestricted border crossing. There are, however, some differences in regulations, and the best way to avoid delays and hassles when crossing the international border is to be prepared.

In either direction, a passport or a birth certificate for each person is required. Usually custom officials will ask you where you live, your citizenship, the purpose of your trip, how long you intend to stay, and if you have any goods to declare. There may be questions about alcohol, tobacco, and firearms. If you made a duty-free purchase, state how much you bought. When returning home, you may be asked what you have purchased, so it's a good idea to save your sales slips and pack your items so they can be easily inspected at the border. Oral declarations are the general rule.

Imagine this: It's July 14, 1932, and you're one of the 50,000 people who have traveled 13 miles north of Dunseith, North Dakota, for the dedication of the *International Peace Garden*—a lavish garden that commemorates peace between Canada and the United States. Dr. Henry J. Moore, a horticulturist from Islington, Ontario, Canada, conceived the idea for the garden when he was on his way home from the 1928 annual meeting of the National Association of Gardeners, a U.S. organization. He thought it was a fitting tribute to the peaceful existence between the two countries.

The proposal was approved at the association's 1929 meeting, and the search began for an appropriate site. Moore liked what he saw when visiting the Turtle Mountains. After a plane ride over the area, he remarked: "What a sight greeted the eye. Those undulating hills rising out of the limitless prairies are filled with lakes and streams. On the south of the unrecognizable boundary, wheat fields everywhere; and on the north, the Manitoba Forest Preserve. What a place for a garden!"

The stone tablet on a cairn of native stone reads: TO GOD IN HIS GLORY . . . WE TWO NATIONS DEDICATE THIS GARDEN AND PLEDGE OURSELVES THAT AS LONG AS MAN SHALL LIVE WE WILL NOT TAKE ARMS AGAINST ONE ANOTHER. The two countries chose a place situated on the longest north-south road in the world and about centrally located on the continent of North America (Turtle Mountains). The Peace Garden is built on the border of North Dakota and Manitoba, with 2,339 acres of land spanning the international boundary.

More than 150,000 annuals grace both sides of the line, a fitting tribute to the tireless friendship the two countries have sustained through the years. The border walk through the Formal Gardens is a one-of-a-kind chance to see an

24-hour ports of entry

Pembina, North Dakota, and Emerson, Manitoba, I–29, (701) 825–6551

Dunseith, North Dakota (International Peace Garden), and Boissevain, Manitoba, U.S. Highway 281, (701) 228–2540

Portal, North Dakota, and North Portal, Saskatchewan, U.S. Highway 52, (701) 926–4241

All other ports of entry are open daily from 9:00 a.m. to 10:00 p.m.

enormous carpet of flowers in bloom across two nations. The 1.5-mile walk takes you past fountains, pools, cascades, the Perennial Garden, Arbor Garden, arboretum, Sunken Garden, the bell tower, and, of course, an enchanting bevy of flowers. If you visit between July 15 and August 15, you'll be dazzled by hundreds of orange and yellow Asiatic lilies. Self-guided driving tours will allow you to see Lake Udall on the United States side and Lake Stormon on the Canadian side.

The park isn't only for the green thumbs in the family; it's the perfect spot for the culturally inclined. The International Music Camp is held annually during early summer at the park, featuring Saturday concerts with guest conductors and an old-time fiddlers' contest.

The International Peace Garden is one of the prettiest spots in the nation for picnicking, camping, or just sitting back and absorbing the scents and beauty of nature. The grounds are open daily, with camping available May through mid-October. Although the garden is perennially gorgeous, August brings its blossoms to their full peak of color. For detailed information call (888) 432–6733 or, in Canada, (204) 534–2510. You can also visit the Web site at www.peacegarden.com. To get to the garden from Bottineau, travel 13 miles east on State Highway 5 until you reach Dunseith; then take State Highway 3 north for 13 miles.

If you drive Highway 3 south back to Dunseith, check out the quirky Wee'l Turtle statue, made from more than 2,000 tire rims. Then take State Highway 5 east approximately 18 miles, which will take you right through Belcourt, near the lovely town of Rolla and the heart of the magnificent Turtle Mountains.

As you head east from the Peace Garden toward Rolla, you'll find a comforting oasis amid the grasslands in the Turtle Mountains. The native people of North Dakota are the Mandan, Hidatsa, and Arikara nations, as well as the Yanktonai, Sisseton, Wahpeton, and other tribes such as the Pembina Chippewa, Cree, and Metis. North Dakota's native people are the descendants of ancient tribes—people who enjoyed years of peace and who survived years of turmoil and change. Their traditions, philosophies, and spirituality have made an unparalleled contribution to the sumptuous cultural landscape of North Dakota.

The Turtle Mountain Band of Pembina Chippewas live in the wooded, rolling hills of north-central North Dakota. The Turtle Mountain Chippewas' ancestors came from the Great Lakes region in the late 1700s, essentially drawn west by the fur-trade business. As trappers, voyagers, entrepreneurs, and caretakers of the land, the Pembina Chippewas formed enduring relations with other indigenous and European peoples, most significantly the Cree and the French. The Chippewa and Metis people built and developed North Dakota's first community: Pembina. The Red River Valley and northern North Dakota were the choice hunting territories of the Pembina Chippewas after the 1800s. As part of the continuing westward migration pattern and following a stir of treaty making, Chief Little Shell III brought his band across the Dakota prairie to the Turtle Mountains, an area much like the woodlands of Minnesota. On December 21, 1882, the *Turtle Mountain Indian Reservation* was established. It is now located on 33,100 acres in Rolette County, where the community of Belcourt is situated.

The reservation is surrounded by the beautiful *Turtle Mountains,* which offer endless recreational opportunities that include cultural centers, gaming facilities, powwows, fishing, swimming, skiing, golfing, and sundry community-sponsored events. Named the Turtle Mountains 200 years ago by explorers, these hills, flecked with lovely lakes, have long been home to native tribes.

The distinctive, colorful history and living traditions of the Pembina Chippewa people are preserved and promoted at *Turtle Mountain Chippewa Heritage Center,* just west of the Turtle Mountains in Belcourt. Through museum exhibits, dioramas, and archives, the history and contemporary culture of the Pembina Chippewas comes alive. Hours are 10:00 A.M. to 5:00 P.M. daily. For information call (701) 477–5688.

TOP ANNUAL EVENTS

International Music Camp,
June–July, International Peace Garden, (701) 263–4390

Norsk Hostfest,
October, Minot, (701) 852–2368

North Dakota State Fair,
July, Minot, (701) 857–7620

Pioneer Days,
third weekend in August, Fargo, (701) 282–2822

Enchanted Forests

The oak and aspen forests of the Turtle Mountain State Forest provide refuge to a variety of birds, including rugged grouse, magpies, and vireos. Also commonly seen are deer, moose, and small mammals such as squirrels, woodchucks, raccoons, and snowshoe hares.

The Indian Gaming Regulatory Act (IGRA), enacted by Congress in 1988, allows tribal governments to conduct gaming operations in states that also permit them off the reservations. For states like both North Dakota and South Dakota, the gaming industry has spurred an economic boom on reservations after a long history of abject poverty and high unemployment.

Two miles north of Belcourt on Highway 5, the **Anishinaubag Intercultural Center** (701–477–5519) offers a hands-on living-history experience in a reconstructed Plains Indian village. In a natural wooded one-hundred-acre setting, visitors can see Native American architecture, villages, a trading post, log cabins, and a log round house, used for dances and meetings. Canoe rental also is available at this exquisite lake setting.

Six miles east of Belcourt on State Highway 5 is Rolla, which rightly calls itself America's Enchanted Outback, and I can't argue with that appellation. In July the town hosts the annual **International Ragtop Festival,** a three-day salute to the convertible, complete with a parade, rock 'n' roll concerts, and other activities. For more information call (701) 477–3610.

Twenty-one miles south of Rolla on Highway 30 is the **Dale and Martha Hawk Foundation Museum,** with North Dakota's largest collection of antique farm machinery and the only known working Hackney Auto Plow. The collection is housed in five historic buildings, including a church, a store, and a schoolhouse. For more information call (701) 583–2333.

Devils Lake and the Rendezvous Region

The emerald waters of **Devils Lake,** located at the crossroads of State Routes 19 and 20, are spring-fed, covering more than 70,000 prairie acres. Flanking the lake are forests of hardwood oak, ash, and elm. The woodland-and-lake combination affords year-round recreation. According to legend it was dubbed Bad Spirit Lake after a group of Sioux were drowned in the lake while returning from battle. Walleye and white bass are the top draws, and yellow perch are found in winter. Migrating geese, ducks, and sandhill cranes take over the skies each spring and fall. Call the Devils Lake Area Welcome Center at (701) 662–4903 for more information on fishing.

At **Sullys Hill National Game Preserve,** swans, buffalo, elk, deer, and other wildlife enjoy a native habitat. The preserve is 12 miles southwest of the town of Devils Lake on State Highway 57, on Devils Lake. Admission is free. Call (701) 766–4272 for information.

Thirteen miles southwest of Devils Lake on State Highway 57, one of the best preserved military outposts in the trans–Mississippi West is found at the **Fort Totten State Historic Site** (701–766–4441; www.state.nd.us/hist). Fort Totten

was built in 1867 to protect the overland route to Montana and was the last outpost before 300 miles of wilderness. Self-guided tours can be enjoyed year-round.

To get a firsthand frontier experience, stay at the **Totten Trail Historic
Inn,** located at the historic site. The bed-and-breakfast inn is furnished in period
style (1870–1910). Rooms are available year-round, with prices ranging from
$80 to $110. A stay includes breakfast and afternoon Victorian tea.

There were two stages for the current renovation and operation of the historic inn. Beginning in 2001 the first floor opened for guests, meetings, receptions, and special events. In 2002 the second floor opened with additional guest
and public rooms. The Fort Totten State Historic Site Foundation with the North
Dakota State Historic Society provided planning and oversight. Furnishings
were made possible through donations from area families, whose names des-
ignate the individual guest rooms. Proceeds from the operation of the inn will
be used to renovate and restore the remaining sixteen original buildings on the
historic site.

The parlor and kitchen are available for special events, meetings, and parties year-round. Some rooms have a private bath, and others share a bath with
one other room. For more information write Totten Trail Historic Inn, P.O. Box
224, Fort Totten, ND 58335.

In the very northeast corner of the state, the four communities of Walhalla,
Pembina, Langdon, and Cavalier form the corners of the so-called Rendezvous
Region. Here traditions and nationalities meld together.

The largest Icelandic settlement in America is located within the region—a
chapter in the rich history of the Frontier West. The towns of Mountain, Gardar,
Hallson, Svold, and Akra were settled in 1873–1879 by Icelanders coming from
a sister colony in Gimli, Manitoba. After traversing the fertile Red River Valley,
the immigrants reached the Pembina Escarpment, a hilly wooded region that
overlooks the valley. They put down roots and thrived here. Quality education
for their children was paramount to the settlers, and the vision was not only to
assimilate into this new world but to be its leaders. Icelandic pioneers and other
ethnic groups are remembered in the Pioneer Heritage Museum, Akra Hall,
Cranley School, and the Gunlogson Homestead at Icelandic State Park near
Cavalier. In Mountain you'll find the oldest Icelandic church in America.

One and one-half miles northeast of Walhalla on State Highway 32, the
Gingras Trading Post State Historic Site (701–549–2775) preserves the home
and trading post established by Metis trader Antoine B. Gingras in the 1840s.
(Gingras was one of the signers of the charter of Winnipeg.) His hand-hewn
oak-log home and store are among the few tangible remains of the fur trade in
the Valley of the Red River of the North. The site is open from May 16 through
September 15 from 10:00 A.M. to 5:00 P.M. daily.

Today Walhalla is more of a vacation outpost. ***Frost Fire Mountain*** is a fully developed ski area, with chairlifts, a lodge, and spectacular views. Summer musicals in an outdoor amphitheater draw audiences from near and far. The covered amphitheater, on the slopes of the heavily wooded Pembina Gorge, sees sellout crowds that like to come early, shop in the crafts barn, and grab lunch before the curtain rises. Call (701) 549–3600 for information.

Located 2 blocks southwest of the intersection of State Highway 32 and County Road 55 in Walhalla, the ***Walhalla State Historic Site*** (701–328–2666) marks the birthplace of Walhalla. The town first was called St. Joseph, after a mission was established near Pembina in 1848 by Father George Belcourt. An original trading post founded by trader Norman Kittson in 1851 was later moved to the site, where a marker is now located.

If you travel 11 miles south of Walhalla on Highway 32, you'll discover a reminder of frontier Protestantism at the ***Oak Lawn Church State Historic Site.*** This site marks the location of a Presbyterian church built by the Reverend Ransom Waite and his congregation in 1885. The church was a prominent landmark until it burned in 1954. A sign and stone marker today represent the faith and fortitude of the church. Call (701) 328–2666 for more information.

Nicknames

- **Peace Garden State.** The International Peace Garden straddles the boundary between North Dakota and the Canadian province of Manitoba. In 1956 the North Dakota Motor Vehicle Department, on its own initiative, added "Peace Garden State" on license plates; the name proved so popular that it was formally adopted by the 1957 legislature.

- **Flickertail State.** Flickertail refers to the Richardson ground squirrels that are abundant in North Dakota. The animal flicks or jerks its tail in a characteristic manner while running or just before entering its burrow. In 1953 the Legislative Assembly defeated Senate Bill No. 134 that would have adopted the Flickertail facsimile as the official emblem of the state.

- **Roughrider State.** This name originated in a state-supported tourism promotion of the 1960s and 1970s. It refers to the first U.S. Volunteer Cavalry that Theodore Roosevelt organized to fight in the Spanish-American war. In fact, the Roughriders, which included several North Dakota cowboys, fought dismounted in Cuba due to logistical problems. In both 1971 and 1973, the Legislative Assembly defeated bills intended to change the slogan from Peace Garden State to Roughrider Country.

- **Dakota.** An attempt to drop "North" from the state name was defeated by the 1974 Legislative Assembly. Again in 1989, the legislature rejected two resolutions intended to rename the state Dakota.

Four miles east of Walhalla on State Highway 5 is Lake Renwick and *Icelandic State Park,* one of the jewels of the park system. Its newest addition is the historic Akra Hall community center, joining the old homestead, a one-room school, and nature trails of the Gunlogson Arboretum, which in winter are groomed for cross-country skiing. The *Gunlogson Homestead and Nature Preserve,* located within the park and the focal point of the Pioneer Heritage Center, elucidates the homesteading days of American history, when immigrants bravely settled land at the edge of the wilderness. The two-story frame homestead was built by Icelandic immigrants between 1882 and 1890. The formidable Pioneer Heritage Center is open mid-May through Labor Day (call 701–265–4561 for information). The six time periods that are featured include the early fur-trapping days, as well as the era of pioneers such as the Gunlogsons.

If you truly want to get away from the madding crowds and savor Dakota hospitality, I highly encourage you to check into the *221 Melsted Place Bed & Breakfast* (701–993–8257; www.melstedplace.com) in nearby Mountain. (To find, travel 1 mile east of Mountain on Highway 3). This elegant bed-and-breakfast is backed by the good words of Olafur Grimsson, the president of Iceland. "It's fantastic; it beats international hotels," observed the president.

The rooms? The Matriarchal Suite, an original bedroom for the maternal grandparents, is appointed with an ornate, gold-leaf headboard and a king-size bed. This is where the Icelandic president stayed in July 1999.

Other rooms are the Melsted Master Suite, with a stained-glass window; the Silhouette Suite, which houses a photo tribute to the original family; and the Ancestral Garden Suite, which delivers a soothing ambience.

Proprietor Lonnette Kelley says she and her husband moved to North Dakota from Omaha, Nebraska, in 1995. "I am a nurse, and we were not thinking bed-and-breakfast until we realized what history and uniqueness this wonderful historic farmstead had to offer." It's no wonder this romantic inn has become a popular place for weddings.

Built in 1910, 221 Melsted Place was originally owned by Sigurdur Magnusson Melsted, an engineer, businessman, farmer, and active citizen. He built the impressive estate for his wife, Rosa, her parents, and their ten children. The home has remained in its original form except for one renovation in the 1950s, when the upstairs verandah was removed and a sloping roof was placed over the roof.

Events at the inn include a Chocolate Festival in February; a Spring Celebration in April, complete with white swans in the pond; October festivities, including a haunted granary; and Christmas events, which promise to be truly magical with sleigh rides, Victorian teas, and festive candlelight dinners.

Room rates range from $80 to $120, which include a full, candlelit breakfast served in the Swan Room from 8:00 to 9:30 A.M. Amenities include a spa, full limousine service, evening bonfires, and a host of nature activities, including bird-watching, stargazing, and berry-picking.

The town of Mountain holds its own treasures: the 1884 Historic Vikur Church, an Icelandic Festival, and the Borg Pioneer Memorial Home.

Two pleasant diversions await travelers heading east on State Highway 5 at Cavalier and the wooded hills of the Pembina Escarpment. The **Pembina County Historical Museum** (701–265–4941), located at Division and Main Streets, features pioneer replica rooms, rotating theme displays, and a research library. Three buildings contain antique pioneer machinery. The museum is open from 1:00 to 5:00 P.M. daily Memorial Day through Labor Day. Four miles west of town is Lake Renwick, a lovely nine-hole golf course.

A second museum in Pembina is the **Pembina State Museum** (exit 215 off Interstate 29; 701–825–6840). Here, visitors can see one hundred million years of history, dating from the Cretaceous Age to modern times, in the permanent exhibit gallery. Or they can view the Red River Valley from the seven-story-high observation deck. Open daily.

North Dakota Heritage

Fortunately for travelers, I–29 runs north-south along the Red River Valley, so travel is easy in the region. If you take the interstate south, you'll land in the heart of Grand Forks, the state's oldest community. Located at the junction of the Red River of the North and the Red Lake River, the forks have traditionally been a meeting place for centuries, first for Native Americans who camped and traded there, then for French, British, and American fur traders who ambitiously peddled their wares around "la Grande Fourches." Across the North Dakota–Minnesota border, East Grand Forks was first established in 1870 by Alexander Griggs, a Missouri River steamboat captain.

Grand Forks began to grow dramatically after the Great Northern Railroad came to town in 1880. From the 1880s to 1910, pine logs were floated down the Red Lake River or brought in by rail to sawmills in the city. Many homes in Grand Forks were built of regal white pine from the immense forests of northern Minnesota.

Grand Forks remains the center of trade and processing for an agricultural area where wheat, potatoes, sugar beets, and livestock are produced. Cream of Wheat is synonymous with childhood—and Grand Forks; here, in 1893, miller Frank Amidon invented the creamy white porridge. Oddly enough, Grand Forks is considered to be the most cosmopolitan city in North Dakota, and its claim to history, a state university, and an air force base most likely have fostered that distinction. Oftentimes national weather forecasts list Grand Forks as the coldest spot in the nation, a chilling fact for the city's promoters.

The Wheat King of America, as Thomas Campbell was known in the early 1900s, was born here, and he earned his nickname because of the enormous farm acreage he owned. Campbell's home, the **Campbell House,** is a white, clapboard structure on 2405 Belmont Road. The house shares space on the old family ranch with an original 1870s post office, a 1920s one-room schoolhouse, a carriage house, the original log Grand Forks post office, and the

passthepasta

North Dakota produces 80 percent of the nation's durum wheat, the main ingredient in most pasta.

In keeping with the fine art of self-promotion, pasta lovers of North Dakota united in 1997 to form the annual Grand Pasta Party on the Prairie. Originally planned as a summer event, the celebration highlights the quality foods that are produced in North Dakota, as well as the people who produce them.

Visitors are encouraged to bring their appetites with them to the two-day festival. A cook-off allows food connoisseurs and chefs to tout their recipes. Area restaurants set up booths and feature their new pasta dishes to be sampled by the public.

Myra Museum. The house and property were deeded to the historical society in 1971. The house has been restored and the Centennial Corner has exhibits devoted to local personalities. The Myra Museum, similar in architecture to that of the Campbell House, was named in honor of John Myra, a Grand Forks County farmer. Dedicated in 1977, the museum houses a wide variety of artifacts from local history. Exhibits are rotated on a regular basis. All buildings are open daily mid-May through mid-September, from 1:00 to 5:00 P.M. The museum also can be toured during the off-season by appointment. Call (701) 775–2216 for more information.

Although Grand Forks lost several downtown buildings to the flood and fire of 1997, many remaining structures reflect the innate style and grace of the architects who shaped the city at the turn of the twentieth century. For instance,

thestateflower

The wild prairie rose (Rosa Blanda or Arkansana) has bright pink petals with a tight cluster of yellow stamens in the center. This rose grows wild along roadsides, in pastures, and in native meadows.

Art Deco style is seen in the 1931 Grand Forks Herald building at 120 North Fourth Street. The building, designed by architect Theo B. Wells, houses the *Herald* newspaper's editorial offices. In Grand Forks, Art Deco, a signature style of the 1920s and '30s, was not common since there was little construction of commercial buildings during the Great Depression. Other architectural styles found in Grand Forks include Classic Revival, Colonial Revival, Romanesque, Greek Revival, and Dutch Colonial. For more information call (800) 866–4566.

The *University of North Dakota (UND),* established in 1883, feeds the minds of its 12,430 students and generously lines the pockets of Grand Forks businesses. Located at the west end of University Avenue, the school is considered the premier liberal arts institution in the state, and it is the largest university in the Dakotas, Montana, Wyoming, and western Minnesota.

The *North Dakota Museum of Art* (701–777–4195) is renowned for its cutting-edge contemporary art. Recent shows have included the "Xu Bing Installations" from China and "The Alphabet of Lily," works on paper by Mike Glier. The museum is open 9:00 A.M. to 5:00 P.M. Monday through Friday and 1:00 to 5:00 P.M. Saturday and Sunday; admission is free.

Also on the UND campus, the *Chester Fritz Auditorium* is a 2,400-seat venue for a wide array of performances, from country acts and classical music to theater. The theater is world renowned for its acoustic brilliance. For more information call (701) 777–3076 or visit www.cfa.und.edu.

A film series of foreign, classic, and rather obscure movies and the highly esteemed annual Writer's Conference are two of the most impressive assets UND brings to the city. Another is the free Geology Museum in Leonard Hall, open weekdays year-round, with fossil and geological displays.

Aerospace progress is carefully chronicled at UND's *John Odegard School for Aerospace Sciences,* located at the intersection of University Avenue and Tulane Drive. Tours of its facilities are available on Tuesday and Thursday at 3:15 P.M. For information or reservations, call (701) 777–2791. If you're still interested in aviation, the *Grand Forks Air Force Base* (14 miles west on US 2) welcomes group tours. *The Heritage Center* on the base displays equipment from World War II through Desert Storm. The center is open Saturday 1:00 to 5:00 P.M. year-round. You can call the Heritage Center and the Air Force Base at (701) 747–5020.

You don't have to stay within the hallowed halls of higher education to find the arts scene in Grand Forks. In addition to the Burtness Theater on the UND campus, the newly restored *Fire Hall Theatre* (yes, it was once a fire station) downtown presents equally high-quality productions. This community theater presents everything from musicals and dramas to classics and comedies year-round. Call (701) 777–2236 for information.

For a scenic afternoon cruise or an evening dinner outing on the James River, hop aboard the **Dakota Queen** (701–775–5656 or 232–2309). River cruises are available daily (except Monday) Memorial Day through Labor Day. Get aboard at 67 South Riverboat Road.

It's Just a Movie

Fargo the town gained a little notoriety when *Fargo* the movie was released in 1996. The witty crime thriller was an independent movie, which seems highly apropos considering the rugged spirit of Dakotans.

The very black comedy was orchestrated by Minnesota natives Joel and Ethan Coen, who filmed in Fargo; Brainerd, Minnesota; and Minneapolis.

Frances McDormand portrays the pregnant Brainerd police chief Marge Gunderson, who is investigating a homicide. McDormand won an Academy Award for her portrayal of the even-tempered, quizzical policewoman.

The film takes a great deal of poetic license with the North Dakota–Norwegian accent and expressions—lines like "You betcha," "You're darn tootin'!," and "Oh yawhhh!"

Having lived in Fargo, my observation is there most certainly is a quaint Dakota accent, but it is greatly exaggerated in the film.

Grand Forks knows how to please shoppers, and the **Columbia Mall** (just off I–29, exit 138, at 2800 Columbia Road) is a buyer's paradise, with more than seventy stores and restaurants and anchor stores such as JCPenney, Dayton's, and Target. The mall (701–746–7383) is open 10:00 A.M. to 9:00 P.M. Monday through Friday, 10:00 A.M. to 7:00 P.M. Saturday, and noon to 6:00 P.M. Sunday.

For an easy weekend getaway, check out **Turtle River State Park** (701–594–4445), located 22 miles west of Grand Forks on US 2 in the breathtaking Turtle River Valley. Camping is a veritable blast here in the summer; if you're brave, try winter camping. The park also is open in winter for cross-country skiing, snowmobiling, sledding, and skating. Camping facilities are available May through September.

Just 45 miles northwest of Grand Forks off State Highway 18 is a Hutterite community known as the **Forest River Colony.** The colony, located near the Forest River and the town of Inkster, allows people to tour its 2,600-acre farm. The tour covers all aspects of the German colony, including the dairy and computerized egg-sorting operation. The tour takes about two hours, and advance notice is required. The cost is $1.00 per person, with a $20.00 minimum. For more information call (701) 865–4112.

If you spend the night in Grand Forks, try the **511 Reeves Bed & Breakfast.** Hosts Bill and Wanda Graveline have three rooms in this historical residence, each with a distinct personality: the Audubon Room, appointed with masculine tastes in mind; the Americana Room, quaint, right down to the plaid dust ruffle; and the Cottage Room, which wistfully recalls the more carefree days of childhood. Call (701) 775–3585 for rates and reservations.

Eden

For another metropolitan stop just get back on I–29 and head south. Fargo, North Dakota's largest city with 90,599 people, has profited immensely from the rich soil in the Red River Valley, where wheat, sugar beets, and sunflowers dapple the landscape. More than a century ago, this land was called Eden, and that appellation still works today. Fargo has been a vital trade and distribution center for the wheat and livestock produced in the surrounding region. Settlers, enticed by the promise of prosperity in the Great West, forded the river in carts. Farm products and by-products keep many factories bustling, and legalized casino gambling has made Fargo a regional tourism center. (Fargo's cousin city, Moorhead, is located just across the state line in Minnesota.)

Fargo was established in 1871 at the point where the Northern Pacific Railway crossed the Red River. Its first name was Centralia, but the town later was renamed to honor William George Fargo, who was founder of Wells, Fargo and Co. and one of the railroad's directors. Low railroad freight rates and the land's incredible wheat-producing potential attracted settlers.

Fargo wears its heritage like a badge of honor. The city has all the accoutrements of culture and higher education in an ambience of small-town hospitality. It gives an earnest tip of the hat to the past with such events as the ***Red River Valley Fair*** and ***Pioneer Days.*** Parades, arts and crafts, and people in period costume set the tone for Pioneer Days, held during the third weekend in August. ***Bonanzaville, USA*** is the backdrop for this event. Bonanzaville is a restored pioneer village from the early twentieth century, and it proudly touts itself as "fifteen acres of valley heritage." More than forty-five buildings are featured, including a train depot, farm machinery buildings, general stores, the Plains Indian Museum, and log cabins. The attraction is open daily from 9:00 A.M. to 5:00 P.M. Memorial Day through Labor Day and from 9:00 A.M. to 5:00 P.M. Monday through Friday in the winter.

The large and well-capitalized Bonanza farms (not to be confused with the ranch of 1960s TV fame) were built by early railroad boosters here and then marketed, to attract settlers, as a slice of Eden in the West. Sure enough, settlers followed with their plows and dreams. Between 1879 and 1886 about 100,000 people, many of them Scandinavian and German, came to live in Dakota Territory. This period became known as the Dakota Boom. Several of the Bonanza farms endured to the early part of the twentieth century—the last threads in the fabric of a powerful era in agriculture. The Bonanza episode is one of the most colorful in this part of the state's history.

Dignitaries such as President Rutherford B. Hayes, journalists from the states and abroad, and businesspeople hurried to the Red River Valley to tour the farms. For more information on Bonanzaville, USA (located 4.25 miles west of I–29 on Main Avenue or via Interstate 94, exit 343), call (800) 700–5317 or visit www.bonanzaville.com.

Children can have their own lesson on the merits of agriculture through the enchanted ***Children's Museum at Yunker Farm,*** at 1201 Twenty-eighth Avenue North in Fargo (701–232–6102; fax 701–232–4605). Here they can see a display of live bees, then crawl through a honeycomb section designed just for them. The exhibits were constructed to involve kids in demonstrations and hands-on experiments. The museum is naturally inviting. It's housed in a reno- vated, century-old redbrick farm house. The fifty-five-acre grounds include a miniature train, a carousel, a playground, a pumpkin patch, nature trails, and a community garden.

Special annual events include an Easter Eggstravaganza, with egg hunting, art, and a petting zoo; the Party in the Pumpkin Patch, which provides families the opportunity to celebrate fall—and kids to select their own pumpkins and decorate them; and the Not-Too-Scary Haunted House, which promises a safe and not-too-spooky Halloween experience.

Admission is $3.00 for children and adults. Thursday is Dollar Day, which means everyone is admitted for $1.00.

Summer hours are 10:00 A.M. to 5:00 P.M. daily, except Thursday (1:00 to 8:00 P.M.) and Sunday (1:00 to 5:00 P.M.). Hours during the school year are 10:00 A.M. to 5:00 P.M. Tuesday, Wednesday, Friday, and Saturday and 1:00 to 5:00 P.M. Sunday.

Fargo's historic downtown district is well preserved, and you can find the ***Fargo Theatre*** (314 Broadway) here—a former vaudeville and silent-film hall, complete with a working Wurlitzer pipe organ. After opening in 1926, vaude- ville acts and silent movies, accompanied by the Wurlitzer, were the main attrac- tions. The next year talking-picture equipment was installed. Early radio and TV programs also originated from the theater. Several renovations of both the the- ater and its entertainment agenda took place in the following years. The inside is decidedly Art Deco, providing the perfect venue for art films, stage plays, and second-run movies. For a current schedule call (701) 239–8385 or visit www.fargo theatre.com.

Another attraction is the ***Fargo-Moorhead Community Theatre*** (701– 235–6778), located at 333 South Fourth Street. The theater offers both amateur and professional live entertainment year-round, with dramas, comedies, chil- dren's shows, musicals, and more.

Swathed in soothing shades of blue inside and outside, ***La Maison des Papillons*** (The House of Butterflies) is an ideal spot for rest and rejuvenation. Proprietor Gracia Fulwiller has taken all the steps needed to ensure guests have a memorable stay at the 1899 bed-and-breakfast on historic Eighth Street South in Fargo.

Appropriately, each of the four guest rooms is named after a butterfly that is native to North Dakota. The Monarch, a double room with a half bath, is located on the north side of the home for solitude. The Swallowtail is also a double room with an exquisite stained-glass window and a bay window. The Fritillary, a single room, overlooks the front yard and nearby park. The Admiral, a double room, adjoins the Fritillary, making the rooms ideal for small groups or families.

Room rates range from $50 to $70. For reservations call (888) 273–3380 between 8:00 A.M. and 8:00 P.M. For more information write La Maison des Papillons, 423 Eighth Street South, Fargo, ND 58103.

If you take I–29 South (actually old U.S. Highway 81, parallel to the interstate), you'll find **Fort Abercrombie,** the site of a six-week siege in 1862. Located at the eastern edge of Abercrombie, this site preserves the military post that served from 1857 until 1878 as the gateway to the Dakota frontier. A museum here interprets the history of the fort and the area. Only one original building remains, but blockhouses and the palisade wall have been reconstructed. The site is open May 16 through September 15 from 8:00 A.M. to 5:00 P.M. daily. For more information call (701) 224–2666.

Near Wahpeton, check out the **Bagg Bonanza Farm,** 45 miles south of Fargo on I–29, Mooreton exit. This twenty-one-building farm is the sole remnant of the boom for "king wheat" in the 1800s, when a 6,000-acre factory farm was not even one of the biggest in the area. This is the last restorable Bonanza farm in the United States. Guided tours are available from noon to 6:00 P.M. Friday through Sunday or by appointment. The season opens Memorial Day weekend and ends Labor Day weekend. Special events are scheduled throughout the season, including the annual Old-Fashioned Fourth of July Celebration. Concessions and a gift shop are on site. For more information call (701) 274–8989.

Gracious living, Dakota style, is exceptionally affordable at **Winsome Manor Bed & Breakfast** in Hankinson, located 30 miles southwest of Wahpeton. (Take I–29 to exit 8 and drive 3 miles west to Hankinson, following the signs.) Proprietors Rick and Sue Oslowski offer a family-style or continental breakfast, and lunch and evening meals, upon request. A leisurely stroll is in order after dinner, with the Winsome Manor offering a southerly view of Lake Elsie. The master bedroom with a private bath is available for $75 per night or $130 for two nights. Additional bedrooms are available, providing guests are willing to share the bathroom facility.

Built by Colonel R. H. Hankinson in 1884, this stately three-story, twenty-room Victorian home—set atop a 9-foot fieldstone basement—is rich with architectural splendor: oakwood details, three fireplaces, and a grand staircase.

Nearby attractions include Lakeview Supper Club, Dakota Magic Casino, Chahinkapa Park Zoo, and the Chahinkapa Park Carousel and Chapel. Outdoor enthusiasts will find a land of plenty, too, with horseback riding, boating, golfing, ice-skating, and snowmobiling available in the area. For more information call (701) 242–0040.

Valley City is the gateway to the Sheyenne Valley. Its amber waves of grain and dairy farms reflect what made the area prosper. The railroad and early settlers arrived here simultaneously, establishing the community first known as Worthington in this densely forested valley.

Two of the Valley area's most prominent features are not always found in North Dakota: trees (North Dakota ranks fiftieth in tree cover, so the Valley is justified in its pride) and winding roadways. In the autumn, the trees turn vibrant shades of gold, yellow, and red. So pretty is this time of year that *Midwest Living* magazine suggested these roadways as a "Fall Color Drive."

The Sheyenne River Valley, from Lake Ashtabula to Lisbon, is designated as a Scenic Byway/Backway by the state of North Dakota, and the route from Valley City to Fort Ransom was listed in National Geographic's *Guide to Scenic Highways and Byways.* Furthermore, Valley City and the Sheyenne River Valley have been featured in North Dakota's *Horizons* magazine, AAA's *Home and Away,* and *Prairie Business* and *Country Discoveries* magazines.

And wait, there's more. Valley City was listed as one of fifteen "Perfect Small Towns" by *Midwest Living* magazine.

If you loved *The Bridges of Madison County,* in book or movie form, with Clint Eastwood and Meryl Streep, then the Valley City bridges are not to be missed. There are such elegantly gracious curves to these bridges, which span

A walking bridge in Valley City

the Sheyenne River. Clearly functional and smartly engineered, the eight Valley City bridges also endear visitors with their Americana charm.

The impressive Hi-Line Bridge, for instance, is a three-span, 255-foot bridge. At 3,860 feet long and 162 feet above the river bed, the Hi-Line Bridge is one of the longest and highest single-track railroad bridges in the nation. The first train officially crossed the trestle on May 12, 1908, and regular train service over the bridge began May 20. Because it was of vital importance in moving supplies and men, the bridge was closely guarded during both World War I and World War II to prevent sabotage.

To receive the beautifully photographed Scenic Bridges and Hidden Treasures brochure, call the Valley City Area Chamber of Commerce at (701) 845–1891 or log onto the Web site at www.hellovalley.com.

Valley City State University, on the south side of town, features a planetarium (702–845–7452), where visitors are treated to an incredible view of the solar system. More history is highlighted at the *Barnes County History Museum* (701–845–0966).

Northwest of Valley City, the *Baldhill Dam and Lake Ashtabula* (701–845–2970) boasts eight recreational areas where you can swim, fish, boat, picnic, and camp. The Valley City Federal Fish Hatchery, one of two such facilities in the state, also is located at the park. On these same grounds the Sibley Resort offers a motel, restaurant, and the expected amenities of resort life, but what makes it unusual is Pederson's Iris Patch. A dazzling array of some 550 varieties of iris qualifies this as much more than a patch; you can catch peak bloom in mid-June. While cross-country skiing and snowmobiling are the major winter activities at the Fort Ransom Ski Area, the facility now boasts a chairlift, a T-bar lift, and a beginner's tow rope. Call (701) 973–4331 for more information.

Thirty miles south of Valley City on State Highway 1, you can steer toward Fort Ransom and *Fort Ransom State Park.* The community and park inherited the name of a 128-year-old frontier cavalry fort, which was situated to protect the settlers' path to the Missouri River. Nowadays, the small Norwegian town of Fort Ransom is regarded as a scenic arts community. *The Ransom County Museum* is open afternoons, May 1 through October. The *Sheyenne Arts and Crafts Festival* is another popular attraction and takes place the last full weekend in September. Call (701) 973–4491 for more information.

Sodbuster Days takes place every summer. Here you can revisit the horse-powered days of threshing, haying, and plowing. Wagon rides and entertainment round out two weekends of living history. For more information call (701) 973–4331.

Land of Louis L'Amour

Jamestown, nestled in the valley where the James and Pipestem Rivers meet, is referred to as the Pride of the Prairie. This thriving community is located midway between Fargo, the state's largest city, and the capital of Bismarck.

Think South Dakota is the only place where buffalo roam? Jamestown gamely presents The **World's Largest Buffalo.** Actually, it's a three-story, sixty-ton concrete sculpture that stands watch on a hill over I–94. Two dozen live buffalo do roam below the giant statue, and the National Buffalo Museum shares the high ground at the Frontier Village Complex, located on I–94 at the south edge of town.

The **National Buffalo Museum** (701–252–8648 or visit www.jamestown nd.com) is dedicated to the history of the American bison, commonly known as buffalo. Displays show the evolution of the regal beast, and you can see a 10,000-year-old buffalo skull. The museum and gift shop are open year-round, with summer hours 9:00 A.M. to 8:00 P.M.; call for winter hours. Admission is $8.00 for families, $4.00 for adults, and $1.00 for students.

While you're at the National Buffalo Museum, meet Mahpiya Ska, the Lakota name meaning White Cloud, a certified albino buffalo. She was born July 10, 1996, on a private farm in Michigan, North Dakota. The nonprofit North Dakota Buffalo Foundation, which owns and operates the National Buffalo Museum, entered a special arrangement with White Cloud's owners so she could join the herd at the museum site.

The white buffalo is sacred to the Lakota people. According to Lakota people, the White Buffalo Calf Woman brought them their most sacred pipe. This beautiful woman in a white buckskin dress spent four days and four nights showing the Lakota how to smoke the pipe, on which a bison calf was carved on one side. As the White Buffalo Calf Woman left, she walked in the direction of the setting sun, stopped, and rolled over four times. The first time, she got up and became a black buffalo, the second time a brown buffalo, the third time

The State Flag

On January 21, 1911, state representative Colonel John H. Fraine introduced H.B. No. 152 designating an official flag for the state of North Dakota. The legislation specifically required that the flag conform to the color, form, and size of the regimental flag carried by the North Dakota Infantry in the Spanish-American War in 1898 and Philippine Island Insurrection in 1899; the only exception was the name "North Dakota" placed on the scroll below the eagle. On March 3, 1911, the Legislative Assembly adopted the North Dakota state flag.

All Creatures Great and Small

As you are traveling along the highways and byways of North Dakota, be on the look-out for small, brown-and-white roadside signs featuring binoculars, which indicate one of the state's eighty-plus roadside viewing areas.

Watch the birds and beasts from a distance with good-quality binoculars, a spotting scope, or a telephoto lens. If the animals you are watching are watching you—with their heads up and ears facing your direction—or are nervous, you are probably too close or moving too quickly.

Obviously, be kind to these bashful critters. Patience will reward you. Keep quiet and wait for animals to return to or enter an area. The early and late hours of daylight are generally the best times to watch and photograph most wildlife.

Call the North Dakota Tourism Department at (800) 435–5663 to order a copy of its *Wildlife Viewing Guide* ($5.95), which has specific directions to more than eighty view-ing areas.

a red buffalo, and the fourth time she rolled over, she became a white buffalo. This buffalo walked on further, stopped, and after bowing to each of the four directions of the universe, disappeared over the hill.

The *Frontier Village* (701–252–6307) details the way humans came to live and learn on the land. A post office, trading post, 1881 church, fire department, and barber house are some of the structures that re-create small-town life in the 1800s. The village is open 10:00 A.M. to 5:00 P.M. May and September and 9:00 A.M. to 9:00 P.M. June, July, and August. Admission is free.

In fact, famed Western novelist and Jamestown native Louis L'Amour's writ-ing shack is one of the featured sites at Frontier Village. L'Amour wrote 117 books and is best known for his Frontier books, such as *Mustang Man, The Sackett Brand, Ride the Dark Trail,* and *The Daybreakers.* More than 30 of his books became movies, including *Hondo,* with John Wayne; *Shalako,* starring Sean Connery; and *The Burning Hills,* which featured Tab Hunter and Natalie Wood.

If you want to learn more about the man who lassoed the American West spirit with words, walk the *Louis L'Amour Trail.* The first stop is the Dakota Territory Courthouse, where L'Amour's father worked as the county and the state veterinarian. He also doubled as a deputy sheriff for several years. The courthouse is located at Fifth Street and Third Avenue Southeast in Jamestown.

The Stutsman County Memorial Museum and the Jamestown City Hall are next along the trail, then the L'Amour Family Home Site. This is where L'Amour's boyhood home was originally located, at 113 Third Avenue Southeast. The home was later moved to the southeast part of Jamestown and structurally changed.

The First United Methodist Church, the Alfred Dickey Library (one of the young boy's favorite places), Franklin Grade School, and Walz Pharmacy, once owned by L'Amour's friend Reese Hawkins and stocked with all of the writer's books, also are highlighted along the trail.

L'Amour's writing reflects his Dakota roots. "The sort of men and women it took to open the West were the kind of whom stories were told. Strongly individual, willing to risk all they possessed as well as their lives, they were also prepared to fight for what they believed was theirs," he wrote in *The Sackett Companion*.

L'Amour is the only writer to receive the Presidential Medal of Freedom and the Congressional Gold Medal. An elephant handler, a professional boxer, a seaman, and a journalist, L'Amour, who died in 1988, is warmly remembered in his hometown.

An attractive brochure charting the Louis L'Amour Trail is available by calling (701) 252–4835.

At the north end of town on U.S. Highway 281 North, the **Fort Seward Historic Site and Interpretive Center** (701–252–6682), which overlooks Pipestem Lake, sheds light on the early military history of the region. The center is open daily April through October. There is also a picnic area on the grounds. Homesteading by covered wagon is commemorated each year in the **Fort Seward Wagon Train** (Web site: covered-wagon.train.com), in which participants don pioneer costumes (which are required) during a one-week wagon train reenactment. The wagon train was first organized in 1969 as a one-time experience, but promoters found it so worthwhile they made it a yearly event. The wagon train starts rolling at the crack of dawn, and it averages 3 to 4 miles per hour. At the end of the day, singing and storytelling around the campfire foster camaraderie, pioneer style—a memorable family affair. It's open from 10:00 A.M. to 5:00 P.M. daily April 1 through Labor Day. For information write to the Registrar, P.O. Box 244, Jamestown, ND 58402.

Just north on US 281 the 840-acre **Pipestem Dam and Lake** offers year-round recreational opportunities, and the lovely lake fascinates bird-watchers, boaters, anglers, and others. Conservation of wildlife and the natural environment is a major objective of the U.S. Army Corps of Engineers, and 4,200 acres of creek valley and rolling upland at Pipestem are home to a wide variety of wildlife and waterfowl. The natural setting has been enhanced by selective planting of more than 250,000 trees around the lake.

Jamestown's more famous firstborns include singer Peggy Lee and the best-selling western author of all time, Louis L'Amour. The **Louis L'Amour Gallery** is open every day, as is **The Arts Center** (115 Second Street Southwest), which features monthly visual-art exhibitions. The **1914 Basilica of St. James,** at 622

First Avenue South, is the only basilica in North Dakota and one of less than fifty in the entire United States. For information on these three attractions, call (800) 22–BISON. The ***North Dakota Sports Hall of Fame*** (located in the civic center at 212 Third Avenue) pays tribute to those who have shaped the growth and development of sports in North Dakota. Hall of Famers include basketball's Phil Jackson, baseball's Roger Maris, and football's Dave Osborn. For more information call (701) 252–3117.

The ***Stutsman County Memorial Museum,*** at 321 Third Avenue Southeast, is housed in the George Lutz mansion, a monument to the early-day history of the area. Four floors in the stately brick museum are devoted to the culture and life of the early pioneers. The first floor, with a complete dining room, kitchen, and butler's pantry, highlights items that a pioneer homemaker might have used. Military life and the railroad's strength in the state are featured on the second floor, and pioneer medicine, wildlife, and church relics round out this eclectic collection on the third floor. A room in the basement has been turned into a claim shanty. The museum is open June 1 through October 1 Monday through Saturday from 1:00 to 5:00 P.M. and 1:00 to 8:00 P.M. Sunday. For more information call (701) 252–6741.

For a special overnight stay in Jamestown, pick the ***Country Charm Bed & Breakfast*** (701–251–1372; fax 701–252–9087), a fancifully decorated farm-house built in 1897. The complimentary full breakfast makes the drive well worth the effort. Room rates are $63 for two people. It's located 6 miles west of Jamestown on I–94, exit 251, 1 mile north, then 0.75 mile east.

For swimming, camping, fishing, and boating, the ***Lakeside Marina and Recreational Area*** (701–252–9200) is just 3 miles north on State Highway 20

Fort Seward Wagon Train

OTHER ATTRACTIONS WORTH SEEING
IN EASTERN NORTH DAKOTA

The Roger Maris Museum, Fargo

Upper Souris National Wildlife Refuge, Minot

Waterworld, Grand Forks

at the Jamestown Dam. Camping and tent and trailer sites are available. There is a fee for some activities. Open early May through late September.

If you go 25 miles northwest of Jamestown on US 281, you'll drive into the 16,000-acre *Arrowwood National Wildlife Refuge* (701–285–3341), where the Jamestown River meanders among marshes and lakes. A self-guided automobile tour affords breathtaking views of duck broods in summer and migrating snow geese in fall. Wildlife officials estimate that fifty-three million birds make North Dakota prairies their warm-weather habitat.

Also north on US 281 is Carrington, which, like most of the communities in North Dakota, can trace its development to the arrival of the railroad. By 1882 the Northern Pacific line ran through the yet unnamed prairie settlement. Agriculture formed the base for Carrington's early and present-day economy. It's home to the state-of-the-art Dakota Growers Pasta Co., which markets pasta made from the durum wheat grown in the region.

History buffs, be sure to check out the *Putnam House* (533 Main Street), an American Foursquare home built in 1907 by Thomas Nichols Putnam, the area's pioneer lumberman, and his wife Clara Belle Putnam. The 4,300-square-foot home is testament to the precise craftsmanship and architecture of the turn of the twentieth century. The grand staircase is a breathtaking focal point, and the dining room features a built-in oak buffet with leaded-glass doors. The first floor is partially preserved and open to the public. The second and third floors are undergoing restoration.

The majestic home can be seen by appointment and from 2:00 to 5:00 P.M. Saturday and Sunday during the summer. For more information about the Putnam House and events, call (701) 652–1213.

Just a few miles southwest of Carrington is *Hawk's Nest,* a 300-foot-high butte standing amid one hundred acres of unfenced land. The area has one of the few remaining stands of buffalo grass and pine oaks. Visitors to Hawk's Nest, which is maintained by the local Kiwanis Club, can hike, camp, and ski there.

In the opposite direction, the tiny town of Kulm is located 38 miles south of Jamestown on US 281, then 16 miles west on State Highway 13. Nearby, a

42,000-acre wetlands district provides the perfect place to hunt, fish, and watch birds. Kulm is also the hometown of actress Angie Dickinson.

One of the more haunting sites in the area is the **Whitestone Hill Battlefield Site.** A day trip from Jamestown can be managed, though it's a little tricky: Go 37 miles south on US 281, then 15 miles west on State Highway 13 to Kulm, then 15 miles south on State Highway 56, then east on an unimproved road.

In September 1863 the Battle of Whitestone, most likely triggered by the 1862 Sioux uprising in Minnesota, marked the beginning of a war between the U.S. Cavalry and the Plains Sioux that lasted for more than twenty years. The tribe was being forced west by European settlers in Minnesota, and the bison herds on the Dakota plains were being decimated.

The Battle of Whitestone Hill lasted for only two hours, but by sunset, an estimated 150 to 300 Sioux had lost their lives and 156 were taken prisoner. The cavalry's death toll was considerably less: Only twenty cavalrymen died, and fifty to sixty were wounded. On a summer day the granite memorial of a bugler gleams starkly against the pure blue skies. A small museum is also on site, as well as a picnic area and playground. The North Dakota Historical Society (701–328–2666) operates the museum. The local Whitestone Historical Society hosts an annual summer event at the site to commemorate the battle.

Germans-from-Russia Pocket

The homelands of the residents in Strasburg, Wishek, Linto, and surrounding areas are no longer in Germany. Around 1804 people from Alsace (then a German province, now a French one) began to emigrate to farm in the Ukraine and escape the Napoleonic Wars. In 1808–1809 another wave of immigration created Roman Catholic communities along the Kutschurgan River in Russia, with names brought from Germany: Strassburg, Baden, and Selz. Those names arrived in North Dakota with yet another wave of immigration, fueled by overpopulation and Russian desires to turn the Germans into Russians. The name *Strasburg* underwent its second spelling change (Strasbourg, Strassburg, Strasburg), and Selz was bestowed upon two towns, the first of which, near Hague, disappeared. The second, in Pierce County, is still a thriving community. Black Sea Germans, or *Russlanddeutsch,* as they are called, are so far removed from Germany that the customs and language they preserve are ancient history in present-day Germany. Whereas French and Scottish immigrants quickly assimilated into North Dakota society, the Black Sea Germans maintained their cultural identity longer and were generally aloof to community involvement.

Nowadays the residents are eager to share their food and festivities. Oktoberfest, a traditional event in Germany, is replicated in many communities in south-central North Dakota, as well as in the western part of the state. The town of Wishek, for instance, has paid homage to fermented cabbage every October for seventy years with its *Sauerkraut Days.* Schoolchildren get out of school early for the free wiener-and-kraut lunch. If kraut's not your style, try *knoephla* soup (spelled many ways, but the soup is always buttery with potatoes and dumplings) and *fleischkuekle,* a beef-filled pasty, or pierogi. The festival is replete with food and drink, and you can hear the oompah-pahs of polka throughout the community.

The family histories of the people who live here are strikingly similar to that of "wunnerful, wunnerful" *Lawrence Welk,* the famous Champagne Music Maker. Welk's father had grown increasingly unhappy with life in Russia, and in 1892 he and his wife came to America. Their voyage was financed by an uncle who ran a store in Strasburg. Lawrence Welk was born in 1903, and he spoke only German until he was twenty-one years old. This was not uncommon for children of German-Russian descent, as parents were reluctant to send their children to school, only allowing them to attend when their work was finished on the farm.

Welk was the sixth of nine children, and on his twenty-first birthday he left for Bismarck. He played his accordion at weddings and dances until his great break came in 1955 when he debuted on national TV.

Welk's birthplace, officially known as the *Ludwig & Christina Welk Farmstead,* is nestled among wheat fields north of Strasburg. Although the home is made of sod, with 3-foot-thick walls, it has white siding on the exterior and wallpaper inside. It is open daily from 10:00 A.M. to 5:00 P.M. May 15 through September 15 and by appointment. Welk died in sunny southern California in 1992, the year the homestead restoration was completed. It's no wonder that Welk's greatest aficionados come from North Dakota and neighboring Minnesota and Iowa. More than 7,000 Welk fans visit the site each year. For more information call (701) 336–7687.

Where to Stay in Eastern North Dakota

BOTTINEAU

Norway House,
1255 Highway SE,
(701) 228–3737

DEVILS LAKE

Comfort Inn,
U.S. Highway 2 East,
(701) 662–6760

Davis Motel,
US 2 East, (701) 662–4927

Super 8,
located on US 2
just east of town,
(701) 662–8656

Totten Trail Historic Inn,
14 miles south of Devils
Lake, P.O. Box 554,
58301, (701) 766–4874,
www.tottentrailinn.com

GRAND FORKS

AmericInn,
1820 South Columbia
Road,
(701) 780–9925,
(800) 634–3444

**Best Western Town
House,**
710 First Avenue N,
(701) 746–5411,
(800) 867–9797

C'mon Inn,
3051 Thirtieth Avenue S,
(701) 775–3320,
(800) 255–2323

Comfort Inn,
3251 Thirtieth Avenue S,
(701) 775–7503,
(800) 228–5150

Days Inn,
3101 South Thirty-fourth
Street,
(701) 775–0060,
(800) 325–2525

Econo Lodge,
900 North Forty-third
Street,
(701) 746–6666,
(800) 424–4777

**511 Reeves Bed &
Breakfast,**
511 Reeves Drive,
(701) 775–3585

Holiday Inn,
1210 North Forty-third
Street, (701) 772–7131,
(800) 465–4329

Lakeview Inn & Suites,
3350 Thirty-second
Avenue S,
(701) 775–5000,
(877) 355–3500

Ramada Inn,
1205 North Forty-third
Street,
(701) 775–3951,
(800) 570–3951

FARGO

**Best Western
Doublewood Inn,**
3333 South Thirteenth
Avenue,
(701) 235–3333

Comfort Inn,
1407 Thirty-fifth Street S,
(701) 280–9666,
(800) 228–5150

Fairfield Inn,
3902 Southwest Ninth
Avenue, (701) 281–0494

Holiday Inn Express,
1040 South Fortieth Street,
(701) 282–2000

**Kelly Inn Thirteenth
Avenue,**
4207 Thirteenth Avenue
SW, (701) 277–8821

Radisson,
201 North Fifth Street,
(701) 232–7363

Super 8 Hotel & Suites,
3518 Interstate Boulevard,
(701) 232–9202,
(800) 800–8000

MINOT

**Dakotah Rose Bed &
Breakfast,**
510 Fourth Avenue NW,
(701) 838–3548

Days Inn,
2100 Fourth Street SW,
(888) 327–6466

International Inn,
1505 North Broadway,
(701) 852–3161

WAHPETON

Holiday Inn Express,
1800 210th Drive,
(701) 642–5000

Where to Eat in Eastern North Dakota

DEVILS LAKE

Cedar Inn Family Restaurant,
U.S. Highway 2 West,
(701) 662–8893

Cove Restaurant,
Highway 19,
(701) 662–5996

Felix's Restaurant & Lounge,
Highway 2 West and Fourth Street,
(701) 662–4941

Mr. & Mrs. J's Restaurant,
Highway 2 East,
(701) 662–8815

FARGO

Twenty-fifth Street Market,
1450 Twenty-fifth Street S,
(701) 451–0870

Basie's On 42nd Street,
1635 Forty-second Street SW, (701) 281–7105

Chili's Grill & Bar,
4000 Thirteenth Avenue SW, (701) 282–2669

Echoz Café,
1638 Thirty-second Avenue S,
(701) 239–9300

Grandma's Saloon & Grill,
4201 Thirteenth Avenue SW, (701) 282–5439

GRAND FORKS

Roadhouse Café,
4720 Gateway Drive,
(701) 772–1273

Applebee's Neighborhood Grill & Bar,
2851 Columbia Road S,
(701) 795–5688

Branigan's Restaurants & Bars,
3451 Thirty-second Avenue S,
(701) 795–6010

Burger Time,
2651 DeMers Avenue,
(701) 775–2776

China Buffet,
3555 Gateway Drive,
(701) 787–0888

China Garden Restaurant, 2550 Thirty-second Avenue S,
(701) 772–0660

Del's Coffee Shop,
South Forks Plaza,
(701) 772–3311

Emerald Grill,
1200 Forty-seventh Street N,
(701) 780–0888

GF Goodribs,
4223 North Twelfth Avenue,
(701) 746–7115

Ground Round Restaurant,
2800 Thirty-second Avenue S,
(701) 775–4646

Happy Joe's Pizza & Ice Cream Parlor,
2909 Washington Street S,
(701) 772–6655

Joe DiMaggio's Sports Cafe,
118 Third Street N,
(701) 775–5699

Royal Fork Buffet Restaurant,
Columbia Mall,
(701) 746–0869

Mexican Village,
1218 Washington Street S,
(701) 775–3653

Muddy Rivers Bar & Grill,
710 First Avenue N,
(701) 787–0733

MINOT

Homesteaders Restaurant,
2501 Highway 2 and 52 Bypass West,
(701) 838–2274

Planet Pizza,
1015 South Broadway,
(701) 852–1700

WAHPETON

China Buffet,
407 Dakota Avenue, (701) 642–6320

Wahpeton Deli,
614 Dakota Avenue, (701) 642–3639

SELECTED CHAMBERS OF COMMERCE

Carrington Area Chamber of Commerce,
P.O. Box 439, Carrington 58421,
(701) 652–2524,
fax (701) 652–2391

Devils Lake Area Tourism Office,
P.O. Box 879, Devils Lake 58301,
(800) 233–8048

Fargo-Moorhead Convention & Visitor Bureau,
2001 Forty-fourth Street SW, Fargo 58103,
(800) 235–7654,
www.fargomoorhead.org

Grafton Area Chamber of Commerce,
432 Hill Avenue, P.O. Box 632,
Grafton 58237,
(701) 352–0781

Jamestown Promotion & Tourism Center,
P.O. Box 389, Jamestown 58402,
(800) 222–4766,
www.jamestownnd.com

Minot Convention and Visitors Bureau,
P.O. Box 2066, Minot 58702,
(701) 857–8206, www.visitminot.org

Valley City Area Chamber of Commerce,
P.O. Box 724, Valley City 58072,
(701) 845–1891, www.hellovalley.com

Wahpeton Visitors Center,
118 Sixth Street North,
Wahpeton 58075,
(800) 892–6673,
www.wahpchamber.com

General Index

Museums

Parks

Lodging

Native American–Related Sites

About the Author

Robin McMacken is an award-winning writer from South Dakota who has been writing about the Dakotas for more than fifteen years. Her articles have appeared in regional magazines and newspapers and national travel books. She has worked as a writer at the *Los Angeles Times* and now freelances for the paper.